Philosophy, *The Federalist,* and the Constitution

The Origin of Dewey's Instrumentalism
Social Thought in America
The Age of Analysis (ed.)
Toward Reunion in Philosophy
Religion, Politics and the Higher Learning
The Intellectual Versus the City (with Lucia White)
Foundations of Historical Knowledge
Science and Sentiment in America
Documents in the History of American Philosophy (ed.)
Pragmatism and the American Mind
The Philosophy of the American Revolution
What Is and What Ought to Be Done
Journeys to the Japanese (with Lucia White)

Philosophy, *The Federalist,* and the Constitution

MORTON WHITE

OXFORD UNIVERSITY PRESS

New York Oxford

OXFORD UNIVERSITY PRESS

Oxford   New York   Toronto
Delhi   Bombay   Calcutta   Madras   Karachi
Petaling Jaya   Singapore   Hong Kong   Tokyo
Nairobi   Dar es Salaam   Cape Town
Melbourne   Auckland

and associated companies in
Berlin   Ibadan

LIBRARY OF CONGRESS CATALOGING-IN-PUBLICATION DATA
White, Morton Gabriel, 1917–
Philosophy, The Federalist, and the Constitution.
Includes index.
1. Federalist.   2. Political science—United States—History.
3. United States—Constitutional history.   I. Title.
JK155.W48   1987   342.73′029   86–5396
ISBN 0–19–503911–4   347.30229
ISBN 0–19–505948–4 (PBK)

2 4 6 8 10 9 7 5 3 1

Printed in the United States of America

TO LUCIA

PREFACE

This work is a sequel to my book *The Philosophy of the American Revolution* (1978), but a sequel which may be read and understood by those who have not read its predecessor. The present work has, for a variety of reasons, taken longer to complete than I expected when I first began the research for it, and I want to say something about the reasons for my delay in bringing it out.

Somewhere in the middle of my journey to the end of this book I came to appreciate the great difficulty of trying to formulate the philosophy of a work such as *The Federalist,* a work which is not exclusively or even primarily philosophical in purpose. The scholar who studies a strictly philosophical text has the advantage of studying one which usually contains an argument that leads to philosophical conclusions, and therefore such a scholar's task may be limited to clarifying that argument and those conclusions. By contrast, my task in presenting the philosophy of *The Federalist* was peculiarly difficult because I sought to extract a philosophy from a work whose authors were not primarily concerned with advocating one. Because I underestimated this difficulty, I underestimated the amount of time it would take to perform the extraction and to clarify some of the historical roots of what I extracted. I was greatly helped by the writings of several scholars who have dealt with individual philosophical topics treated in *The Federalist,* but, so far as I know, no other philosopher has ever presented a synoptic view of the major philosophical ideas in *The Federalist.* The resulting absence of this kind of secondary literature deprived me of another advantage that historians of philosophy usually have when working on philosophical texts.

However, though I lacked certain advantages while preparing this work, I also had an incomparable one—the assistance of my wife, Lucia White. As usual, she helped me immensely in the preparation of this work by carefully reading it in its many different versions, by advising me about many points of substance and of style, by lifting my spirits at times when they were very low, and by patiently tolerating occasionally stubborn resistance on my part. To express my loving gratitude for all of her help, I have dedicated yet another book to her, knowing full well that the dedication hardly constitutes an adequate expression of my gratitude.

I also want to thank Hugh Benson, my research assistant during the academic year 1984–85. He brought many books to me from local libraries, checked the accuracy of my quotations and citations, and gave me the benefit of his reaction to certain parts of the book. In addition, I want to record my debt to Bernard Bailyn and Deane Montgomery for helping me clarify my ideas about a part of *Federalist Number 10*. I am grateful to Albert Furt- wangler for informing me of the existence of certain works about *The Feder- alist* that I might otherwise have missed, and to Sebastian de Grazia for dis- cussing with me some of my ideas about *The Federalist*. I am also grateful to Harvard University for appointing me as Visiting Scholar in Philosophy for short periods in 1984 and 1985, during which I did some of my research and writing. I thank the librarians of The Institute for Advanced Study for quickly acquiring books that I required and I thank my lucky stars for being a mem- ber of the faculty of the Institute. No other academic position would have provided me with the assistance that I needed while trying to produce this book. Most of the words I have written were expertly processed—if that is the correct verb—by Laura Schuckmann Glück and by Felicia Schuckmann; I thank them warmly.

Readers who would like to find out quickly how I conceive the total phi- losophy of *The Federalist* may wish to read Chapter 12 after reading Chap- ter 1 and before reading Chapter 2.

Princeton, N.J.   M. W.
July 3, 1985

CONTENTS

I

INTRODUCTION

1

The Role of Philosophy
in *The Federalist*

Writing to a correspondent in May of 1790, Thomas Jefferson characterized *The Federalist* in a manner that continues to influence almost every scholar who studies that great defense of the Constitution of the United States. Jefferson's letter to Thomas Mann Randolph, Jr., penned about two years after the last number of *The Federalist* had appeared in a New York newspaper, contained some striking bibliographical advice which concluded with a comment on *The Federalist*. Jefferson began by calling Adam Smith's *Wealth of Nations* the best book in political economy; he went on to say more cautiously that in the science of government Montesquieu's *Spirit of the Laws* "is generally recommended" but that any reader "must be constantly on his guard" because of "the mixture of truth and error found in this book"; he added significantly that Locke's "little book on government"—meaning his *Second Treatise of Government*—"is perfect as far as it goes"; and then wrote his most important sentence from our point of view. "Descending from theory to practice," he declared, "there is no better book than the Federalist."[1]

We need not spend too much time trying to discover how Jefferson was using the word "descending." He may have been writing ironically or he may have been expressing a conventionally hierarchical view of the logical relationship between theories and statements about practice, but whatever he meant, he was certainly correct in regarding *The Federalist* as a practical work by comparison to some of the other books he had mentioned. For one thing, *The Federalist* was practical because it was written with a concrete political purpose in mind. The authors, Alexander Hamilton, John Jay, and James Madison, urged their readers to support the ratification of the Constitution that had been first proposed to the Philadelphia Convention in September of 1787 and then vigorously attacked in New York newspapers during late September and early October of the same year. But *The Federalist* was not only written in a practical effort to rally support for the Constitution; it also defended some very practical detailed propositions in law and politics.

3

Although its authors used much rhetoric, they also argued logically in support of various political devices provided for in the Constitution; for example, separation of powers, a bicameral legislature, certain methods of raising revenue, and many other political devices which had drawn the fire of those who opposed ratification. *The Federalist* was a brilliant collection of connected political pamphlets, written hastily in defense of a shrewdly drawn legal document. It was therefore very different from works in what we usually call theoretical science or in philosophy.

The idea of Jefferson that *The Federalist* was a practical work was repeated—but with a certain anti-intellectualistic bias—by one of its most ardent admirers in the twentieth century, Charles Beard. The eminent historian and political scientist remarked sarcastically that "the authors of *The Federalist,* poor fellows" failed to "have the benefit of modern sociology, psychology, economics, and political science,"[2] and that they "did not . . . discuss the problems of epistemology, or 'appearance and reality,' which have long occupied the attention of armchair philosophers."[3] Beard seems to have thought even less of armchair philosophers than he did of twentieth-century social scientists when he contrasted both groups of thinkers with Hamilton and Madison. Since the latter had taken an active part in the war for independence and in the founding of the Republic, Beard believed they would "stand forever in striking contrast to the ideologues and theoreticians so influential in the Western world." Accordingly Beard dismissed Locke as "essentially a speculative thinker, at home mainly, if anywhere, in theology and psychology" and testily declared that Rousseau was even less a political philosopher than Locke— "indeed, no political philosopher at all." Both of them, Beard went on, had exerted enormous influence in Western history, but, he sighed, "it is, of course, not uncommon for writers on great and complicated subjects to be entirely devoid of practical experience in the matters on which they discourse. . . ." Unlike Locke and Rousseau, Beard added, Hamilton, Madison, and Jay "were not closet philosophers. They were not dust sifters engaged in dissecting the ideas of other dust sifters."[4]

In the face of all this, why should one inquire into the philosophy of *The Federalist?* Why examine the epistemology, the ethics, the philosophy of history, or the theory of human nature espoused by authors who were mainly interested in the machinery of government and who therefore did not produce a book in theoretical social science or in philosophy? One reason for doing so is that the authors of that work often used language and expressed ideas which must be examined philosophically if we are to understand the authors adequately. The point is that they frequently used philosophical terms such as "reason," "human nature," "science," "experience," "truth," "duty," "good," "passion," and "interest" without saying very much about *how* they were using them. In short, the very failure of Hamilton, Madison, and Jay to write more expansively when using philosophical terms makes it necessary to find out what they had in mind when they used them. Their silence about such matters may explain why Charles Beard, who says he first read *The Federalist* at the turn of the century and then reread parts or all of it nearly every year for fifty years, was astonished at each reading "by the discovery of ideas and suggestions which [he] had previously overlooked or had failed to grasp in their full meaning."[5] Perhaps Beard's distorted interpretation of Madison's *Number 10* would have been less distorted if he had not only reread that number regularly but had occasionally read certain essays by the philosopher David Hume, several of which are recommended as "good" in the letter in which Jefferson praises *The Federalist* to T. M. Randolph, Jr.[6] Had Beard read Hume, he might have found it easier to see—as Douglass Adair has shown—that Madison, like Hume, did not think that the various and unequal distribution of property was the *only* source of factions. Beard might have also hesitated to claim Madison as an anticipator of Marx's philosophy of history.

It is even more evident that Beard might have improved his understanding of some of Hamilton's explicitly held philosophical views if Beard had known more than he seems to have known about Locke's epistemology. Beard's low opinion of Locke may have prevented Beard from seeing that the man he dismissed as a closet philosopher very probably influenced the fundamental ideas of Hamilton's *Number 31,* a paper which plays an important part in Beard's Introduction to *The Enduring Federalist.* There Beard referred to Hamilton's notion of a "primary truth" as one which contains "an internal evidence which, antecedent to all reflection or combination, commands the assent of the mind," but Beard did not seem to realize that Hamilton's notion of primary truth was very probably an echo of Locke's notion of self-evident or intuitive truth, an echo of rationalism that still remained in Locke's generally empiricistic philosophy. Had Beard known this, he might not have written without qualification that the primary truths mentioned by Hamilton in *Number 31* were derived by Hamilton and Madison "from studies of historical experience and from their own observations of the politics in which they participated, as responsible leaders and actors."[7] Although the authors of *The Federalist* certainly relied on historical experience when arguing for many of their beliefs, and although they often revealed their attachment to British empiricism as that was conceived by Hume, Hamilton's references to primary truths which are established by internal evidence and his occasional remarks about some propositions in political science being susceptible of absolute demonstration show that he was also under the influence of the *un*Humeian, rationalistic view that all moral principles and even some proposions about matters of fact can be rationally "demonstrated." This meant that they could be established, *without* appealing to historical experience, by deducing them from self-evident, intuitive primary truths which may be seen to be true merely by examining the ideas expressed in them.

All of this goes to show that even though *The Federalist* is a practical work on government, it invites rather than precludes philosophical analysis, that is to say, an effort to clarify the thought of Publius—the collective pseudonym of Hamilton, Jay, and Madison. At times such clarification may require no more than careful reading and rereading of *The Federalist,* the sort of reading that a systematic philosopher might do while studying any work in political science, whether it be written in 1787 or yesterday. However, as soon as we find Hamilton referring to "primary truths" and "internal evidence" for them, we realize that we must know something about the history of philosophy to understand his technical terminology, and that being a philosophical analyst of occasionally archaic English is not enough. In any case, no amount of cant about how practical and active Publius was and how dusty, closeted, and impractical Locke was should prevent us from using philosophy and the history of philosophy while trying to understand *The Federalist*. Nor should we be turned aside from using them by the notion that only "a decent respect for the proprieties of political discussion required" the founders at the Philadelphia Convention to make "at least occasional reference to Locke and Montesquieu," or that "such excursions into political philosophy as were made are to be regarded rather as purple patches than as integral parts of the proceedings."[8] It may well be that philosophical terms were often used by the framers in purple patches, but in those very same patches we find them logically defending some very important provisions of the Constitution. For example, Hamilton used his view of primary truths in order to defend the unqualified power of the federal government to levy taxes. And it is ironical that when the twentieth-century historian R. L. Schuyler made light of the purple-patched philosophy which had been used in defense of the Constitution, he supported his anti-intellectualistic view by citing some exceedingly philosophical words that John Dickinson used at the Convention while defending the power of the lower house to initiate bills of revenue, namely: "Experience must be our only guide. Reason may mislead us."[9] To cite this remark of Dickinson's while arguing that the founders did not make serious use of philosophy is ironical indeed. No pair of words played a larger part in the vocabulary of eighteenth-century philosophy than "reason" and "experience"; and no pair of words played a larger part in the total argument of *The Federalist*.

Although I have so far mentioned only the use of methodology or epistemology in *The Federalist,* I want to stress that other parts of philosophy were also employed by Publius. Substantive views in the doctrine of natural law were on his mind in several parts of his work, and these views are views in normative ethics because they assert, for instance, that men have the *rights* of life, liberty, and property. These substantive moral views stand in contrast to the epistemological thesis that it is a *self-evident* or primary truth that all men have a right to life or to liberty. Publius's views in normative ethics and in the epistemology of normative ethics are in turn distinguishable from his views in the theory of human nature, views in which he describes the different motives or springs of human action. Today Publius's theory of human nature would be called a part of psychology since it describes the causes of human action without telling us what men ought to do or what they have a right to do; in the eighteenth century, however, the theory of human nature was regarded as a philosophical discipline. In fact, when Hume called his major work *A Treatise of Human Nature,* he virtually equated philosophy with the study of human nature. But no matter how broadly we use the word "philosophy" when discussing *The Federalist,* it will be useful to distinguish between Publius's epistemology, his normative ethics, and his theory of human nature on the one hand, and, on the other, the main subject of *The Federalist,* which Publius called "political science."

Political science was regarded by Publius as a discipline in which one asserts and defends descriptive propositions about the causes of factions and the effects of having a large republic, as well as practical or technological propositions about what ends would be accomplished by a separation of powers, by checks and balances, and by the division of the government into state and federal jurisdictions. Because Publius supported many of his views in both descriptive and practical political science by appealing to a more fundamental theory of human nature, this theory has been a central concern of those students of the work who have tried to give more than a summary of what Publius believed about the nuts and bolts of constitutional law. They have discoursed endlessly about Publius's view of human motivation, thinking that in doing so they have squeezed out virtually all of the philosophy to be found in *The Federalist.* And because Madison discussed the causes of factions in a way that Beard found similar to the way in which Marx discussed the origin of classes, Beard thought that Madison was an economic determinist and therefore a philosopher of history. In short, many scholars think that philosophy entered *The Federalist* only by way of a theory of human nature and a view of history. This, however, is not true. Discussing these two philosophical subjects has brightened the days of many scholars who rightly see *The Federalist* as more than a treatise on constitutional law, but there is more explicit and implicit philosophy in the book than that, philosophy which is seriously used and not merely displayed in purple patches.

In my view, therefore, a thorough understanding of *The Federalist* requires us to see that it contains or relies upon a theory of knowledge, a doctrine of normative ethics, a psychology of motivation, a theory of the causes of factions which can be called a speculative philosophy of history only by misunderstanding Madison, and even some metaphysics and theology—all of them used in different ways to support the adoption of the Constitution. My primary aim in this study will therefore be to expose such philosophical elements of Publius's thinking, those that are close to the surface and those that are not. In doing so I shall sometimes write as an historian of philosophy and sometimes as a philosopher of the political science advocated in *The Federalist.* I shall sometimes call attention to the influence of major philosophers, notably Locke and Hume, on the thought of Publius, and sometimes I shall use the tools of systematic philosophy while trying to clarify what Publius says. Naturally, there will be places in this study in which I shall be doing both of these things at the same time, places where I cite the influence of a major philosopher while I also logically analyze statements made by the authors of *The Federalist.*

When I cite the influence, or probable influence, of certain philosophers on Publius, I do not wish to suggest that we can explain the formation of the Constitution merely by citing, amplifying, or tracing the history of philosophi-

cal ideas. Nor do I wish to suggest that we can in this way give a complete explanation of why the authors of *The Federalist* supported the Constitution.
Obviously some of them were prompted by motives which, as Hamilton said
in *Number 1,* would remain in the depository of their own breasts. On the
other hand, I am anxious to illuminate *The Federalist* by examining the fundamental ideas that appear in it, ideas which I think we must understand if
we are to understand the work in more than a superficial way. I hope, therefore, that this work will be judged as a study which is primarily concerned to
show the part that philosophy played in *The Federalist*'s defense of the Constitution. How *big* a part I leave it to others to say, to others who are ingenious enough to measure in a clear way the relative importance of intellectual
and nonintellectual factors in that defense. I hope that the present work will
be of some use to them, and that it will be of use to any readers who are concerned with the way in which philosophy is linked with other ideas in the history of American thought.

I know that some historians are wary of relying exclusively on intellectual history when trying to explain why Publius wrote *The Federalist,* and
rightly so. They also properly insist that the same expression in different
mouths may mean different things, and therefore argue that we cannot say
that just because Madison and Hume happened to use the same expression,
they meant the same thing by it. But sometimes the same expression *is* used
in the same, or in a very similar way by an earlier and a later thinker; and
sometimes when we can show this we can improve our understanding of the
later thinker. That is why, as we shall see, Douglass Adair's discovery of certain similarities between Hume's essay "Of Parties in General" and Madison's *Number 10* is so illuminating. It is, of course, unfortunate that some
writers who have tried to link certain views in *The Federalist* with those of
earlier writers have made exaggerated claims and have slipped into the so-
called pitfalls of intellectual history. But the fact that some scholars have
slipped into those pitfalls is no argument against efforts by others to illuminate
one text by showing its connections with another text in a responsible, scholarly manner. Indeed, for every pitfall that lies ahead of the historian of ideas
who tries to explain a text by reference to other texts, there is an equally deep
and treacherous pitfall that lies ahead of the historian who is so obsessed with
describing the extra-intellectual forces exerted on a writer such as Publius
that the historian cannot bring himself to dissect any argument that contains some philosophy. The moral of this is obvious. Students of intellectual
history need to understand the philosophical ideas they confront in a work
such as *The Federalist* if they want to locate it in the total context of the life
of colonial America. And there are at least two ways of trying to understand
such ideas, two ways that are not mutually exclusive. One is to read *The Federalist* with what Hume called "a strict philosophic eye"—something that even
an unlearned philosopher can often do successfully. The other is to read *The
Federalist* with one strict philosophic eye on the text of Publius and the other
on any philosophical text which influenced him when he was writing.

Before closing this chapter, I want to emphasize that in the eighteenth century philosophy was a much broader subject than it is today, and so, in one sense, extracting the philosophy of Publius would amount to extracting virtually everything he said that was general or theoretical in character. For this reason I must make a disclaimer. I do not plan to deal with everything that Publius said which was philosophical in the eighteenth-century sense. Instead, I plan to deal with ideas of Publius that have remained within the purview of philosophy as we now know it: with his theory of different kinds of knowledge, with his substantive moral philosophy, with what has been misleadingly called his philosophy of history, with parts of his psychology that continue to interest philosophers, with what would today be called his theory of action, and even with a part of his metaphysics. The task of extracting and explicating Publius's views in these different fields is ambitious, but I think it is necessary to undertake it if we are to understand his major contributions to what he called political science, the discipline of most concern to him.

Virtually all of the disciplines that I have labeled philosophical were employed by the authors of *The Federalist*. They freely used terms that appeared in those disciplines—for example, "reason" and "experience"—and they freely assumed propositions contained in those disciplines, much as the physicist uses the terms of logic and arithmetic and also assumes laws of those disciplines. Consequently, anyone who tries to understand what Publius meant by some of his statements without understanding certain expressions in the theory of knowledge or ethics is like someone who tries to understand physics without knowing any arithmetic or any logic. I state the point of studying the philosophy of Publius in this way only to emphasize the need to understand what may be called the philosophical context of *The Federalist,* a context which a serious scholar will neglect at his peril even if he is ultimately bent on locating *The Federalist* in the total life of colonial America. After all, the total life of colonial America contained a philosophical life in which authors of *The Federalist* participated as cultivated lawyers, and one of the methods that a historian can use in illuminating that philosophical life is to expound the ideas of John Locke and David Hume, who influenced it so much. With this in mind I shall now consider certain views of theirs on reason, experience, morals, and history—views that I think will be of use even to social and political historians of America in the period when the Constitution was formed. In focusing on the views of Locke and Hume, I do not mean to imply that they were the only philosophers to influence Publius. They were, however, the most important philosophers to influence him, and I think they influenced him in dramatically different ways.

II

THE DIFFERENT
LEGACIES OF
LOCKE AND HUME

2

Hume's Experience and
Locke's Reason

In this chapter I am not particularly interested in trying to show that the founding fathers derived all of their philosophical ideas from Locke and Hume. Yet I am concerned to explain the terminology of the latter and their philosophical views in order to help the reader gain a better notion of what Madison, Hamilton, and Jay may have had in mind when they used such terms as "history," "reason," "experience," and "primary truths," and when they made certain statements containing these terms. I do not mean to imply that the American thinkers were directly propelled into saying what they said by reading their philosophical betters. Generally speaking, the assertions of pamphleteers and practical politicians cannot be accounted for simply by reference to the assertions of philosophers, but it is obvious that if we wish to improve our understanding of what intellectual borrowers thought, we can be helped greatly by knowing something about what their intellectual creditors said.

The two philosophers whose views I shall discuss in this chapter exerted their main influence on different parts of *The Federalist*. Locke exerted a profound influence on Publius's normative theory of natural rights as well as on his epistemological reflections about how to support that theory. Hume, on the other hand, not only influenced the political technology and the political science of *The Federalist* but also seems to have provided the authors with methodological or epistemological views concerning both of these experimental disciplines. Since political science, as opposed to normative ethics, was the central concern of *The Federalist,* I shall begin with a brief presentation of Hume's epistemology of science before turning to the relevant views of Locke and Hume in the epistemology of normative ethics. What I have to say is familiar to most students of the history of British philosophy, but it is best said here in order to illuminate certain parts of *The Federalist* for readers who may not be familiar with the epistemological views of Locke and Hume on these subjects.

Hume on Reason and Experience in Science

Unlike Beard, many commentators on *The Federalist* who came after him have recognized how much influence Hume exerted on Madison and Hamilton in political technology or science, but no matter how much these commentators have contributed to our understanding of *The Federalist* on such topics as the size of a good republic, or the separation of powers, or checks and balances, they have not provided us with an altogether satisfactory understanding of such words as "reason," "experience," and "history" as they are used in *The Federalist*. For this reason I want to present a brief discussion of these and related terms as they are used in the writings of Hume, a discussion which will ultimately clarify some of the things said in *The Federalist* even though at first sight it may not seem to do so.

The first thing to observe is that Hume distinguishes between the use of demonstrative reason or reasoning in pure mathematics, which concerns what he calls the relations between ideas, and the use of experimental reason or reasoning in, say, physics, which concerns what he calls matter of fact or existence. He says that these are two *kinds* of reasoning.[1] For our purposes it is perhaps enough to add that, according to Hume, we use demonstrative reasoning when establishing arithmetical propositions as well as geometrical propositions such as "the square of the hypothenuse is equal to the squares of the other two sides,"[2] whereas we use experimental reasoning to show that fire burns or "that a body at rest or in motion continues for ever in its present state, till put from it by some new cause."[3] We need not enter the difficult subject of what Hume means by the word "ideas" when he says that mathematics concerns the relations of ideas; suffice it to say that he distinguishes ideas from "external objects" such as fires, animals, plants, or parts of the human body. Hume calls these external objects matters of fact and existence as opposed to ideas; and, he says, when we reason experimentally and arrive at beliefs about such matters of fact and existence, we appeal to experience. The important thing to bear in mind is that, according to Hume, beliefs in the sciences which employ experimental *reasoning* are also said by him to be supported by *experience*. With this in mind, I now want to deal with Hume's own statement that one and the same belief may be established by what he is willing—with certain important qualifications—to call a priori reasoning and also by experience in experimental disciplines, including the main discipline pursued in *The Federalist,* namely, that of political science.[4]

Hume held that it was erroneous—or at least superficial—to suppose that even when using reason to establish a truth about a matter of fact, we dispense with making any appeal to experience. He presents his view on this while expounding and criticizing certain unnamed writers in experimental sciences such as politics. They find it useful, he says, "to distinguish between *reason* and *experience,* and to suppose, that these species of argumentation are entirely different from each other." Hume represents these writers as holding that argumentation in which we use reason is carried on by our "intellectual faculties" while considering *"a priori* the nature of things, and examining the effects, that must follow from their operation." This is how, Hume's opponents say, we use a priori reason to establish principles. According to Hume, however, these same writers believe that when we use experience in argumentation, we use only sense and observation, "by which we learn what has actually resulted from the operation of particular objects, and are thence able to infer, what will, for the future, result from them."

To illustrate what he regards as this erroneous or superficial view of the different methods of reason and experience in experimental science, Hume presents an example of special interest to readers of *The Federalist*. He says that his epistemological opponents maintain that we may defend the limitations and restraints of civil government and a legal constitution in two *entirely* different ways. One of these ways is by using the method of reason—for example, by "reflecting on the great frailty and corruption of human nature"—in which case we allegedly come *without* using experience to the conclusion "that no man can safely be trusted with unlimited authority." Here the words "reflecting" and "reason" are employed by Hume's unnamed opponents in order to characterize the method of the supposedly a priori thinker. These opponents also say, however, that we can use the allegedly different method of experience or history to inform ourselves of the enormous abuses that ambition in every age and country will produce if we *do* trust some men with unlimited authority. In short, Hume's opponents say, when we use the method of experience or history, we observe the behavior of human beings, something we allegedly do not do when we use the method of reason and argue from the supposedly a priori principle about the great frailty and corruption of human nature to the conclusion that no man can be safely trusted with unlimited authority.

Hume denied that the so-called method of reason was as nonempirical as his opponents said that it was. While he was prepared to acknowledge that by using the method of reason one could establish truth in experimental science, he balked at the idea that when using the method of reason in the example offered by his opponents, we do *not* rely on experience at all. Hume asserts that even though this version of the distinction between the method of reason and the method of experience is "universally received, both in the active [and] speculative scenes of life," he does "not scruple to pronounce, that it is, at bottom, erroneous, [or] at least, superficial." He says, furthermore, that if we examine any argument which is said to lead by the use of reasoning and reflection alone to the conclusion that no man can be safely trusted with unlimited authority, that argument will be found to rest on propositions "for which we can assign no reason but observation and experience." Hume insists therefore that even when we use the so-called method of reason to defend the proposition that no man can be trusted with unlimited authority by deriving this proposition from the proposition that human nature is frail and corrupt, the *latter* proposition is itself based on our experience of human beings. We learn of its truth by observation and then we infer from it and other true factual statements that no man can be trusted with unlimited authority. Our next step is to infer that we should impose the limitations and restraints of civil government and a constitution on any man with governmental authority. Therefore, according to Hume, the so-called a priori method of reason cannot dispense with observation about human nature when supporting a general premise about it from which we infer our practical political beliefs.

Hume adds that when we use the so-called method of "pure experience" or history in establishing that no man can be trusted with unlimited authority, we rely on a narrower kind of experience. We examine the careers of actual monarchs who have been trusted with unlimited authority—for example, Tiberius and Nero—and, on the basis of our historical examination, we conclude that such monarchs become tyrants when freed from the restraints of laws and senates. However, Hume wants us to bear in mind that observation or experience of any fraud or cruelty in private as opposed to public life would be enough, "with the aid of a little thought," to give us the same apprehension that we derive from studying the past histories of Tiberius and Nero. By observing the behavior of ordinary men around us today we can also come to a generalization about the corruption of human nature, and therefore about the danger of "reposing an entire confidence" in any men, and therefore in monarchs who are not limited. In short, Hume maintains that whether we use the so-called method of reason while making inferences from the observed corruption of men around us, or the method of pure experience which is based on observation of the lives of past monarchs such as Tiberius and Nero, "it is experience which is ultimately the foundation of our inference and conclusion" that no man can be trusted with unlimited authority.[5] By contrast, Hume insisted that, unlike the truths of an experimental science such as politics, the truths of mathematics can be established without appealing to experience insofar as they can be established merely by examining relations between *ideas* as opposed to examining human beings.

It was in 1748 that Hume made his point about the fundamentally empirical character of all testing in political science, but John Stuart Mill made a statement on the same general issue in 1836 which more clearly conveys the methodological or epistemological message of Hume on matters of concern to Publius. Even though Mill's view was published almost a half-century after *The Federalist* had appeared, I present it here because it may help the reader understand more clearly what the authors of *The Federalist* meant when they said—as we shall see they said—that one can support the same proposition by an appeal to reason or one's knowledge of human nature *and* by an appeal to experience or history. Mill held that so-called practical men who reason on social and political questions require specific experience "and argue wholly *upwards* from particular facts to a general conclusion; while those who are called theorists aim at embracing a wider field of experience, and, having argued upwards from particular facts to a general principle including a much wider range than that of the question under discussion, then argue *downwards* from that general principle to a variety of specific conclusions." Mill offers an illustration which is similar to Hume's:

Suppose, for example, that the question were, whether absolute kings were likely to employ the powers of government for the welfare or for the oppression of their subjects. The practicals would endeavour to determine this question by a direct induction from the conduct of particular despotic monarchs, as testified by history. The theorists would refer the question to be decided by the test not solely of our experience of kings, but of our experience of men. They would contend that an observation of the tendencies which human nature has manifested in the variety of situations in which human beings have been placed, and especially observation of what passes in our own minds, warrants us in inferring that a human being in the situation of a despotic king will make a bad use of power; and that this conclusion would lose nothing of its certainty even if absolute kings had never existed, or if history furnished us with no information of the manner in which they had conducted themselves.

The statement that an absolute king is likely to employ the powers of government for the oppression of his subjects is the Millian counterpart of Hume's statement that no man can safely be trusted with unlimited authority. And Hume's statement about the frailty and corruption of human nature might have served as an example of what Mill's "theorist" might have offered if pressed to make his most general assumption more explicit. The Millian theorist might well have asserted what Hume had asserted about man's frailty and corruption when the theorist described "the tendencies which human nature has manifested in the variety of situations in which human beings have been placed," that is to say, the tendencies that would warrant him in inferring that a human being in the situation of a despotic king will make a bad use of power. Furthermore, one methodological or epistemological idea of Hume was well expressed by Mill when he said that the method of those he called the practicals was that of induction *by itself,* this being what Hume meant by the method of "pure experience." Second, Mill followed in Hume's footsteps when he referred to what Hume called the method of reason as "a mixed method of induction and ratiocination." And, third, although Mill, like Hume, was prepared to use the terminology according to which the method of the practicals is called a posteriori whereas the method of the theorists is called a priori, Mill went on to make Hume's central epistemological point in the passage I discussed earlier. Mill made the point when he said that he was aware that the expression "a priori" was "sometimes used to characterize a supposed mode of philosophizing, which does not profess to be founded upon experience at all. But," Mill continued, "we are not acquainted with any mode of philosophizing, on political subjects at least, to which such a description is fairly applicable. By the method a posteriori we mean that which requires, as the basis of its conclusions, not experience merely, but specific experience. By the method a priori we mean (what has commonly been meant) reasoning from an assumed hypothesis. . . ."[6] However, according to Mill, this assumed hypothesis is also founded on experience, just as Hume said it was and just as Publius thought it was in spite of certain lapses that we shall describe later. Broad generalizations about all men, like narrower generalizations about all despotic kings, must be supported by experience—that was the fundamental message of Hume, a message that Publius took quite seriously, as we shall see.

Mill's application of the word "practicals" to those who use only direct induction and his application of the word "theorist" to those who occupy a different position in the intellectual world was not unconnected with some other remarks by Hume that should interest the student of *The Federalist*. Hume noted that "in all our deliberations concerning the conduct of life . . . the experienced statesman, general, physician, or merchant is trusted and followed; and the unpractised novice, with whatever natural talents endowed, neglected and despised."[7] When Hume said this, he had in mind the view of those who held that "practicals" use pure experience whereas "an unpractised novice" allegedly uses no experience at all and relies on reason or theory alone. However, Hume, in keeping with his view that not even a youthful theorist can dispense with experience, wrote: "There is no man so young and unexperienced, as not to have formed, from observation, many general and just maxims concerning human affairs and the conduct of life."[8] But, Hume added, when a young man comes to put these maxims into practice, he will be liable to error unless he enlarges them on the basis of further experience and learns how to apply them properly. In other words, further experience may lead the theorist to make his theory more complex by adding qualifications, and it will also make him more careful about applying his theory. Thus, the theorist may begin with the belief that all dry paper bursts into flame when ignited, but then come to believe on the basis of further experience that all dry paper *which is surrounded by enough oxygen* bursts into flame when ignited. Moreover, he will use experience to see that a certain piece of paper has all the properties mentioned in his more complex generalization before concluding that it will burst into flame. All of this led Hume to say that "an unexperienced reasoner could be no reasoner at all, were he absolutely unexperienced; and when we assign that character to any one, we mean it only in a comparative sense, and suppose him possessed of experience, in a smaller and more imperfect degree."[9] One cannot help feeling that in 1787, Hamilton, born in 1755, Madison, born in 1751, and Jay, born in 1745, would have been encouraged—if they had read this passage in Hume—to think that they had enough experience to discover certain principles about human nature and to apply them successfully while making and defending the Constitution.

I now want to add some further remarks about philosophical terminology in order to make a point that will help us understand certain passages in *The Federalist*. It is clear from what we have seen in the writings of Hume that an appeal to what he called "pure experience" in establishing a political maxim was an appeal to history. For him, history supplied experimental or empirical evidence for general propositions in political science but was not to be confused with the latter discipline. According to Hume, there are two kinds of experimental reasoning. One discovers what he calls particular facts and the other discovers general facts; for example, history discovers particular facts but political science discovers general facts. Like physics and medicine, political science inquires into "the qualities, causes and effects of a whole species of objects."[10] In further explication of his view of the relationship between history and those sciences that discover general facts about man, Hume tells us that the chief use of history

> is only to discover the constant and universal principles of human nature, by showing men in all varieties of circumstances and situations, and furnishing us with materials from which we may form our observations and become acquainted with the regular springs of human action and behaviour. These records of wars, intrigues, factions, and revolutions, are so many collections of experiments, by which the politician . . . fixes the principles of his science, in the same manner as the physician or natural philosopher becomes acquainted with the nature of plants, minerals, and other external objects, by the experiments which he forms concerning them.[11]

Hume makes the same point more succinctly in his more popular essay "Of the Study of History," where he writes that "history is not only a valuable part of knowledge, but opens the door to many other parts, and affords materials to most of the sciences."[12] In the same essay, Hume distinguishes between what Machiavelli says when he talks as a "politician"—meaning a political scientist—and what he says "when he speaks as an historian, in his particular narrations."[13] It is important to recognize, therefore, that although Hume says that the chief *use* of history is to discover the constant and universal principles of human nature, he does not think of those principles as propositions *in* the discipline of history but rather as propositions in what later came to be called the generalizing sciences such as psychology or political science.

Because I have been expounding Hume in order to illuminate certain parts of *The Federalist*, I think that it would be best to sum up those views of Hume that will be most useful when I try to cast some philosophical light on the American document which is my primary concern. (1) The first point to bear in mind is Hume's distinction between reasoning in the demonstrative science of mathematics—which is *not* in his view experimental or empirical—and reasoning in what he called experimental science—which *is* based on experience. The former sort of reasoning concerns relations between ideas whereas the latter concerns what Hume calls matter of fact and existence. He held, therefore, that we do *not* need to study anything but the relations between ideas when establishing mathematical truths, but we *do* need to appeal to experience in order to establish propositions in the experimental or empirical sciences. (2) Hume said that some writers make a false or at least superficial distinction between truths in political science which are established by a priori reasoning and truths which are established by "pure experience" or by "sense and observation." He argued that both the so-called a priori method and the a posteriori method appeal to experience, albeit in different ways. (3) Hume distinguished between experimental reasoning in political science, where we deal with general facts, and experimental reasoning in history, where we deal with particular facts.

The relevance of all of this to the method of *The Federalist* will become more evident in later chapters, but it will be helpful to say a few words here in anticipation of what will emerge, I hope, with greater clarity later on. By and large, the authors of *The Federalist* had little occasion to use the method of demonstrative science as conceived by Hume since they were not engaged in mathematical inquiries. On the other hand, there is no doubt that they tried to defend many general political beliefs by appealing to experience in a manner about which Hume could not complain on epistemological grounds. Sometimes they defended such beliefs by using what Hume and Mill called the (ultimately empirical) a priori method, sometimes by using the method that Hume called the method of pure experience or history and Mill called the a posteriori method or the method of direct induction, and sometimes by using both of these methods to lend double support to one and the same belief. In spite of an occasional lapse in the direction of rationalism when they claimed to be "demonstrating" truths in political science as if they were mathematical truths, the authors of *The Federalist* were overwhelmingly Humeian in their methodology or epistemology of political science. When they used the a priori method and operated as what Mill called "theorists," they made generalizations about human nature that they regarded as ultimately based on experience.

Hume vs. Locke on Morality as a Demonstrative Science

However, there is no hint in *The Federalist* that Publius subscribed to Hume's views in ethical theory. There is no evidence to show that Publius maintained, as Hume had, that virtue is *by definition "whatever mental action or quality gives to a spectator the pleasing sentiment of approbation;* and vice the contrary." In accepting this definition, Hume implied that any statement in which we attribute "a blemish, a fault, a vice, a crime" is synonymous with a statement which asserts that something gives a spectator the painful sentiment of disapprobation. The most important thing about Hume's definition from our point of view is that it converts a statement about the virtue or moral criminality of an action into a statement about a spectator's *sentiment,* and that is why Hume's view may be regarded as inconsistent with what appears to be Publius's view of ethical statements. If he had accepted Hume's definition, he would have been forced to say that any statement about the virtue of an act or of an individual was synonymous with a statement about the sentiments of a spectator, but I think it is clear that neither Madison nor Hamilton would have accepted this view; they would not have agreed with Hume's appeal to sentiment in defining "vice" or "virtue."[14]

It is a curious fact that students of *The Federalist* who stress the influence of Hume on that work, and especially his influence on Madison, rarely consider the implications of another passage in Hume that is a commonplace among philosophical students of Hume's ethics. It occurs in Appendix I of his *Enquiry Concerning the Principles of Morals* and contains an exchange in which a man is asked why he takes exercise, to which he replies that he desires to keep his health. When he is asked why he desires his health, he is said to reply that he does so because sickness is painful. But, Hume says, "If you push your enquiries farther, and desire a reason *why he hates pain,* it is impossible he can ever give any. This is an ultimate end, and is never referred to any other object."[15] Ultimate ends of human actions can never, Hume also says, "be accounted for by *reason,* but recommend themselves entirely to the sentiments and affections of mankind, without any dependance on the intellectual faculties."[16] So far as I can see, there is no evidence in *The Federalist* or in other writings of Hamilton or Madison that they were prepared to accept the views that Hume expressed in this passage. A twentieth-century commentator on Hume's ethical views has plausibly argued that one consequence of Hume's view "is that every dispute on questions of right and wrong is capable of being settled completely by the simple method of collecting statistics," and it is highly unlikely—as we shall see later—that Madison would have accepted Hume's ethical views if he had interpreted them in this way.[17] The idea that we determine the justness or unjustness, the rightness or wrongness, or the virtue or vice of an action by seeing whether it produces certain sentiments was probably anathema to Madison, who believed that an action could be unjust even if many persons were thoroughly pleased by it. Madison and Hamilton were, as we shall see, sympathetic to the rationalistic views of Locke on the foundations of ethics. Consequently, I want to say something further about Locke's views by comparison with Hume's in the theory of ethical knowledge.

Unlike Hume, Locke believed that morality could be shown to be a demonstrative science like mathematics. Locke realized that in order to construct a demonstrative science of morality, he would have to set forth self-evident or intuitively known primary truths or axioms, and from these, through the use of deduction, derive the principles of morality, which contained the doctrine of natural law as a part. And although he never succeeded in constructing the science of morality he thought possible, he tried to describe what an axiom of such a science would be like. It would have to be a self-evident truth, namely, a truth to which we assent immediately upon hearing the terms that it contains. In saying that such a truth is intuitively known, he meant that the mind can, as he put it, immediately perceive the agreement or disagreement of the ideas expressed by the terms. In this way, he said, we see that white is not black, that a circle is not a triangle, that three is greater than two. His point is that we do not have to introduce any other idea between the idea of a circle and the idea of a triangle to see that the former excludes the latter. This kind of knowledge, he pointed out, "is irresistible, and like the bright Sun-shine, forces it self immediately to be perceived, as soon as ever the Mind turns its view that way; and leaves no room for Hesitation, Doubt, or Examination, but the Mind is presently filled with the clear Light of it."[18] Such intuitively known or self-evident truths could, Locke thought, be used as axioms from which we might then deduce ethical truths in the theory of natural law. Even the Golden Rule, which Locke did not think was self-evident, could, he thought, be deduced from axioms which, however, he never produced in any system of ethics of the kind he thought possible.[19]

I need not say much more at this point about Locke's views about a demonstrative science of morality but I do want to emphasize that Hume did not agree with them. Hume denied that morality was a demonstrative science and, at certain places in his writing, even denied that it was an experimental science. I think Hume was inconsistent when he denied that ethics was an experimental science and also held that we examine a plain matter of fact in deciding whether an action is virtuous or vicious. But since Hume is not my main subject here, I need not say more about that inconsistency. No matter what affirmative doctrine of morals Hume held, we must remember that he attacked Locke's doctrine in a way that did not command the agreement of Madison and Hamilton. Hume wrote, as he clearly referred to Locke and others like the philosopher Samuel Clarke without mentioning them by name: "There has been an opinion very industriously propagated by certain philosophers, that morality is susceptible of demonstration; and tho' no one has ever been able to advance a single step in those demonstrations; yet 'tis taken for granted, that this science may be brought to an equal certainty with geometry or algebra. Upon this supposition, vice and virtue must consist in some relations [between ideas]; since 'tis allow'd on all hands, that no matter of fact is capable of being demonstrated."[20] Hume flatly denied that morality could be established merely by comparing ideas, and this is the important thing for the student of *The Federalist* to keep in mind. There is no evidence that the authors of that work agreed with Hume's criticism of Locke's rationalism in ethics even though they agreed with Hume on the methodology or epistemology of political science and on other matters. Locke's moral doctrine of natural law was accepted by Publius, and the views he advanced on the epistemology of that doctrine were Lockeian rather than Humeian. In this chapter, I have tried to prepare the way for showing the hybrid nature of the philosophy to be found in *The Federalist*—how it appeals to Locke's ethics and theory of ethical knowledge as well as to Hume's experimental political science and his epistemology of experimental science. I am mainly concerned to stress the eclectic nature of Publius's thinking on certain philosophical questions and to show how questionable it is to trace it all to Locke, or all to the Scottish philosophy, or all to Hume, or all to any one philosopher or school of philosophers. Like many debating politicians, Hamilton, Jay, and Madison were often willing to pick up whatever philosophical muskets they could respectably shoot at those who attacked the Constitution they sought to defend.[21]

III

THEORY
OF KNOWLEDGE

3

Using Abstract Reason
in Morals and Politics

Although I have been emphasizing up to now that Jay, Madison, and Hamilton were predominantly Humeian empiricists in their epistemology of political science and Lockeian rationalists in their views on morals, I believe there are signs of what I have called rationalism in their defense of political as opposed to moral truths. There are, I mean, places at which Hamilton maintains that he can demonstrate by abstract reasoning what Hume would have called a belief about political fact. In other words, Hamilton maintained that he could logically deduce some truths in the science of politics from self-evident or intuitively known axioms, meaning propositions which Hamilton thought could be certified merely by examining the relationship between ideas. Let me say parenthetically that not every appeal to "reason" in *The Federalist* should be taken as a sign of anti-Humeian rationalism. Sometimes the word "reason" was used by Publius in the manner described by Hume when he allowed that certain principles of experimental science may be supported by reason as distinguished from "pure experience"; and in the next chapter I shall present some examples of this nonrationalistic use of the a priori method in *The Federalist*. In the present chapter, however, I want to show how rationalistic Publius could sometimes be when discussing the epistemology of morals, and how rationalism could even creep into his epistemology of political science. Before doing so, I want to call attention to passages which show that the authors of *The Federalist* accepted the substantive moral doctrine of natural rights and the theory of the social contract.

Natural Law and Natural Rights:
Publius's Substantive Moral Philosophy

A. O. Lovejoy once wrote that "the ablest members of the Constitutional Convention were well aware that *their* task—unlike that of the Continental Congress of 1776—was not to lay down abstract principles of political philosophy, not to rest the system they were constructing simply upon theorems about the 'natural rights' of men or of States, though they postulated such rights. Their problem was not chiefly one of political ethics but of practical psychology. . . ."[1] Although natural rights were not discussed at length in *The Federalist*, Lovejoy was quite correct when he said that some members of the Convention had postulated them; the moral ideas of the Declaration of Independence had not disappeared when it came time to make the Constitution, even though very little of *The Federalist* was given over either to substantive or to epistemological discussion of natural law and natural rights. And it is easy to see why. *The Federalist* was written very hastily in order to expedite the ratification of the Constitution. Therefore, the authors must have thought it unnecessary and even dangerous to devote too much space to highly technical problems of philosophy by trying to define the difficult concept of a natural right or trying to state the conditions under which we may say that we have such a right. After all, readers of *The Federalist* were quite familiar with examples of the concept of natural right such as the right to liberty and the right to property, both of which are frequently mentioned in *The Federalist*—familiar enough to make it unnecessary for the authors to become entangled in efforts to define natural rights or to state the grounds for believing that men have them. Such abstract philosophical discussion might well have confused some of Publius's readers while it gave others the opportunity to engage in what he regarded as irrelevant controversy and logic-chopping. On the other hand, a philosophical historian of ideas—unlike those running readers of 1787 who snapped up issues of *The Independent Journal, The New York Packet, The Daily Advertiser,* or *The New-York Journal and Daily Patriotic Register*—has a right, and even a duty, to say something about the doctrine of natural law and of natural rights as that was understood by Publius. For this reason, I want to give a brief account of what the authors of *The Federalist* believed about natural rights and natural law, however glancingly they may have dealt with these matters in their very practical work. In trying to show what they believed, I shall refer not only to what they said in *The Federalist* itself but also to views they expressed in other places, views they continued to hold while writing *The Federalist*.

Early in *The Federalist*, namely, in *Number 2*, John Jay wrote that nothing is more certain than the necessity of government and, furthermore, that it is equally undeniable that whenever and however government is instituted, "the people must cede to [government] some of their natural rights, in order to vest [government] with requisite powers."[2] But, with characteristic philosophical brevity, Jay made no attempt to say what natural rights are, nor did he bother to expound the theory of the social contract which he was assuming.

Jay's brief reference to natural rights in *Number 2* is matched by Madison's equally brief remark in *Number 43* concerning "the great principle of self-preservation; . . . the transcendent law of nature and of nature's God, which declares that the safety and happiness of society are the objects at which all political institutions aim, and to which all such institutions must be sacrificed."[3] Here, of course, we find direct echoes of the Declaration of Independence in the phrase "law of nature and of nature's God" and in the word "happiness"; and an indirect echo of the Declaration's right of life in Madison's word "self-preservation." However, we find no analysis of the concepts expressed by these words even though we find Madison making a moral assertion about the conditions under which we have a right to supersede a compact. Madison asks: "On what principle [can] the confederation, which stands in the solemn form of a compact among the States, . . . be superceded [*sic*] without the unanimous consent of the parties to it?"[4] And his answer to this question reminds us of an ethical passage in the Declaration of Independence. Madison says that "the absolute necessity of the case"[5] will justify superseding the confederation, that is, the states' compact with each other, without the unanimous consent of the parties to that compact. I have in mind that part of the Declaration which says that governments long established should not be changed for light and transient causes; that a long train of abuses and usurpations evinces a design to subject the colonies to absolute despotism; and that it is not only their right but their *duty* to throw off such a government. At this point, it will be recalled, the Declaration says: "Such has been the patient sufferance of these colonies, and such is now the *necessity* [my emphasis] which constrains them to alter their former systems of government." Thus the Declaration's moral "necessity" or duty to make the revolution corresponds to the "absolute necessity" that Madison thinks would justify superseding a compact without the unanimous consent of the parties to it.[6] In this part of *The Federalist* Madison makes an ethical statement just as the Declaration does when it speaks of *duty* and of the moral *necessity* which *constrains* the colonies to rebel.[7] In 1787 Madison accepted a Lockeian moral philosophy of natural rights and natural duties even though he did not systematically defend that moral philosophy in *The Federalist*.

This is especially evident in *Number 51* when Madison writes about the anarchy that reigns in a society where the stronger or majority faction can readily unite and oppress the weaker or minority faction. In that number Madison compares this anarchy with that in a state of nature, where the weaker *individual,* as opposed to the weaker *group* in civilized society, is not secured against the stronger. Madison observes that in a state of nature even "the stronger individuals are prompted by the uncertainty of their condition, to submit to a government which may protect the weak as well as themselves." This observation is reminiscent of Locke's observation in his *Second Treatise* that individuals will give up some rights that they have in a state of nature because the enjoyment of such rights "is very uncertain, and constantly exposed to the Invasion of others."[8] And when Madison goes on to say in *Number 51* that a majority faction in a small, nonfederal republic will be prompted by an uncertainty like that of a strong individual in a state of nature "to wish for a government which will protect all parties, the weaker as well as the more powerful," Madison seems to exploit an analogue of a Lockeian idea in order to buttress his own idea that majority factions will be induced to seek an extended federal republic which will prevent majority factions themselves from forming and oppressing others. Here, then, Madison predicts that the self-interest of factious oppressors will lead them to do something which he thinks they are morally obligated to do, namely, to avoid acting tyrannically.

Madison's view in *Number 51* that a state of nature is one in which anarchy may be said to reign is also reminiscent of Locke's view that in a state of nature *"every one has the Executive Power* of the Law of Nature" and therefore that in such a state men will "be Judges in their own Cases."[9] Madison shows that he morally condemns such a state when he says in *Number 10* that the most important acts of legislation in modern government are acts in which legislators serve as judges as well as advocates and parties, thereby introducing the evil spirit of faction into the necessary and ordinary operations of government. Madison also says in *Number 10* that precisely because legislative factions act as judges in their own cases, the stronger faction, rather than justice, must be expected to prevail.[10] This contrast between strength and justice was as fundamental in Madison's thinking as it was in Locke's. Madison believed that a society in which natural rights are not safe is not a just society, and he held that the transcendent law of nature and nature's God declares that societies should protect private rights and promote the public good. But how does Madison support this "transcendent law"? Though he does not tell us in *The Federalist,* I think that he, like Hamilton, would have associated himself with Locke by calling the law of nature and of nature's God a self-evident proposition or one that could be derived from a self-evident proposition.

The influence of Locke on Hamilton's substantive doctrine of natural rights—as well as on his epistemology of morals—may be seen in views which he had advocated as a young revolutionary, views which he continued to advocate in *The Federalist.* Replying in 1774 to a pseudonymously published pamphlet by "A. W. Farmer," Hamilton writes as follows in "A Full Vindication of the Measures of Congress, etc.": "All men have one common original: they participate in one common nature, and consequently have one common right. No reason can be assigned why one man should exercise any power, or pre-eminence over his fellow creatures more than another; unless they have voluntarily vested him with it."[11] It may be noted here that Hamilton's idea that "all men have one common original" is similar to Locke's remark in his *Second Treatise of Government* that all men are "the Workmanship of one Omnipotent, and infinitely wise Maker."[12] Hamilton's idea that all men "participate in one common nature" is similar to Locke's idea that men are "Creatures of the same species and rank promiscuously born to all the same advantages of Nature, and the use of the same faculties."[13] And Hamilton's inference from the fact that men have one common nature and origin to the conclusion that they have "one common right" reminds one of Locke's inference from the fact that men are "Creatures of the same species and rank promiscuously born to all the same advantages of Nature, and the use of the same faculties," to the conclusion that men *should* also be "equal one amongst another without Subordination or Subjection, unless the Lord and Master of them all, should by any manifest Declaration of his Will set one above another, and confer on him by an evident and clear appointment an undoubted Right to Dominion and Sovereignty."[14]

It will be observed that Hamilton, as he moves from "one common nature" to "one common right," does not repeat Locke's stipulation that having one common nature implies equality without subordination only if God does not clearly set one man above another. However, in the very next sentence Hamilton introduces a different stipulation which *is* Lockeian: he says that no man should have more power or preeminence over his fellow creatures than another *unless* the *fellow creatures* of that man have voluntarily vested him with it. Locke, of course, held that such creatures could cede that *"equal Right* that every Man hath, *to his Natural Freedom,* without being subjected to the Will or Authority of any other Man."[15] They could do so by vesting the power or preeminence of which Hamilton speaks in what Locke calls a "Judge on Earth, with Authority to determine all the Controversies, and redress the Injuries, that may happen to any Member of the Commonwealth; which Judge is the Legislative, or Magistrates appointed by it."[16] This vesting is part of Locke's theory of the social contract, which Hamilton seems to have adopted in the passage I have quoted from his "Full Vindication" of 1774. In that piece Hamilton's agreement with Locke is indicated not only by Hamilton's acceptance of the theory of the social contract but also by his condemnation of his opponents as "enemies to the natural rights of mankind" who "wish to see one part of their species enslaved by another."[17] In his "Full Vindication" he declares that "self preservation is the first principle of our nature."[18] And in "The Farmer Refuted," published by Hamilton in 1775 as a rebuttal to "The Farmer's" reply to "A Full Vindication," Hamilton said: "Apply yourself, without delay, to the study of the law of nature. I would recommend to your perusal, Grotius, Pufendorf, Locke, Montesquieu, and Burlamaqui."[19]

As we read on in "The Farmer Refuted," we can see further evidence of Hamilton's Lockeian attachment to natural law, natural rights, and the social contract, as well as evidence of his disapproval of Hobbes, whom he criticized as the defender of the "absurd and impious doctrine" that virtue is a purely artificial contrivance of politicians for the maintenance of social intercourse. Hobbes, Hamilton went on, accepted this doctrine because he was an atheist who "disbelieved the existence of an intelligent superintending principle, who is the governor, and will be the final judge of the universe." By contrast to Hobbes, said Hamilton, good and wise men have in all ages "supposed, that the deity, from the relations, we stand in, to himself and to each other, has constituted an eternal and immutable law, which is, indispensibly [*sic*], obligatory upon all mankind, prior to any human institution whatever."[20] This eternal and immutable law, Hamilton continued in by now predictable fashion, "is called the law of nature." He then quoted an appropriate passage from Blackstone's *Commentaries* and announced that "upon this law, depend the natural rights of mankind." Hamilton insisted that to deny the principles of natural law "will be not less absurd, than to deny the plainest axioms,"[21] thereby anticipating something he came to say in *Number 31* about "primary truths."

Before leaving Hamilton's "Full Vindication" and his "Farmer Refuted" it may be well to mention a few other passages in which he reveals the extent of his attachment to natural law and natural rights. He says, for example, to his opponent: "The fundamental source of all your [Farmer's] errors, sophisms and false reasonings is a total ignorance of the natural rights of mankind. Were you once to become acquainted with these, you could never entertain a thought, that all men are not, by nature, entitled to a parity of privileges. You would be convinced, that natural liberty is a gift of the beneficent Creator to the whole human race. . . ." He also says: "The right of colonists, therefore, to exercise a legislative power, is an inherent right. It is founded upon the right of all men to freedom and happiness."[22] And after a long legal discussion of the charters of the colonies, in which he tries to refute "The Farmer's" views, Hamilton tells his reader: "There is no need, however, of this plea: The sacred rights of mankind are not to be rummaged for, among old parchments, or musty records. They are written, as with a sun beam, in the whole *volume* of human nature, by the hand of the divinity itself; and can never be erased or obscured by mortal power."[23] Finally, I quote a passage in which Hamilton says something very much like what Madison says in *The Federalist* and what Jefferson says in the Declaration about the moral right and even the moral duty or necessity of superseding a compact under certain circumstances by appealing to the law of nature. Hamilton declares:

> When the first principles of civil society are violated, and the rights of a whole people are invaded, the common forms of municipal law are not to be regarded. Men may then betake themselves to the law of nature; and, if they but conform their actions, to that standard, all cavils against them, betray either ignorance or dishonesty. There are some events in society, to which human laws cannot extend; but when applied to them lose all their force and efficacy. In short, when human laws contradict or discountenance the means, which are necessary to preserve the essential rights of any society, they defeat the proper end of all laws, and so become null and void.[24]

A dozen years later Hamilton continued to accept the general principle of this Lockeian outburst. In *Number 28* he said that if the representatives of the people betray their constituents by failing to put down an insurrection, "there is then no resource left but in the exertion of that original right of self-defence, which is paramount to all positive forms of government."[25]

Rationalism in Publius's Theory of Ethical Knowledge

In 1787, therefore, Hamilton was still an advocate of the natural rights about which he had written so passionately before the Revolution. No matter how constructive the framers of the Constitution and the authors of *The Federalist* had become, they continued to believe in the natural rights upon which they had rested their rebellion against Great Britain, even though they did not think that their chief problem was one of political ethics. Hamilton plainly revealed that he continued to accept Locke's theory that morality could become a demonstrative science and that he, Hamilton, was prepared to use it against opponents of the Constitution with all the vehemence he had summoned when using it against opponents of the Revolution. In *Number 31,* as we know, Hamilton says that moral statements which he calls primary truths or first principles "contain an internal evidence, which antecedent to all reflection or combination commands the assent of the mind." In this respect, he goes on to say, moral maxims resemble maxims in geometry such as "The whole is greater than its part; that things equal to the same are equal to one another; that two straight lines cannot inclose [*sic*] a space; and that all right angles are equal to each other."[26] Hamilton's primary truths express what Locke called intuitive knowledge. They are truths, Locke said, which forced themselves irresistibly on the mind like bright sunshine and which can be established merely by examining the ideas expressed by the words appearing in them, without the intervention of any other idea. To deny them, Hamilton said in 1787, as he had said in 1774 and 1775, would be absurd.

According to Hamilton in *Number 31,* there are ethical maxims of this kind, such as the maxim that "the means ought to be proportioned to the end."[27] In one respect, Hamilton thinks that this maxim resembles the principles of natural law that he had asserted in "The Farmer Refuted" and in "A Full Vindication," principles that he said were "written, as with a sun beam, in the whole *volume* of human nature, by the hand of the divinity itself."[28] But it is equally important to observe that, insofar as Hamilton agrees with Locke that there are self-evident ethical maxims which can be established merely by examining relations between *ideas,* Hamilton sharply diverges from Hume's views in the epistemology of morals. Hamilton does not appeal to Humeian matters of fact or to Humeian sentiment when he treats maxims of morals as he treats maxims of geometry.

Neither does Madison appeal to them in one of his best-known expositions of the natural right to religious freedom, his *Memorial and Remonstrance against Religious Assessments* of June 1785. He begins his argument by asserting "a fundamental and undeniable truth" which he quotes from an article of the Virginia Declaration of Rights, an article he helped draft.[29] Before quoting that truth, I want to remark that in calling it "undeniable," Madison characterized it partly as Jefferson had characterized his "self-evident" truths in the Rough Draft of the Declaration of Independence, where Jefferson had called them "sacred and undeniable" truths.[30] It would seem that Madison not only agreed in his *Memorial and Remonstrance* with some of Locke's substantive views on the relations between church and state, but also, as Jefferson did, with Locke's conception of morality as a demonstrative science that contains undeniable propositions like those in mathematics.[31] The fundamental and undeniable truth which was asserted by Madison and quoted by him from the Virginia Declaration of Rights was "that Religion or the duty which we owe to our Creator and the manner of discharging it, can be directed only by reason and conviction, not by force or violence." Madison goes on to say, as he presumably derives a consequence of this undeniable truth, that "the Religion then of every man must be left to the conviction and conscience of every man; and it is the right of every man to exercise it as these may dictate."[32]

According to Madison, "this right is in its nature an unalienable right," and in support of this statement he gives two reasons which deserve our attention. The first is that the opinions of men—all kinds of opinions—depend only on the evidence contemplated by their own minds and consequently cannot follow the dictates of other men. Therefore, A cannot transfer to B the right of A to judge for himself what opinions to hold, since A can make such a judgment only on the basis of the evidence that A himself contemplates. Certainly, the argument runs, B cannot contemplate that evidence for A and that is why A cannot transfer to B the right to form A's opinions for A. Madison's second reason for asserting the unalienability of the right is that "what is here a right towards men, is a duty towards the Creator." He says that "it is the duty of every man to render to the Creator such homage and such only as he believes to be acceptable to him." This means that A owes it to God to render to God not *any* sort of homage, but only homage that A believes will be acceptable to God.[33] Therefore, A, who has this duty, cannot transfer to B his right to decide for himself what he believes will be regarded by the Creator as acceptable homage. That is what Madison has in mind when he says that the unalienability of the right of religious freedom is based on a connection between that right and a duty that men have to the Creator.

Madison's idea that this right of A is unalienable because of A's duty towards the Creator deserves special notice by anyone interested in Madison's view of how statements about natural rights are to be established. This duty to the Creator is called by Madison a duty which "is precedent, both in order of time and in degree of obligation, to the claims of Civil Society." Before any man can be regarded as a member of "Civil Society," Madison holds, he must be regarded as a subject of "the Governour of the Universe." And just as a member of "Civil Society" who enters into any subordinate association must always do it "with a reservation of his duty to the General Authority," so—to an even greater degree—"must every man who becomes a member of any particular Civil Society, do it with a saving of his allegiance to the Universal Sovereign." Every man's allegiance to the "Universal Sovereign" is what requires "every man to render to the Creator such homage and such only as he believes to be acceptable to him"; and this allegiance or duty to the "Universal Sovereign" is fundamental in Madison's argument for the right of religious freedom. It leads him to insist "that in matters of Religion, no mans [sic] right is abridged by the institution of Civil Society and that Religion is wholly exempt from its cognizance."[34] In short, the statement that every man has the unalienable right of religious freedom is logically derived from the "fundamental and undeniable truth" that every man has a certain duty towards the Creator. Therefore, if this fundamental truth is self-evident, any logical consequence of it is demonstrable in the sense in which Locke thought that all moral principles are demonstrable.

It is important to recognize that, according to Madison, religion consists of speculative or theoretical beliefs and of practical beliefs about the manner in which one should worship God. This helps elucidate a crucial phrase in the "undeniable truth" that Madison quoted from the Virginia Declaration of Rights, the phrase "Religion or the duty which we owe to our Creator and the manner of discharging it." Since Madison held that the word "religion" refers to speculative beliefs about, for example, the existence and attributes of God, and to practical beliefs about the manner in which we ought to worship God, Madison also held that both of these kinds of beliefs "must be left to the conviction and conscience of every man," just as Locke held in his (first) *Letter concerning Toleration.* There Locke says that "whatever profession we make, to whatever outward worship we conform, if we are not fully satisfied in our own mind that the one is true, and the other well-pleasing unto God, such profession and such practice, far from being any furtherance, are indeed great obstacles to our salvation" because they lead to "hypocrisy, and contempt of his Divine Majesty."[35]

Since Madison held that the right to exercise one's religion as one's conviction and conscience dictate is an unalienable natural right, we can see why any attempt to give a so-called operational definition of that right or of its unalienability will run counter to what Madison says in his *Memorial and Remonstrance.* (I say this in anticipation of an extended discussion of this matter in Chapter 11, below.) Because Madison holds that religion is a duty we owe to our Creator, he must hold that the right to exercise that duty will be without anything like an operational definition so long as his term "Creator" is not given an operational definition. Madison's *Memorial and Remonstrance* therefore fortifies the view presented in the previous chapter that a statement which attributes an unalienable natural right to every man was not construed by Madison as a statement in experimental science as conceived by Hume. On the contrary, Madison regarded it as a statement in the abstract science of morality as viewed by Locke, derivable from intuitively known and allegedly self-evident primary truths.

Furthermore, Madison's view of the logical connection between man's rationally discernible duties to God and man's unalienable right to religious freedom was generalized by American colonists so as to apply to other unalienable rights. The general principle, as we have seen, is that if a man has a duty to do something, then he not only has the right to do it but he has an unalienable right to do it. The point is that one cannot transfer to another, or even renounce, a right which follows from a duty that one has. That is why the rights to preserve one's life, to preserve one's liberty, to pursue one's happiness, to arrive at one's own opinions of any kind, and to exercise one's religion in accordance with one's own conviction and conscience were so often said to be unalienable rights in colonial times. They were thought to follow from duties that every man has to his Creator and therefore were not attributed to men in empirical statements but rather in statements which the Lockeian Jefferson, the Lockeian Madison, and the Lockeian Hamilton regarded as truths which could be axioms or theorems in a demonstrative science of morality that Locke thought was constructible but never constructed.[36] Unlike Locke, Hume did not think that such a science of morality was possible but Publius seemed to agree with Locke that it was, and that he could use it quite effectively in his effort to show that the Constitution ought to be adopted. There is no truth that can be more useful to a politician than an allegedly self-evident or undeniable truth when he is trying to win an argument, as anyone may see by reading the Declaration of Independence or *The Federalist.*

Rationalism in Publius's Theory of Political Knowledge

We can see this with particular clarity in *Number 31,* where Hamilton goes as far as he could possibly go in diverging from the epistemology of Hume, for in *Number 31* Hamilton holds that there are primary truths in *politics* which "contain an internal evidence"; and politics, it must be remembered, was for Hume an experimental science which was founded on experience of external objects and therefore could not rest on truths like those to be found in the demonstrative mathematical sciences. It is obvious that in *Number 31* Hamilton diverged from the views of Hume when Hamilton argued for the existence not only of moral but also of political maxims which could be established merely by examining ideas. I grant that the influence of Hume may be seen in many other parts of *The Federalist,* but the difference between Hume's views and those of Hamilton in the epistemology of morals and politics must be faced by any student of *The Federalist* who is tempted to exaggerate the influence of the great Scottish philosopher upon Publius.

The political truth for which Hamilton argued in *Number 31* was the necessity of a general power of taxation in the government of the union, a subject I have discussed at length in another place.[37] Hamilton's departure from Hume's epistemology in trying to deduce this from allegedly self-evident propositions may be made more obvious by turning once again to some of Hume's statements. "It seems to me," Hume says, "that the only objects of the abstract science or of demonstration are quantity and number, and that all attempts to extend this more perfect species of knowledge beyond these bounds are mere sophistry and illusion."[38] And after Hume says that "all the objects of human reason or enquiry" may be divided into two kinds, namely, relations of ideas and matters of fact, he explicitly denies that matters of fact are ascertained in the same manner as that in which we ascertain truths in mathematics, which "are discoverable by the mere operation of thought." Our evidence of the truth of propositions about matters of fact, however great, he continues, is not "of a like nature" with our evidence for the truths demonstrated by Euclid.[39] Yet, in spite of this declaration by Hume and in spite of the admiration that Hamilton expressed for Hume in *Federalist Number 85,* where he called him a writer who was "equally solid and ingenious," there is an argument in that very number which diverges from Hume's philosophy in the direction of rationalism. I have in mind Hamilton's belief that we can demonstrate at least some truths about matters of fact and thereby support such truths with the same sort of evidence that a mathematician can adduce in support of his truths about the relations between ideas. In *Number 85,* Hamilton says that there are instances "in which a political truth can be brought to the test of mathematical demonstration." To be sure, he says that such instances are "rare," but a devout Humeian would never have granted that there could be *any* exceptions to one of the most fundamental principles of Hume's epistemology.[40]

What political truth in *Number 85* does Hamilton think can be mathematically demonstrated and how does he think that it can be demonstrated? Once again the proposition concerns a very important political matter on which Hamilton wished to be as persuasive as possible. In *Number 85* Hamilton tried to answer critics of the Constitution who said that it lacked, among other things, a formal bill of rights and a provision about the liberty of the press. In the course of his answer he urges the adoption of the Constitution as drafted and says to its critics that it would be "far more easy to obtain subsequent than previous amendments to the constitution." And this, he says, appears to him "susceptible of absolute demonstration" for the following reasons. Any alteration in the Constitution he was defending, he says, would have to be approved by thirteen states because it would become, for purposes of adoption, a new Constitution. However, if it were adopted as it then stood, it could be altered, according to the method of amendment specified in Article V of the Constitution, by only nine or ten states. Article V first says that the Congress, whenever two-thirds of both Houses shall deem it necessary, shall propose amendments. Alternatively, on the application of the legislatures of two-thirds of the states, the Congress shall call a convention for proposing amendments. Article V goes on to say that once amendments are proposed, they become valid parts of the Constitution when ratified by the legislatures of three-fourths of the states, or by conventions in three-fourths of the states—depending on which mode of ratification may be proposed by Congress. Two-thirds of thirteen is treated by Hamilton as equal to nine; three-fourths of thirteen is treated as equal to ten. That is why Hamilton says that *nine* or *ten* states may amend the Constitution after ratification; it is nine when one considers *proposal* and ten when one considers *ratification.* After having pointed this out, Hamilton transforms his proposition that it would be "far more easy to obtain subsequent than previous amendments to the constitution"[41] into a probability statement, namely, that "the chances are as thirteen to nine [or ten] in favour of subsequent amendments, rather than of the original adoption of an intire [*sic*] system."[42] This probability statement is the one that he regards as capable of absolute demonstration; it appears to be the same "political truth" that can, in Hamilton's view, "be brought to the test of mathematical demonstration."

I do not wish to discourse at length about the philosophical cogency of Hamilton's view on this matter. However, I do wish to point out that Hamilton's equation of a factual statement about the greater ease with which something can be done in the real world with an allegedly mathematical truth is what leads him to say that at least one political truth is capable of mathematical demonstration. On the face of it, of course, if thirteen votes are legally required to accomplish one thing whereas ten votes are legally required to accomplish another, then *within that legal system* the chances of accomplishing the second thing by comparison to accomplishing the first thing are in the ratio of thirteen to ten. But it is one thing to say what will happen within an artificially constructed legal system and another to say what will happen in the world. Therefore, when Hamilton moves from a constitutional stipulation to a statement about *the ease with which something will happen in the real world of politics,* he would be required, according to a consistent Humeian, to regard the Constitution as *obeyed* in the real world. For that reason, Hume would not have regarded Hamilton's so-called mathematical demonstration of a political truth as a demonstration of a truth in what Hume would have called the experimental science of politics. If Hamilton thought it was, then he was thinking in a manner that he often criticized in *The Federalist,* namely, confusing what is true "on parchment" with what is true of the political world itself.

It is ironical that after allegedly demonstrating a political truth in a mathematical manner, Hamilton not only refers to Hume as a solid and ingenious writer, but favorably quotes the following statement by Hume in his essay "Of the Rise and Progress of the Arts and Sciences": "To balance a large state or society, whether monarchical or republican, on general laws, is a work of so great difficulty, that no human genius, however comprehensive, is able, by the mere dint of reason and reflection, to effect it. The judgments of many must unite in this work: experience must guide their labour: time must bring it to perfection: and the feeling of inconveniences must correct the mistakes which they inevitably fall into, in their first trials and experiments."[43] Hamilton's favorable quotation of Hume in *Number 85* is ironical for obvious reasons. To call upon Hume's statement that experience should guide the labor of those who make constitutions after purporting to show that one can establish a political truth by mathematical demonstration is to praise a master's empiricist teachings immediately after abandoning them.

It is true that Hume writes as follows in his essay "That Politics May Be Reduced to a Science": "So great is the force of laws, and of particular forms of government, and so little dependence have they on the humours and tempers of men, that consequences almost as general and certain may sometimes be deduced from them, as any which the mathematical sciences afford us."[44] But it will be noted that Hume describes these consequences as being *almost* as general and certain as any which the mathematical sciences afford us; he does not go any further in the direction of violating his sharp distinction between the experimental science of politics and the mathematical sciences. By contrast, Hamilton definitely violated that distinction in *Num-*

ber 85. In doing so, he showed that he could be an anti-Humeian in his epistemology of political science as well as in his epistemology of morals. He used what Hume called abstract reasoning in two areas where Hume thought it could not be used: in morals and in politics.[45] And this is what I meant when I said at the beginning of this chapter that Publius was a rationalist in the epistemology of moral knowledge and that he occasionally succumbs to the influence of rationalism in his defense of some political truths.

4

Using Experience and History in Politics

While Hamilton made occasional appeals to self-evidence and to the alleged mathematical demonstrability of political truth in a rationalistic manner, the authors of *The Federalist* usually argued in a Humeian fashion by resting their political beliefs on history and experience and not on the relationship between ideas. Thus, although Madison used elementary mathematics in *Number 10,* he did not say there that he was *demonstrating* a truth in political science. In the same spirit, a Humeian empiricist would not have concluded that physics was a demonstrative science simply because physicists used arithmetic. In spite of their rationalistic views of natural law and their occasional lapses into rationalism when defending certain political truths, the authors of *The Federalist* were primarily empiricists in the epistemology of political science. They appealed to different kinds of experience in support of their political beliefs. They appealed to their broad experience of how all men behave; they appealed to a narrower experience of how specific kinds of men behave under certain circumstances; they appealed to experience of past individual events; and they appealed to experience of current individual events. They tended to equate experience with history and, like Hume, they thought that history dealt with particular facts whereas political science dealt with general facts. The significance of these observations about the views of Publius will, I hope, become clearer in what follows.

Reason Without Rationalism in Politics

We may see how Madison could *use* mathematics without thinking that he was engaged in mathematical demonstration by examining an argument he offered in what has become the most famous of all the papers, *Number 10.* There he tries to show that a large republic, by which he means a large representative democracy or one that contained a large number of citizens,

38

was more likely to elect a good body of representatives than a small republic. He says, first of all, that however small a republic may be, the representatives must be raised, as he puts it, "to a certain number, in order to guard against the cabals of a few." And, second, he says that however large the republic may be, the number of representatives must have some upper limit "in order to guard against the confusion of a multitude." But now Madison tries to derive some conclusions from these and other factual assumptions or hypotheses. He says that because the number of representatives has a lower and an upper limit, the ratio of representatives to constituents will be greater in a smaller republic. No matter how small the republic is, the fact that its representatives cannot, by hypothesis, drop below a certain number will keep the ratio of representatives to constituents relatively large. On the other hand, in a larger republic, or one with many constituents, the fact that the number of representatives cannot, by hypothesis, exceed a certain number will make for a smaller ratio of representatives to constituents. Furthermore, Madison says, if the proportion of "fit characters" to the number of constituents is not smaller in the large republic than it is in the small republic, the probability is greater that a large republic will choose a superior group of representatives. The main point is that the relatively small number of representatives' seats will be open to a larger number of able persons in a large republic.[1]

After reflecting on this passage in *Number 10,* we may ask, as we did when considering Hamilton's efforts in *Number 31* and *Number 85,* whether Madison *mathematically demonstrated* a political truth in the sense in which Hamilton claimed to have done so in *Number 85.* It seems obvious to me that Madison did not, though I should add that, unlike Hamilton, Madison never said that he had. The point is that in the course of arriving at his conclusion Madison assumes certain propositions, as Hume would have said, about matters of fact. Madison assumes that there is a maximum and a minimum number of representatives in the hypothetical republics about which he speaks; he also assumes that the proportion of fit characters is not less in a large than in a small republic. And because he makes at least one assumption that is, in Humeian terminology, not mathematical but factual, he is not able to produce a mathematical demonstration of the factual "political truth" that "extensive Republics are most favorable to the election of proper guardians of the public weal."[2] At best we may think of him as having offered the sort of argument that Hume described when he allowed that in political science we can sometimes deduce empirical conclusions from premises that are themselves empirical. In other words, Madison offers an argument that uses reason but not in a way that would justify our calling his argument rationalistic.

The argument of Madison that I have just examined is not the only example in his writings of the use of reason without rationalism in politics. Therefore I want to present another example of his which shows more readily how he could make an explicit appeal to reason in order to support a factual political truth, but without being committed to the sort of anti-Humeianism that Hamilton occasionally adopts. In *Federalist Number 63* Madison tries to rebut the view of those who opposed Article I, Section 3, paragraph 1 of the original Constitution, which dictates the appointment of senators for six years by state legislatures and therefore not directly by the people. Opponents of the unamended Constitution argued that a senate formed in this way "must gradually acquire a dangerous preeminence in the government, and finally transform it into a tyrannical aristocracy."[3] Madison replies in *Number 63* that this suspicion should not be harbored, and says that both reaon and experience condemn it.[4]

How does *reason* condemn it? Madison answers that reason can show that if a transformation of the planned government into a tyrannical aristocracy were to be made, the senate would first have to corrupt itself, then corrupt the state legislatures, then corrupt the house of representatives, and finally corrupt the people at large; but, he continues, the senate could not be expected to accomplish all of these four tasks.[5] In saying that *reason* can show all of this, Madison is certainly not engaged in what Hume called demonstrative argument while trying to establish a political truth about matters of fact. No proposition asserted here by Madison has the status of a pure arithmetical truth as viewed by Hume. No one of them would have been regarded by Madison, or by Hume, as supportable merely by examining ideas or relations between ideas. Madison did not think that merely by examining *the idea* of a plotting senator, or *the idea* of corrupting all of the other mentioned sorts of individuals, he could establish that such a senator would have to behave in a certain way in order to produce a tyrannical aristocracy. Nor did Madison regard his belief that a plotting senator could not accomplish the four mentioned tasks as one which was *not* based on experience but rather on an examination of the relations between ideas.

What, then, did Madison have in mind when he said that *reason* condemned the belief that a senate which was indirectly elected for six years could and, indeed, *must* create a tyrannical aristocracy? The first step in any attempt to reply to this question is to point out that, according to Madison, reason supports the subjunctive conditional proposition that if any senate elected according to the originally proposed Constitution were to transform the government into a tyrannical aristocracy, that senate would have to perform four successive but different acts of corruption. So we must first ask how reason would, according to Madison, establish this proposition, and it is here that our earlier discussion of the views of Hume and Mill comes in handy. It will be recalled that when Mill argued, in the manner of Hume, that there was an a priori or rational method as well as an a posteriori method of establishing the factual proposition that a human being in the situation of an absolute king will oppress his subjects, Mill said that by using the a priori method one could show this to be true even if absolute kings had never existed or if history furnished us with no information about the manner in which they conducted themselves. Mill thereby indicated that we might equate this proposition about absolute kings into one having the form "If any human being were an absolute king, he would oppress his subjects"; and this subjunctive conditional statement resembles in a crucial respect what may be attributed to Madison in *Number 63*.

How, we may ask, does Mill's example help us understand what Madison meant when he said that *reason* could establish his own subjunctive conditional statement? For one thing, it helps us see that Madison, through the use of reason, was trying to establish a factual proposition that was supposedly true even though the group of senators mentioned in Madison's proposition never existed. How *could* they have existed before the Constitution had been put into operation? For another thing, Mill's example and what he says about it show that he thought that his proposition about absolute kings could be deduced from more general propositions about human beings. He believes that *any* human being with unlimited power over others would oppress them; he then adds the premise that absolute kings would be human beings with unlimited power over others; and from these two premises he concludes that absolute kings would oppress their subjects. I suggest that Madison meant something analogous when he held that reason could establish his subjunctive conditional statement about an indirectly elected senate. Madison seemed to believe that any human being—or group of human beings—who wished to establish a tyrannical government while working within legal limits such as those imposed by the Constitution would, as a matter of fact, have to perform four acts of corruption. His additional premise was simply that senators bent on tyranny were—or constituted a group of—human beings of this kind; and his conclusion from both premises was that such senators would have to perform four acts of corruption. In other words, Madison thought that he could *deduce* the subjunctive conditional statement in question *by reason* from certain general factual propositions about human beings in certain circumstances *and* certain factual propositions asserting that senators were in such circumstances.

Here it may be helpful to recall something that Mill said when describing the a priori method, namely, that when we appeal to generalizations about human nature, we may appeal to "what passes in our minds."[6] Therefore, in the case of senators, operating within the limits set by the proposed Constitution, Madison seems to ask us to perform a "thought-experiment" which would lead us to see that, as human beings with a certain goal who are in certain circumstances, they would have to perform four acts of corruption in order to achieve their goal. It should be noticed, however, that whatever the premises to which Madison appealed when he called upon "reason," they would have to be what Hume would have called propositions about matters of fact and existence, and therefore Madison could not have used them as premises in a demonstration of the kind to be found in mathematics as viewed by Hume.

Now we must ask about Madison's use of "reason" in showing that it would be impossible to overcome all of the obstacles to tyranny that he mentions. Why does he believe they are insuperable? He does not give a deductive argument for his belief. He simply expresses astonishment that any man might seriously persuade himself "that the proposed senate can, by any possible means within the compass of human address, arrive at the object of a lawless ambition, through all these obstructions."[7] In other words, Madison seems to hold that no matter how corrupt or clever the indirectly elected senators might be, they could not *in fact* surmount the obstacles to tyranny that were put before them in the proposed Constitution. If, in saying that *reason* condemned opposition to the indirect election of senators, Madison thought that the insurmountability of these obstacles could be deduced by reason from certain premises, we must observe, as we did in the case of the subjunctive conditional discussed earlier, that he does not present the premises from which he draws his conclusion about insurmountability. He simply asks the reader to contemplate the obstructions and to recognize that no man could overcome them. Once again he may have been inviting us to perform a thought-experiment and to conclude from it that human beings who were senators, however corrupt and clever they might be, would not perform the four successive acts of corruption required of them by the Constitution and their goal. However, Madison would have been hard pressed to produce fully articulated premises from which this conclusion might have been deduced, just as he would have been hard pressed to write out a full deductive argument for his statement that any group of indirectly elected senators who were bent on establishing aristocratic tyranny would have to surmount the four obstacles that Madison regarded as insuperable. In any event, by keeping in mind the views of Hume (and the later but similar views of Mill), I think we can get a better idea of what Madison may have had in mind when he said that *reason* condemns the suspicion that an indirectly elected senate would produce a tyrannical aristocracy. In effect, I think he was deducing this condemnation from Hume's idea that man was corrupt and frail, but that in this instance man's frailty was too great to permit him to overcome the obstacles that the Constitution had put in the way of his corruption.

Now it is time to say what Madison had in mind when he said that "the same sentence is pronounced by experience."[8] His use of the word "experience" is also illuminated by referring once again to the epistemological views of Hume as formulated in the more explicit language of Mill. It will be recalled that when Mill spoke of the use of direct induction in confirming the statement that absolute kings were likely to employ the powers of government for the oppression of their subjects, he said that this statement could be confirmed by our experience of such kings. As I have said earlier, however, Madison was obviously not in a position to call upon our experience of United States senators in order to show that if indirectly elected for six-year terms, they would achieve tyranny only through surmounting the insurmountable objects put in the way of nonexistent senators by an as yet unratified Constitution. Therefore, Madison could not use what Mill called direct induction or what Hume called pure experience when Hume said "the history of a Tiberius or a Nero makes us dread a like tyranny, were our monarchs freed from the restraints of laws and senates."[9] But Madison thought he could appeal to pure experience about other legislative bodies that he regarded as analogous to the as yet nonexistent senate of the United States.

Madison's argument from this experience of analogous legislatures begins with his citing "the most apposite example" of Maryland, where the senate was, as the federal senate would be according to the Constitution, chosen indirectly; where the senate filled its own vacancies within the term of its own appointment; and where there was no rotation of the kind proposed for the federal senate. In addition, Madison says, some other features of the senate in Maryland would expose it to objections that could not be leveled against the federal senate. So Madison concludes by saying: "If the federal senate therefore really contained the danger which has been so loudly proclaimed, some symptoms at least of a like danger ought by this time to have been betrayed by the senate of Maryland; but no such symptoms have appeared." In fact, Madison goes on to say, critics of Maryland's constitution who had offered arguments like those offered by critics of the proposed federal senate, have been shown to have been excessively anxious. Moreover, Madison adds, the constitution of Maryland has developed an unrivaled reputation for excellence precisely because of the salutary operations of that part of it which concerns the choice and term of its senate.[10] After saying this, Madison cites the examples of Britain, ancient Greece, ancient Rome, and Carthage, where senates did *not* behave as tyrannically as critics of the Constitution thought that the proposed senate would be likely to behave. He points out that the British senate is an hereditary assembly of opulent nobles rather than a senate elected for a term of six years; and that the British house of representatives, instead of being elected for two years by the whole body of the people, is elected for seven years by a relatively small proportion of the people. And yet, so far from leading the nation into a tyrannical aristocracy, even the British upper house, Madison went on, had been unable to resist the continual encroachments of the lower house. While appealing to antiquity on the same subject, Madison tries to offer further reinforcement for his argument from "experience."[11] At the end of *Number 63* he refers to "the conclusive evidence resulting from this asemblage of facts"[12] that he has presented to his reader; and "facts" were, according to Hume, what political science was all about.

Since we have been examining Madison's arguments from an empiricistic conception of reason and from experience, it might be instructive to add that whereas his argument from *reason* is directed at showing that it would be *impossible* for the indirect election of senators to lead to tyrannical aristocracy, his arguments from experience are directed at showing something weaker, namely, that this method of electing senators *would not necessarily* lead to a tyrannical aristocracy.

I want to emphasize that my discussion—in the present and the preceding chapter—of Publius's use of philosophical terms such as "reason," "experience," "primary truths," and "mathematical demonstration" is intended primarily to clarify what Publius was trying to say when he used such terms, and also to show that he was not consistently Humeian in his epistemology of political science. I am inclined to think—though I cannot show this conclusively—that even though all three of the authors of *The Federalist* were Lockeian rationalists in their view of the normative principles of natural law, Hamilton was more conspicuously hospitable than the others to a non-Humeian mode of argument when trying to establish truths in political science. However, in fairness to Hamilton, I must repeat that he was aware that he was straying into non-Humeian rationalism in *Number 85.* Just after he entered what he must have regarded as dangerous philosophical territory, he said the following about his argument against "previous" as opposed to "subsequent" amendment of the Constitution: "If the foregoing argument is a fallacy, certain it is that I am myself deceived by it; for it is, in my conception, one of those rare instances in which a political truth can be brought to the test of mathematical demonstration."[13] In a related expression of hesitancy about political rationalism, Hamilton said in *Number 80:* "If there are such things as political axioms, the propriety of the judicial power of a government being co-extensive with its legislative, may be ranked among the number."[14] The word "axiom," it should be pointed out, is equivalent to the phrase "primary truth" as used by Hamilton in the very rationalistic *Number 31,* and yet here we find Hamilton expressing doubt as to whether there are any such political axioms.

Hamilton's remark on the *rarity* of the instances in which a political truth may be supported by mathematical demonstration and his doubt as to whether there are such things as political axioms show that although he was not a complete Humeian empiricist in his theory of political knowledge, he comes very close to being one. In *Number 6* Hamilton's attachment to empiricism is evident, because there he employs three varieties of experience in support of his belief that the private passions of leading individuals sometimes produce "great national events, either foreign or domestic."[15] He does not say that private passions serve as the only causes of hostility among or within nations but he insists that they have caused disruptions of both kinds. In establishing his causal propositions, he freely appeals to historical experience. Hamilton says that Pericles, in compliance with the resentments of a prostitute, attacked, vanquished, and destroyed the city of Samos; and he adds that the same Pericles, moved by other considerations, "was the primitive author" of the Peloponnesian war. Hamilton goes on to argue that Cardinal Wolsey, motivated by a desire to be Pope, precipitated England into a war with France, and then Hamilton tells similar tales about Madame de Maintenon, the Duchess of Marlborough, and Madame de Pompadour.[16] After Hamilton stops marshaling these historical examples—which, he says, can be supplemented by similar examples that are familiar to his audience—he goes on to say that "those who have a tolerable knowledge of human nature will not stand in need of such lights, to form their opinion either of the reality or extent" of the role of personal considerations in the production of national events.[17] Here we find Hamilton adducing a second kind of experience, the kind to which Hume appealed when he described the fundamentally empirical character of the so-called a priori method in political science. Hamilton maintains here that any individual with an empirically supported knowledge of human nature would agree with him that the passions of leading individuals sometimes play a major part in bringing about national events. But then Hamilton says, as he adds a third kind of confirmatory experience: "Perhaps however a reference, tend-

ing to illustrate the general principle, may with propriety be made to a case
which has lately happened among ourselves. If SHAYS had not been a *des-
perate debtor* it is much to be doubted whether Massachusetts would have
been plunged into a civil war" in 1786–87.[18] Shays's Rebellion is here presented in confirmation of Hamilton's idea that one cause of domestic strife is
to be found in the private passions of individuals. The recency of Shays's
Rebellion led him to speak of "the concurring testimony of *experience* [my
emphasis], in this particular,"[19] but we should not conclude from this that
Hamilton regarded his earlier historical examples, or the observation which
supports knowledge of human nature, as *non*experiential. On the contrary,
Hamilton was using what he regarded as three varieties of experience: that
which supports our general knowledge of human nature, that which supports
causal statements about past historical events, and that which supports causal
statements about current historical events. In this respect his views parallel
those of Madison in *Number 63*. As we have seen, when Madison appealed
to "reason" there, he was ultimately resting on the sort of experience that
supported general knowledge of human nature. And although Madison used
the word "experience" when referring to the contemporaneous example of
Maryland, according to a wider use of that word, examples in the British and
ancient past could also be called objects of experience.[20]

Reason, Long Experience, and Short Experience

With this in mind I want to return to a remark that I quoted in an earlier
chapter, a remark made at the Constitutional Convention by John Dickinson: "Experience must be our only guide. Reason may mislead us."[21] This,
it will be recalled, was also quoted by R. L. Schuyler when trying to show
that the "practical" Madison, like the "practical" Dickinson, did not rely
very much on studies of ancient history, and that it was not Madison's
"classical lucubrations" nor his familiarity with philosophy but rather "his
experience in public life and his wide knowledge of the conditions of his
day . . . that bore fruit at Philadelphia."[22] I have previously noted the irony
of Schuyler's citing Dickinson's highly philosophical remark in order to show
that Dickinson and his colleagues did not seriously rely on philosophy while
they were making the Constitution. What I am more interested in now is what
Dickinson had in mind when he made his remark, and how it is connected
with what I have been saying about the role of experience and reason in
The Federalist.

To get some idea of what Dickinson had in mind, we must turn to the
context in which he was speaking on August 13, 1787. The issue under debate was whether revenue bills should originate only in the lower house of
the legislature. James Wilson and Madison had argued against this, saying
that it had proved to be a source of altercation in every American state where
it had been established in the years after 1776. Dickinson tried to rebut the
views of Wilson and Madison with a lengthy argument that followed his

striking remark that "experience must be our only guide. Reason may mislead us." He elaborated as follows:

> It was not Reason that discovered the singular & admirable mechanism of the English Constitution. It was not Reason that discovered or ever could have discovered the odd & in the eye of those who are governed by reason, the absurd mode of trial by Jury. Accidents probably produced these discoveries, and experience has given a sanction to them. This is then our guide. And has not experience verified the utility of restraining money bills to the immediate representatives of the people. Whence the effect may have proceeded he could not say; whether from the respect with which this privilege inspired the other branches of Govt. to the H. of Commons, or from the turn of thinking it gave to the people at large with regard to their rights, but the effect was visible & could not be doubted. Shall we oppose to this long experience, the short experience of 11 years which we had ourselves, on this subject.[23]

There are two distinctions in this passage that should be kept separate. The first is the distinction between reason and experience; the second is the distinction between long experience and short experience. Since Dickinson does not say enough in his speech about these subjects to permit us to be very confident about what he had in mind, to understand him as well as possible we have to rely on our knowledge of eighteenth-century philosophical usage as well as on our knowledge of what other founding fathers said. I believe that when Dickinson said that reason may mislead us, he probably meant that the a priori method as accepted by Hume and later by Mill was not to be trusted *in the case at hand.* One might easily imagine that Dickinson would hesitate to defend the origination of revenue bills in the House of Representatives by the use of Hume's a priori method. After all, Hume himself, in the very passage that Hamilton cites so praisingly in *Number 85,* says that no one human genius can make a constitution merely by using reason and reflection and that "experience must guide [the] labour" of those who make one.[24] Here Hume was saying in effect that the method of pure experience was the only available method in certain cases. This was the method used by "the experienced statesman, general, physician, or merchant,"[25] the method of the so-called empiric in medicine, which did not proceed by deducing maxims from principles of human nature and other premises. And Dickinson, I submit, was expressing a preference for the method of pure experience when he said that experience must be our only guide and that reason may mislead us. That was probably what he had in mind when he referred to the English Constitution as a singular and admirable mechanism that was not discovered by reason, thereby echoing Hume's remark that "to balance a large state or society, whether monarchical or republican, on general laws, is a work of so great difficulty, that no human genius, however comprehensive, is able, by the mere dint of reason and reflection, to effect it."[26] Hume used the mechanical figure of balancing a complex state on laws, whereas Dickinson used the similar figure of a singular and admirable mechanism in order to emphasize the difficulty that a human reasoner would have in constructing the English Constitution out of his own head, so to speak. And when Dickinson said that "accidents probably produced" the discovery of the English Constitution and trial by jury, he did not mean that they had *no* causes but rather, as Hume might have said, that their causes were unknown because of their complexity.

Having suggested what Dickinson had in mind when he said that reason may mislead us and therefore that experience must be our *only* guide, I now come to the different question as to what Dickinson meant when he said that the Convention should appeal to what he called "long experience" as opposed to "short experience" when trying to decide whether revenue bills should be initiated only in the House of Representatives. Dickinson maintained that the long favorable experience of Great Britain—where the privilege of originating such bills was given to the House of Commons—outweighed the short unfavorable experience of eleven years during which this practice had, according to Madison and Wilson, proved a source of altercation in the American states. However, if we take Dickinson to believe that giving the lower house the power to initiate revenue bills *always* has favorable consequences, then it would seem obvious that Wilson and Madison could refute Dickinson's claim merely by citing the counterexamples provided during the eleven years from 1776 to 1787. If Dickinson held that giving the lower house of a bicameral legislature the power to initiate revenue bills would always have good consequences, then his universal proposition could have been refuted by citing counterexamples from any period of time, past or present.

What, then, shall we say about the views of Dickinson on the relative weight of a long historic experience as against a short recent experience? Once again we may improve our understanding of Dickinson by turning to a passage in which Hume tells us that "though experience be our only guide in reasoning concerning matters of fact; it must be acknowledged, that this guide is not altogether infallible, but in some cases is apt to lead us into errors." Hume illustrates his point by saying that a person who, "in our climate," should expect better weather in any week of June than one in December, would reason correctly and in conformity with experience. But, Hume goes on to say, "it is certain, that he may happen, in the event, to find himself mistaken." In other words, it may turn out that a particular week in June will not afford better weather than a particular week in December. But this, Hume continues, should not give us cause to complain of experience, which itself tells us of the uncertainty involved in predicting weather with complete accuracy. In reasoning about matters of fact, therefore, we can have different degrees of assurance, ranging from certainty to its opposite. In some cases we may expect an event with the highest degree of assurance, but in other cases, Hume says, we must be more cautious; and it is at this point that Hume says things which seem to bear closely on Dickinson's inclination to give more weight to long historic experience than to a short recent experience. Hume tells us that the wise, cautious man weighs the opposite experiments: He considers which side is supported by the greater number of experiments: to that side he inclines, with doubt and hesitation; and when at last he fixes his judgement, the evidence exceeds not what we properly call *probability*. All probability, then, supposes an opposition of experiments and observations, where the one side is found to overbalance the other, and to produce a degree of evidence, proportioned to the superiority. A hundred instances or experiments on one side, and fifty on another, afford a doubtful expectation of any event; though a hundred uniform experiments, with only one that is contradictory, reasonably beget a pretty strong degree of assurance. In all cases, we must balance the opposite experiments, where they are opposite, and deduct the smaller number from the greater, in order to know the exact force of the superior evidence.[27]

This passage in Hume illuminates, I think, Dickinson's willingness to grant that although his view about revenue bills was not in conformity with eleven years of American experience, it was nevertheless correct. If pressed, he might have said that he was merely trying to predict with a high probability that allowing the lower house to initiate revenue bills would have more "utility" than an opposed course of action. Past *English* experience, he might have replied, had provided him with a large number of experiments "on one side"—namely, his own side—whereas recent American experience had provided a small number of experiments on the side of Wilson and Madison. In that case, however, the decision of Dickinson to give less weight to recent American experience would be based not on its *recency* but on the small number of experiments that recent time had provided against initiating revenue bills in the lower house. Analogously, he would be forced to abandon any notion that the *pastness,* so to speak, of past experience gave it greater value as evidence.

The main lesson to be drawn from this excursion into the views of Dickinson is that although Publius and other founding fathers appealed to past historical examples, they do not seem to have regarded them as evidentially superior to current examples when they regarded the examples as equally authentic. They thought that a man who believes that the sun rises every morning may give as strong support to his belief by pointing out that the sun rose on a day twenty years ago as he may by pointing out that it rose on a day last year; and they thought that something analogous was true of the method of supporting probability statements. For them, the fact that a coin turned up head a year ago was on a par with the fact that it turned up head a week ago when they were trying to determine the probability that that particular coin would turn up head. By parity of reasoning, Hamilton's belief that private passion is a cause of national events could be supported, with equal strength, by his citing the behavior of Pericles or by his citing the more recent behavior of Shays. Perhaps Hamilton thought that the vividness of Shays's Rebellion might have made a stronger impression on some of his readers than Pericles's attack on Samos, and perhaps Madison thought that by referring to Maryland's senate in *Number 63* he achieved a similar effect on some readers. On the whole, however, Publius showed no inclination to favor examples on the basis of their recency or their pastness, so long as he accepted the examples as authentic. I grant, of course, that if Publius had been more of a philosopher than he was, he might have worried about the reality of *all* past examples; but there is no sign of *that* sort of epistemological worry in *The Federalist*. In concluding this part of my discussion, I merely wish to point out that Dickinson contrasts "long experience" with "short experience"; he does not contrast "long historic experience" or "long past experience" with "short contemporary experience" or "short present experience." Length is different from being past and shortness is different from being present. It *happens* that the long experience of the House of Commons was in the past whereas the short experience of the American states was in the present for those living in 1787, but that fact was not crucial to Dickinson's argument from long experience. For him, long British experience was a long run of experiences that outweighed the short run of American experiences with regard to originating bills of revenue.

Experience, History, and Political Science

We have seen that the more philosophically minded members of the Constitutional Convention distinguished different kinds of experience in different ways. They distinguished between the extensive experience that would support the most general principles of human nature and the more specific experience that would support less general principles about certain kinds of men; they distinguished between experience of what happened in the past and experience of what was going on during their lives or before their eyes; and they distinguished between a long experience of many events and a short one of fewer events when trying to estimate the probability that a certain political device should be adopted. When they made such distinctions, they used the word "experience" much as Hume had used it, that is, to distinguish between what he called "experimental reasoning" and what he called "demonstrative reasoning." For Hume, all truths in the experimental sciences are supported by experience in this broad sense, though Hamilton, as we have seen, excepted those few political truths that he thought could be demonstrated.

Sometimes the word "history" is used by Publius as an equivalent of "experience," and when he does he reminds one of Locke. In the *Essay Concerning Human Understanding,* after Locke indicates that it is impossible—or at least extremely difficult—to arrive at what he calls the "real essence" of any kind of physical body such as gold, he says that in order to determine whether gold is resistant to heat, "I must apply my self to *Experience.*" He then refers to what he calls "this *way* of getting, and *improving our Knowledge in Substances only by Experience* and History." Here the words "experience" and "history" seem to be interchangeable, so that appealing to experience and appealing to history in this broad sense come to the same thing.[28] Moreover, appealing to them is very different from appealing to a "real essence."

To illustrate these remarks about Publius's empiricistic terminology, I shall begin by referring to some passages that show the extent to which Publius used the word "history" in a general way. When Hamilton tried to dispel the view that the pursuit of a firm and efficient government was carried out by men who sought despotic power and who were hostile to the principles of liberty,[29] he announced that "history will teach us" that those who have paid obsequious court to the people begin as demagogues and end as tyrants, and that members of the party of liberty have done more to bring about despotism than those who have favored firm and efficient government.[30] This kind of appeal to history occurs throughout *The Federalist*. It is a rhetorical device in which the authors merely tip their hats to history without producing any concrete examples to support the general proposition they assert. A somewhat more specific appeal to history in support of a statement about groups of people (as opposed to individuals) may be seen in *Number 5*. In that number Jay says that if America were divided into states or confederacies, there would be a danger that some of these separate bodies might remain neutral when one of their sisters was attacked by a foreign power. They might, he adds in explanation, be flattered into neutrality by false foreign promises or seduced by too great a fondness for peace to come to the aid of neighbors of whom they have been jealous and whose importance they might be content to see diminished. In support of this view of what the separate bodies would do and why they would do it, Jay declares that it would be natural, that the histories of the states of Greece and of other countries abound with instances of such behavior, and that "it is not improbable that what has so often happened, would under similar circumstances happen again."[31] Nothing more is said about the relevant states of Greece and of other countries, so once again no specific evidence is offered for the asserted proposition. It is defended by the use of analogy, but the historical analogue is left in vagueness. A little later Jay shows by his use of classical examples that he was in accord with Hume's observation that mankind is so much the same in all times and places, that history informs us of nothing new or strange with regard to the sentiments, inclinations, course of life, and actions of different nations at different times.[32] Continuing to show his typically colonial penchant for appealing to classical analogies, Jay asks rhetorically: "How many conquests did the Romans and others make in the characters of allies, and what innovations did they under the same character introduce into the Governments of those whom they pretended to protect?"[33] However, once again the historical analogue is very briefly described: "The Romans and others" made conquests while serving as allies; therefore, a danger existed that such a thing might happen again.

I turn now to Publius's tendency to use the word "experience" in a rather general way. Experience is called "that best oracle of wisdom" by Hamilton.[34] In a similar vein, Madison writes that "experience is the oracle of truth; and where its responses are unequivocal, they ought to be conclusive and sacred";[35] Hamilton tells us without further ado that "the experience of all ages" has attested to the truth that the people are always most in danger when the means of injuring their rights are in the possession of those of whom they entertain the least suspicion;[36] Madison says that the errors which may be contained in the plan of the Constitutional Convention resulted from "the defect of antecedent experience" on such a complicated and difficult subject, and not from a want of accuracy or care in investigating it;[37] Madison also says that "a dependence on the people is no doubt the primary controul [*sic*] on the government; but experience has taught mankind the necessity of auxiliary precautions";[38] he advises: "Let us consult experience, the guide that ought always to be followed, whenever it can be found."[39]

The reader of *The Federalist* who keeps his eye on "history" and "experience" will therefore note that these words are often used by Publius merely to show us that he is, for the most part, a philosophical empiricist. In such contexts Publius will refer to history and experience without actually citing historical examples or experiences that seriously support his beliefs in political science. This is a form of epistemological rhetoric which is accompanied by celebration of the achievements of what Hume called the experimental science of politics. In this congratulatory spirit Hamilton announced with satisfaction that

> the science of politics . . . like most other sciences has received great improvement. The efficacy of various principles is now well understood, which were either not known at all, or imperfectly known to the ancients. The regular distribution of power into disinct departments—the introduction of legislative ballances [*sic*] and checks—the institution of courts composed of judges, holding their offices during good behaviour—the representation of the people in the legislature by deputies of their own election—these are either wholly new discoveries or have made their principal progress towards perfection in modern times. They are means, and powerful means, by which the excellencies of republican government may be retained and its imperfections lessened or avoided.[40]

Adair quite rightly maintained that Publius tried to use past history in support of his beliefs in "the science of politics." Adair was especially anxious to stress this in order to refute Schuyler's anti-intellectualistic view that the delegates to the Constitutional Convention did not make serious use of past history and that Madison, for example, relied primarily on "his experience in public life and his wide knowledge of the conditions of his day."[41] This is why Adair seized on Dickinson's appeal to the "long experience" of Great Britain in his speech to the Convention on August 13, 1787. However, in order to make his point, Adair was forced to treat Dickinson's appeal to long experience as an appeal to long *historic* experience and also to blur the difference between history and the precepts of history by appealing to the fact that Publius had been influenced by Hume's writing on this subject.[42] In my opinion, however, this was misleading as an account of what Hume or of what his followers among the founding fathers thought. We have seen that Hume regarded history as a discipline which concerned "particular facts," whereas politics or political science concerned "general facts," and Hume obviously held that precepts or maxims express general facts. By contrast, Hume held that history records particular events such as wars and intrigues which may be recent or remote and which may be cited in support of general propositions that are not in the science of history but rather in politics or political science. Perhaps the difficulty lies in the preposition "of" in the phrase "precepts *of* history." A precept *of* history should not be understood as a proposition *in* the science of history as understood by Hume; it is rather a general proposition in politics which is discovered or established by examining the particular facts studied by the historian. In stressing this I certainly do not dispute Adair's view that Hume and the founding fathers relied on history conceived as experience in supporting many of their political generalizations. Moreover, I heartily agree with Adair when he says that the authors of *The Federalist* were not anti-intellectualists who paid no attention to theory or past history while defending the Constitution. My main concern is to delineate more accurately their conception of the relationship between theory and history.

I hope it is now clear what I think that conception was. I also hope that in the present chapter and in the preceding one I have shown more generally how the authors of *The Federalist* used philosophical terms like "demonstrate," "reason," and "experience" in trying to establish what they regarded as important truths in political science. Although, as I have pointed out, they relied predominantly on history and experience in that enterprise, I have tried to show that Hamilton, for one, did not hesitate to haul up the guns of rationalism to "demonstrate" the necessity for a federal power of taxation or the wisdom of "previous" as opposed to "subsequent" amendment of the Constitution. It is impossible, in my opinion, to gain a thorough understanding of Publius's argument for the truths that were of most concern to him as a practical politician unless we are familiar with his use of certain philosophical terms. They are crucial components of Publius's argument and are not to be dismissed as decorative verbiage nor as what dust sifters find after "dissecting the ideas of other dust sifters." Indeed, even if they were used as mere ornaments—and I do not think they all were—a serious student of *The Federalist* would want to understand them. For how could he show that they were used as mere ornaments or as purely rhetorical embellishment unless he understood them?

IV

PHILOSOPHY
OF HISTORY

5

The Causes of Factions
and the Question
of Economic Determinism

Madison's seemingly empirical view of the causes of factions in *Number 10*
has often been regarded as the most philosophical view expressed in *The
Federalist*. It has been said that this view contained his philosophy of history
and, moreover, that this view anticipated a philosophy of history that is
usually associated with the name of Karl Marx. Before examining this claim,
I want to make a terminological remark about the phrase "philosophy of
history." Contemporary philosophers of history sometimes distinguish between a theory of historical knowledge and a speculative philosophy of
history. The former, they say, is concerned with the nature of history as a
discipline, with the method or methods used in testing historical statements,
and with the relationship between history and other disciplines; the latter
they regard as a general theory about historical events themselves. And since
I have dealt with the theory of historical knowledge that seems to be implicit
in *The Federalist* while discussing the role of history, reason, and experience
in testing the political beliefs held by Publius, I want now to consider some
views of his that have been thought to form part of a speculative philosophy
of history as that term has come to be used.[1]

Such views emerge most conspicuously when Madison discusses the
causes of faction, and they prompt us to ask whether in *Number 10* he
adopted the speculative philosophy of history that Charles Beard attributed
to him in *An Economic Interpretation of the Constitution of the United
States*. In that work of 1913, Beard seems to have regarded Madison as more
of a theoretician than he gave him credit for being when Beard published
The Enduring Federalist of 1948. In *An Economic Interpretation of the
Constitution* Beard said that in *Number 10* Madison had advocated "the
theory of the economic interpretation of history," thereby showing that it was
not a "European importation." In effect, therefore, Beard put Madison's

views in the same discipline as those of Marx, Engels, and others who confidently issued highly general statements about the whole course of history. Exactly which European thinkers Beard was most concerned to deprive of their supposed originality when he praised Madison is of relatively little concern to me here, but I am concerned to say whether we can extract anything as grand and general as a speculative philosophy of history from Madison's observations on the causes of factions.[2] My conclusion is that we cannot; and while defending it I shall have occasion to deal in some detail with Charles Beard's interpretation of *Number 10,* with the links between Madison's views and those of Hume, and with Douglass Adair's illuminating discussion of those links.

Factions in Madison's "Philosophy of History"

When Madison presented what some have called a philosophy of history in his discussion of the causes of factions, he appears to have thought that he was presenting a doctrine about what Hume called general as opposed to particular facts. Madison himself would probably have called his theory of factions a contribution to experimental political science or politics, because he, like his fellow authors, thought that politics inquired into—according to the succinct formula of Hume—"the qualities, causes and effects of a whole species of objects."[3] It is obvious that factions constituted a whole species of objects for Madison and equally obvious that he was interested in their qualities, causes, and effects. He presents what he seems to think is their defining quality early in *Number 10.* "By a faction," he says, "I understand a number of citizens, whether amounting to a majority or minority of the whole, who are united and actuated by some common impulse of passion, or of interest, adverse to the rights of other citizens, or to the permanent and aggregate interests of the community."[4] The effects of factions are also mentioned early in *Number 10.* They are said to be mischievous and vicious because they produce instability, injustice, and confusion, "the mortal diseases under which popular governments have every where perished."[5] And once Madison says that factions produce political disease, he is moved to inquire into their causes. His discussion of their causes earned him Beard's praise for having offered "a masterly statement of the theory of economic determinism in politics."[6] According to Beard, Madison's crucial statement is that

> the most common and durable source of factions has been the various and unequal distribution of property. Those who hold, and those who are without property, have ever formed distinct interests in society. Those who are creditors, and those who are debtors, fall under a like discrimination. A landed interest, a manufacturing interest, a mercantile interest, a monied interest, with many lesser interests, grow up of necessity in civilized nations, and divide them into different classes, actuated by different sentiments and views.[7]

This statement is a pivotal part of Beard's effort to attribute a descriptive speculative philosophy of history to Madison, but we must bear in mind that "faction" as used by Madison might well be regarded as a moral epithet. We must recall that factions, according to what seems to be Madison's definition of them, are actuated by impulses which are adverse to what he sometimes calls the private rights of other citizens or to what he calls the public good. Therefore we must recognize that even though we shall be concerned in this chapter with his view of the causes of factions—and to that extent with what he thinks is a view in experimental or descriptive political science—his own definition of the term "faction" seems to make it a moral term, in which case it might be argued that Madison's fundamental thesis was ethical in character. The point is that the private rights to which the impulses of a faction might be adverse were natural or moral rights for Madison, and the permanent and aggregate interests of the community to which factious impulses might also be adverse in his view were identified by him with the public good. In that case, Madison's thesis about the causes of factions might be regarded as an ethical thesis insofar as it presents the causes of a morally objectionable phenomenon and is therefore not a thesis which contains only descriptive terms. I repeat, however, that Madison himself seems to have regarded his thesis about the causes of factions as an experimental thesis which could be established by history and by appealing to general facts about human beings. Therefore, I shall treat it as such in this chapter and will reserve for a later chapter the questions raised by the ethical character of the term "faction" as defined by Madison.[8]

When Madison says that the various and unequal distribution of property has been the most common and durable source or cause of factions, he implies what he says explicitly in other parts of *Number 10,* namely, that there are other causes of factions besides this economic cause.[9] In order to show why factions should be dealt with by controlling their effects—that is, by preventing them from acting oppressively rather than by removing their causes—he argues against any effort to remove their causes; and I am primarily concerned in this chapter with what he says about these causes. To those who might try to remove political liberty—which is essential to the formation of factions—he says that such a remedy would be worse than the disease itself. To those who might try to remove factions "by giving to every citizen the same opinions, the same passions, and the same interests," he says that this would be "impracticable," meaning impossible to accomplish.[10] And it is during his discussion of the impossibility of giving every citizen the same opinions, the same passions, and the same interests that he expresses beliefs which demonstrate, according to Beard, that Madison is an economic determinist. Beard arrives at his mistaken view by focusing almost exclusively on what Madison says about the impossibility of giving every citizen the same economic interests. Consequently Beard disregards what Madison says about the impossibility of giving every citizen the same opinions and the same passions, and in this way disregards Madison's belief that some factional differences are based on the fact that men will inevitably have different or opposed opinions and that some are based on the fact that men will inevitably have different or opposed passions.

In order to show that factions cannot be eliminated by giving every man the same opinions, the same passions, and the same interests, Madison first argues that we cannot give every man the same opinions. He says that as long as the reason of man continues to be fallible and he is at liberty[11] to exercise his reason, he will form *different* opinions on various subjects. When Madison used the phrase "as long as," I do not think he intended to suggest that there might come a day when the reason of man would *not* be fallible. On the contrary, I think he meant to suggest that the reason of man would continue forever to be fallible. He also seems to think that man's liberty to exercise reason in the formation of opinions would continue to exist forever. So, given the perpetual continuation of man's capacity to err as well as the perpetual continuation of man's freedom to exercise that capacity, men, Madison held, would continue to adopt *different,* that is to say, *opposed* opinions on a given subject.

Because Madison is so brief at this point it is hard to see how he arrives at this conclusion. Why should man's free exercise of his fallible reason lead to *different* opinions on a given subject? Why should it not lead to a uniformity of erroneous opinion? One possible answer is that Madison thought some men would exercise their fallible reason freely to arrive at true opinions on a given subject whereas others would exercise their reason freely to arrive at false opinions on the same subject, thereby arriving at different or opposed opinions on that subject. But difference of opinion does not prevail only when one man has a false opinion on a subject and another has a true opinion on the same subject. Two men may both have false opinions on a given subject and differ, as when they confront each other by asserting what logicians call contrary, rather than contradictory, opinions. One may say that all men are six feet tall and another may say that no men are six feet tall, in which case they will have opposing opinions that are both false. The important thing to observe is not the truth or falsity of the opinions, but the fact that they are different in the sense of opposed. It is the *difference* of opinion between factions that Madison says is inevitable while he is trying to show that the causes of faction are ineliminable.[12]

Madison's next step is to show that *different passions* will also persist throughout history. Once again he uses that phrase "as long as," asserting that "as long as the connection subsists between [man's] reason and his self-love, his opinions and his passions will have a reciprocal influence on each other; and the former will be objects to which the latter will attach themselves."[13] Whatever specific connection between man's reason and his self-love was in Madison's mind when he wrote those words, Madison believed that a man's passions will attach themselves to his opinions, and this, for Madison, is enough to insure the existence of opposing passions once he has shown that men will have opposing opinions. For example, one man may become passionately attached to one proposition while the second becomes passionately attached to the contrary *or* contradictory of that proposition.

And since Madison thinks that opposing passionate attachments to opposing opinions will continue throughout man's history, Madison thinks he has now shown the impracticability of eliminating *different passions* as a way of eliminating factions.

Madison's final step in this part of his discussion—the part upon which Beard concentrates—is to show the impracticability of eliminating *different interests* which arise from "the various and unequal distribution of property." He tries to show this by pointing to the diversity in the faculties of men, to their different abilities. One man—and here I use Locke's famous illustration—may be able to gather more acorns than another; furthermore, one man may be more gifted at gathering acorns while another is more gifted at picking apples. In this way we can see what Madison meant when he referred to "different and unequal faculties of acquiring property": the acorn-gatherer and the apple-picker have *different* faculties of acquiring property whereas the superior acorn-gatherer and the inferior acorn-gatherer have *unequal* faculties of acquiring property. Madison uses neither Locke's example of the acorn-picker nor mine of the apple-picker, but the crucial point in this part of his argument may be illustrated by saying that he believes that the first object of government is to protect such different and unequal faculties of acquiring property by letting the acorn-gatherer acquire acorns if he wishes, letting the apple-picker acquire apples if he wishes, and letting the superior person in either group acquire as many acorns or apples as he wishes. Once government protects these different and unequal faculties, Madison says, "the possession of different degrees and kinds of property immediately results." In other words, there will be men who will possess more acorns than others, and there will be men who will possess acorns as well as men who possess apples simply because they have been allowed through the protective devices of government to exercise their different and unequal faculties.[14] Madison may be interpreted as holding that the fact that men have different—in the sense of distinct—degrees of property and different—in the sense of distinct—kinds of property will have an influence on "the sentiments and views of the respective proprietors"[15] that will produce a division of society into different—in the sense of opposed—interests and factions. All of this goes to show, Madison holds, that there is "an insuperable obstacle to a uniformity of interests."[16] And once Madison reaches this point, he has completed his effort to show that we *cannot* give each citizen the same opinions, the same passions, and the same interests, from which he thinks it follows that we cannot eliminate factions by eliminating their causes.

Since economic interest is, for Madison, the most common and durable source of factions, I want to focus now on the part of his argument in which he tries to show the impracticability of giving every citizen the same economic interests. He begins by asserting that the diversity in the faculties of men is an obstacle to a uniformity of interests; but in order to show that it *is* an obstacle, he must, as we have seen, use additional premises. One is that the object of government is to protect the diversity in the faculties of men so that they can and will exercise their different and unequal faculties; another premise—which is tacit—is that government will in fact accomplish its object. Only by assuming that government successfully protects man's different and unequal faculties of acquiring property will Madison be able to show that "the possession of different degrees and kinds of property immediately results" and therefore that factions based on *different interests* will inevitably exist in society. Consequently, although Madison says that "the latent causes of faction are . . . sown in the nature of man," we must not forget that in his view factions based on economic interests can exist only after government has been established, namely, at a time after man has left the state of nature.[17]

When Madison said that the latent causes of faction are sown in the nature of man, after having said that the first object of government is to protect one of these latent causes—namely, the diversity in the faculties of men from which the rights of property originate—I do not think he meant that governmental protection of man's different and unequal faculties of acquiring property had itself existed from the beginning of man's history. Since Madison accepted the theory of the social contract, he could not have meant that and did not mean that, as is evident from what he says in his famous letter to Jefferson of October 24, 1787.[18] Man may have had different and unequal faculties from the beginning of his history, but government could not have protected, and therefore permitted, the exercise of those faculties from that beginning, simply because government did not exist that early according to the view that the social contract was an actual historical event. Therefore, when Madison explains the origin of factions, he appeals not only to attributes of man which are sown in his nature—such as the fallibility of his reason and his different and unequal faculties of acquiring property—but also to certain events which take place only after government has been instituted. The existence of different property interests is consequently a phenomenon of civil society whose origin or cause is located by Madison in the natural diversity of man's faculties, but in explaining the existence of different interests, he assumes the existence of government and civil society. The diversity in man's abilities to acquire things, according to Madison in *Number 10,* must be protected by government if that diversity is to give rise to "the possession of different degrees and kinds of property."

Madison's views on property may be instructively compared with those of the Swiss jurist Burlamaqui, who exerted so much influence on American revolutionaries. Burlamaqui's right of property is said by him to be adventitious because it does not immediately arise from the primitive constitution of man as God himself established it, independently of any human act. It emerges only after man himself has done something to bring mankind into a new state.[19] The idea that Madison's different amounts and kinds of property arise after civil society has arisen is borne out by what Madison says after telling us that the various and unequal distribution of property is the most common and durable source of factions, namely, that "a landed interest, a manufacturing interest, a mercantile interest, a monied interest, with many lesser interests, grow up of necessity in *civilized* [my emphasis] nations, and divide them into different classes, actuated by different sentiments and views." Madison says that these different property-based interests grow up of necessity *in civilized nations;* he does not say that they grow up of necessity in a state of nature. And this leads me to correct or at least to qualify something that I wrote many years ago, namely, that whereas Marx held that class societies are transient, Madison thought that they were permanent because they were rooted in human nature.[20] Leaving aside the fact that Madison's conception of a faction should not be identified with Marx's conception of a class, I now think it was misleading to say that because Madison's economic factions are rooted in human nature, they were therefore not transient. It is true that in a certain sense of "rooted in," Madison's economic factions may be said to be rooted in human nature because one of their latent causes is a "diversity in the faculties of men." But since Madison says that this latent cause manifests itself in different interests, and therefore in opposed economic factions, only after the intervention of government, it would appear that there was a time when Madison's economic factions did not exist. Furthermore, it would seem to follow that they might cease to exist at such time as government might cease to exist. For these reaons, I am not now inclined to say that, according to Madison, factions are not transient merely because he holds that their latent cause is the diversity of man's abilities. Property-based factions may not exist at certain stages in man's history, according to my present reading of Madison, and in that sense they are not, for him, permanent fixtures of man's history but, at best, permanent fixtures of man's civilized history.

Was Madison an Economic Determinist?

Now that we have some idea of Madison's central views about the different causes of faction, we may discover more easily whether we can extract from *Number 10* what Beard sometimes calls "the theory of economic determinism in politics" and at other times calls "the theory of the economic interpretation of history." To begin with, we had better avoid treating these phrases as though they referred to the same thing. A theory of economic determinism in *politics* is obviously not a theory of all history, so to speak. According to an economic interpretation of all history, the economic basis of a society determines the whole of society's so-called superstructure—which consists of law, philosophy, politics, literature, art, and other elements in what is sometimes called "ideology"—but a theory of economic determinism *in politics* is, on the face of it, more modest in scope.[21] Presumably, it merely asserts some causal connection between economics and politics alone. Yet when Beard attributed a theory of economic determinism in politics *and* a theory of the economic interpretation of history to Madison, he neglected to call attention to this difference even though his own summary of Madison's theory of economic determinism in politics is quite different from the theory of the economic interpretation of history that he cites as authoritative, namely, that presented by E. R. A. Seligman. According to Beard, Seligman said something which was as "nearly axiomatic as any proposition in social science can be," namely:

> The existence of man depends upon his ability to sustain himself; the economic life is therefore the fundamental condition of all life. Since human life, however, is the life of man in society, individual existence moves within the framework of the social structure and is modified by it. What the conditions of maintenance are to the individual, the similar relations of production and consumption are to the community. To economic causes, therefore, must be traced in the last instance those transformations in the structure of society which themselves condition the relations of social classes and the various manifestations of social life.[22]

However, when Beard characterized certain of Madison's words in *Number 10* as a masterly statement of the theory of economic determinism in politics, he attributed the following view to Madison:

> Different degrees and kinds of property inevitably exist in modern society; party doctrines and "principles" originate in the sentiments and views which the possession of various kinds of property creates in the minds of the possessors; class and group divsions based on property lie at the basis of modern government; and politics and constitutional law are inevitably a reflex of these contending interests.[23]

If I were inclined to use the word "axiomatic" freely, I should say that it is axiomatic that the theory that Beard attributes to Madison is different from the theory that Beard quotes from Seligman, and equally axiomatic that Madison did *not* subscribe to the doctrine summarized by Seligman. Nowhere in *Number 10* does Madison say or imply that "economic life is . . . the fundamental condition of all life." And nowhere in *Number 10* does Madison say or imply that "to economic causes . . . must be traced in the last instance those transformations in the structure of society which themselves condition the relations of social classes and the various manifestations of social life." Madison never says anything about economic causes in general. He limits himself to a statement about the causes of *one* manifestation of social life—faction in his sense—a statement in which he says that its most common and durable cause is the various and unequal distribution of property.

Does Beard's summary of the theory of economic determinism in politics accurately represent what may be found in *Number 10?* Like many other readers of Madison and Beard, I think not. When Beard implies without qualification that, according to Madison in *Number 10,* party doctrines and principles—meaning factional doctrines and principles—originate *only* in the sentiments and views which the possession of various kinds of property creates in the minds of the possessors, Beard blatantly disregards other things that Madison said in *Number 10* about opinions or ideas in political life.[24] True, Madison did say that from the influence of different degrees and kinds of property "on the sentiments and views of the respective proprietors, ensues a division of the society into different interests and parties"; and to this extent

Madison may be interpreted as holding that *some* opposing factional "views" or opinions may be linked with the different degrees and kinds of property held by members of opposed factions. For example, Madison says that a difference of opinion may arise about a law concerning private debts in which creditors, who constitute one economic faction, may be pitted against debtors, who constitute an opposed faction. Another difference of opinion may arise over whether domestic manufactures should be encouraged by imposing restrictions on foreign manufactures, and here two economic factions, "the landed and the manufacturing classes," may be on different sides of the question. The apportionment of taxes on different kinds of property is an even more obvious example of an issue that may, according to Madison, produce "different sentiments and views" that are directly based on different economic interests. Nevertheless, these examples in *Number 10* are not enough to justify Beard's flat statement that, according to Madison, "party doctrines and 'principles' originate in the sentiments and views which the possession of various kinds of property creates in the minds of the possessors," as if Madison held that party doctrines and principles originate *only* in this way. The fact is that Madison allowed for the formation of factions on the basis of differences of religious and political belief that were not economically motivated when he plainly implied in a passage *not* quoted by Beard that "a zeal for different opinions concerning religion, concerning Government and many other points" may divide mankind into factions even in the absence of any difference in the kind or amount of property held by members of the factions. Nonetheless, in *An Economic Interpretation of the Constitution,* Beard says without qualification that, according to Madison, "the theories of government which men entertain are emotional reactions to their property interests."[25] Here Beard simply disregarded Madison's remark that factions may be caused by opinions about government that are not necessarily based on economic interests. Beard gives the impression in *An Economic Interpretation of the Constitution* and in *The Economic Basis of Politics* that Madison regarded "frivolous and fanciful distinctions" as the only intellectual matters that Madison contrasted with differences of economic interests.[26] But Madison refers to these frivolous and fanciful distinctions only after asserting that a nonfrivolous and nonfanciful zeal for different opinions about religion and government has divided mankind into noneconomic factions. Beard incorrectly seizes upon "frivolous and fanciful distinctions" as the only things to be contrasted with economic differences because he does not recognize that, according to Madison in *Number 10,* a nonfrivolous intellectual difference about government or religion can arouse men's passions and thereby split them into factions which are not based on economic interests.

In Madison's view, possessing different kinds or amounts of property can cause opposed economic factions to have correspondingly opposed opinions on government, but, as we have seen, he would not have identified the possession of different kinds or amounts of property as "the most common and durable source" of factions if he had thought it was *the only* source of factions. We must also remember that his definition of "faction" allows for opposed factions that are caused by opposed passions as well as for those that are caused by opposed interests, since he defines a faction as a number of citizens who are united and motivated by "some common impulse of passion, *or* of interest."[27] In this definition Madison deliberately allows for factions whose sources or causes are noneconomic motives that he calls "passions," and a zeal for an opinion about government is such a passion. Unfortunately, however, Madison says two different things in *Number 10* about the role of "opinions" or "views," and this, understandably, may have misled Beard. On the one hand, Madison says that opposed political opinions arising from man's free use of his fallible reason cause opposed passionate attachments, which in turn cause factional differences based on these passionate attachments; on the other hand, Madison says that the various and unequal distribution of property causes opposed factional economic interests, which in turn cause opposed opinions. In other words, one Madisonian causal route proceeds from (1) a difference of opinion to (2) a difference of passion to (3) a factional difference, whereas a second causal route proceeds from (1') a difference in degree or kind of property to (2') a difference of factional interest to (3') a difference of "views." If Madison's words "opinions" and "views" are synonymous—and I think they are—then, although opinions occupy a different position in each of these two routes described by Madison, Beard does not see that two such routes *are* described in *Number 10* because he focuses exclusively on the second route, which begins with a difference in degree or kind of property. He fails to see that, according to Madison, not all factional differences of political opinion arise from factional differences of economic interest. Madison holds that *some* factional differences about government may arise independently of economic differences whereas other factional differences about government arise from economic differences.[28]

If this reading of a brief section of *Number 10* is correct, Madison does not advocate a very general theory of the economic interpretation of history, nor a less general—but nevertheless quite general—theory of economic determinism in politics. All that we can attribute to Madison in this area of thought is just what he says, namely, that the various and unequal distribution of property is the most common and durable source of factions in civilized society. From a logical point of view, the structure of Madison's thesis is comparable to a very mundane twentieth-century thesis about the causes of automobile collisions. One might say to begin with that different automobile collisions are caused by different things: by slippery roads, by worn tires, by faulty brakes, by drunken driving, and so on. But then one might go further and say that the most common and durable cause of automobile collisions is the slipperiness of roads. To establish this thesis one would presumably make a statistical study of automobile collisions. One would examine them in order to discover the cause of each collision and then count in order to discover the most frequent cause. One might also try to support one's statement that slippery roads constitute the most durable or most persistent cause of collisions throughout the history of automobile driving.

If this thesis about collisions and Madison's thesis are logically analogous, then it is obvious why we should not think the latter presents an economic interpretation of history in which Madison attempts to trace the "various manifestations of social life" to economic causes. Just as our student of automobile collisions does not try to explain all phenomena associated with automobile driving, so Madison restricts himself with comparable modesty in what he tries to explain about society. To say that one cause or source of factions is the most common and most persistent is obviously very different from saying that such "ideological" elements as the metaphysics and the painting of a society are determined "in the last instance" by economic causes. Madison not only refrains from explaining *all* of what Marx somewhere calls celestial, meaning ideological, phenomena; Madison even refrains from explaining the rise of *one* general idea such as political democracy. Therefore, he not only does not advocate an economic interpretation of *all* history but does not even advocate what Beard calls economic determinism in politics if we think of the latter as a theory that does try to explain the rise of an idea such as that of political democracy. When Madison explains the emergence of what may be called political "ideas," he limits himself to relatively specific ideas such as why creditors and debtors hold different views on laws concerning private debts and why landowners and manufacturers might disagree about encouraging domestic manufactures by restricting foreign manufactures. Causally explaining the existence of such political "views" is quite different from causally explaining the emergence of, say, the theory of the social contract in political thought. That highly general theory or view was not typical of what Madison had in mind when he said that opposed economic factions were "actuated by different sentiments and views."

Finally, I should say that although I have stressed the analogy between Madison's thesis and a thesis about the most common and durable source of automobile collisions, I have not forgotten my earlier observation that Madison's term "faction" is, according to what appears to be his definition of it, a moral epithet. Although a statement about what caused an automobile collision would be thought by many philosophers to be a purely descriptive statement, these same philosophers would say that a statement about the most common and durable cause of a Madisonian faction is not purely descriptive because it requires reference to a group's being united and actuated by an impulse of passion or of interest adverse to such moral entities as private natural rights or the public good. Still, we must bear in mind that Madison's statement about factions is structurally similar to a statement about the most common and durable source or cause of automobile collisions even if Madison's term "faction" is regarded as moral whereas the term "automobile collision" is not.

Madison and Hume on the Method
of Supporting a Theory of Factions

Madison's theory of the causes of factions may be clarified by examining it in the light of ideas that were commonly accepted in the eighteenth century, ideas that we have discussed in previous chapters. Some of these ideas were methodological or epistemological but others were substantive. I want to begin by comparing Madison's method of supporting his relatively modest theory of economic factions with methods advocated by Hume. Part of Madison's theory was supported by the use of what Hume called the method of reason as used in experimental, but not in demonstrative, sciences. Madison, as we have seen, began with certain preliminary assertions about human nature that might well have been regarded by Hume as "general and just maxims" that could have been formed a priori in Hume's sense even by young and relatively inexperienced novices who would not be obliged to present explicit evidence for them from past or present experience, or from history conceived as comprising current events.[29] For this reason, Madison did not supply large lists of confirming examples to show that human beings differ in their abilities to acquire things; that government would protect them so that they could exercise those different abilities; that once they exercised them, different kinds and amounts of property would come to exist among men; and that these differences would sometimes cause men to divide themselves into opposed economic factions or interest groups having opposed sentiments and views. Madison seems to have thought that his readers would have agreed with him on these points and therefore needed no confirming examples from him. He felt no need to pile up historical examples in order to convince his reader of the modest proposition that *some* divisions of men into factions are caused by their having different amounts or kinds of property. In *Number 10* Madison wrote as though he believed—to use a few of Hamilton's words in *Number 6*—that those who have a tolerable knowledge of human nature would not stand in need of examples to persuade them that some factional differences are economic in origin.

Now let us examine a part of Madison's argument where he shifts gears from a methodological point of view. At a certain point he stops uttering "general and just maxims" and makes his statement that the various and unequal distribution of property has been the most common and durable source of factions. Here Madison goes beyond saying merely that *some* factions originate in the various and unequal distribution of property and, what is more important for us, he ceases to regard what he says as though it were made so obvious by deducing it from generally accepted principles about all men as to need no supplementary historical support. Therefore he tells us that those who hold and those who do not hold property have "ever" formed distinct interests, meaning opposed interest groups or factions in civilized society. Here he uses the word "ever" in order to substantiate his contention that the unequal distribution of property has been a "durable" source of factions. He adds further historical support for the same contention by telling us that creditors and debtors "fall under a like discrimination," meaning that the former hold large amounts of money, that the latter hold small amounts of money, and that they therefore have always formed opposing factions in civilized society. Finally, he tries to marshal historical support for that part of his fundamental thesis which concerns not *the amount* but *the kind* of property that men hold, saying that a faction of landholders, a faction of manufacturers, a faction of merchants, a faction of "monied" men—all "grow up of necessity" in civilized nations.

To be sure, Madison remains on a relatively general level when supplying historical evidence for his thesis that the various and unequal distribution of property is the most common and the most durable cause of factions. After telling us that those who hold and those who do not hold property have always formed distinct factions in civilized society, he does not go on to name specific historical oppositions originating in the fact that members of one faction held property whereas members of the other did not. Nor does he get down to individual historical cases when he speaks in a general way about factions composed of creditors being opposed to factions composed of debtors. Nevertheless, he does make progress in his effort to substantiate his general thesis in an inductive way. Having said that the holding of different *amounts* of property is the most common cause of factional difference, he cites two subclasses of factional differences which are caused by the holding of different amounts of property: those in which the holders of *some* property are pitted against the holders of *no* property and those in which the lenders of money, who presumably have a lot of it, are pitted against those who borrow it and therefore have less of it as their property. Madison's appeal to history and experience is made in a similar way when he mentions the factions of landholders, of manufacturers, and of merchants that grow up of necessity in civilized nations.

Once again the method of historical confirmation is wholesale and not illustrated by presenting the proper names, so to speak, of different groups of landowners in different nations at different times. This is quite understandable when we reflect on the nature of certain factions. Not all of them, especially those that arise out of economic differences, bear names like those of the Guelphs and Ghibellines. Some of them may never gather together in one place or create a formal organization bearing a name. Hence "a landed interest" in Madison's terminology refers in a general way to any group of individuals who all own land in a given nation and who may form an interest group. He might have cited different economic interest groups in different nations at different times, but it is understandable why he did not cite them in the small amount of space at his disposal. He must have believed that he had already given enough support to his general thesis even without naming historical names. A very demanding critic might argue that Madison does not present nearly enough historical evidence to support his belief that the various and unequal distribution of property is *the most common* or *the most durable* cause of factions. But no critic can deny that Madison *tries* to support that belief by adducing historical evidence, even though he offers such evidence in general language. Therefore, one can say that Madison's argument for his fundamental thesis about the most common source of faction appeals to general principles about human nature and to more specific truths about past historical events. When Madison appealed to reason and also to history in *Number 10,* he was quite in accord with Hume's views on the method of experimental science and, more particularly, with Hume's views in the method of political science. However, Hume's epistemological views about the roles of reason and experience in political science were not the only views on the causes of factions that influenced Madison in *Number 10,* as Douglass Adair has conclusively shown.[30] Hume also held substantive views on the causes of factions that influenced Madison, and by comparing these substantive views we can see even more clearly that Madison did not advocate a speculative philosophy of history of the kind that Beard attributed to him.

Madison's and Hume's Substantive Views on Factions

Because Hume's substantive views on factions are similar to and yet different from Madison's, an examination of what Hume has to say about factions will help us see how Madison diverged from Hume when discussing the causes of factions in *Number 10.* Hume begins his essay "Of Parties in General" with a two-part distinction in which he calls some factions "personal" and others "real." Personal factions, he says, are predominantly based on personal friendship or animosity among those who compose the factions. By contrast, Hume's real factions are predominantly based on what he calls "some real difference of sentiment or interest,"[31] though, as we shall see, this characterization of real factions is amplified in a later section of Hume's essay. Hume observes that we seldom find factional differences that are purely personal or purely real, and therefore that personal as well as real differences exist in some degree whenever men separate into opposed factions. For this reason, his distinction between personal and real factional divisions depends on whether the fundamental difference is predominantly personal or predominantly real.[32] We must bear in mind that Hume thinks of a personal faction as one in which the members of one faction may personally hate the members of the other faction and conversely, also that members of one personal faction may be friendly to each other just as members of the opposed personal faction may be friendly to each other. One reason for emphasizing this will become evident when we later consider how Hume viewed what he called the real faction of affection. In contrasting personal factions and real factions, Hume does not wish to say that the sentiments of friendliness and hostility underlying personal factions are not real because they do not *exist.* His main point in distinguishing personal factions from real ones is that when two groups of people oppose each other as factions because of personal feelings of friendliness or animosity that constituent members of the factions have, their factional difference is not based on substantial, objective, or important differences. That is why Hume uses the language of comparison when he distinguishes personal factions from those "which are founded on the most real and most material difference."[33] He might have said therefore that whereas personal factions oppose each other because of relatively intangible differences like mutual animosity, real factions oppose each other because of the most tangible, solid, or substantial differences.

In order to illustrate his concept of personal factions, Hume presents examples of factions in the small republics of Florence, Genoa, and Rome, where every domestic quarrel, he says, became an affair of state and where any passion might produce a public division. He also cites two factions in the Greek empire, the *Prasini* and the *Veneti,* whose mutual animosity originated in a "trivial" difference of livery colors in horse races. He refers to the tribal dissension between the *Pollia* and *Papiria* in Roman history and to the later history of the conflict between Guelph and Ghibelline, when any "real difference" between them had vanished.[34] He says a number of other interesting things about what he called personal factions, but they need not be discussed any further here. They confirm what I have already suggested, namely, that Hume was contemptuous of people who divide themselves into factions primarily on the basis of merely personal, as opposed to what he regarded as real or weighty, differences.

With this in mind, I want to take up Hume's three-part distinction among *real* factions, a distinction which is more importantly connected with what Madison has to say on this subject. According to Hume, some real factions are based on "interest," some on "principle," and some on "affection."[35] When illustrating the concept of a faction from interest, he points to the nobles and the people in situations where each of these groups has a different sort of authority in a government that is not very accurately "balanced and modelled." Hume holds that such factions naturally have different interests and that we cannot reasonably expect them not to have different interests, "coinsidering that degree of selfishness implanted in human nature." It should be observed, however, that whereas in *Number 10* Madison seems to limit factions based on interest only to those based on *economic* interest, Hume illustrates his idea of factions based on interest by mentioning a factional difference between the nobles and the people, and one between soldiers and merchants, where only one of the factions mentioned would seem to be definable in terms of a kind or degree of property, namely, merchants. The nobles may in fact have held more property than the people, but Hume did not *define* the difference of interest that divided them by reference to a difference in the amount of property they held. In the same essay, Hume denies that "the *landed* and *trading* part of the nation" constituted factions in the England of his day, thereby showing how much Madison diverged from Hume's views when Madison explicitly identified a landed interest and a mercantile interest as factions in every civilized nation.[36]

Furthermore, Hume maintains that the rise of factions based on interest may be prevented by a skillful legislator, and that any faction in a free society may be eradicated by a legislature using the steady application of rewards and punishments.[37] By contrast, Madison thought that factions based on interest are not preventable in civilized nations and did not assert in *Number 10* that a free legislature could eradicate them. Finally, when Madison said that the various and unequal distribution of property was the most common and durable source of factions, he said nothing that could be found in Hume's essay. True, Hume held that factions based on political and economic interest are the *most reasonable and most excusable* ones; but this remark was quite different from Madison's causal thesis about economic factions in *Number 10*.[38] Plainly, Madison diverged in important ways from Hume's views on factions founded on interest, no matter how much Madison may have absorbed while reading Hume's essay "Of Parties in General." When comparing what Hume has to say about factions with what Madison has to say on this same subject, we must be cautious. We must be aware of difficulties in identifying certain similarly named items in their different classificatory schemes. In order to show what these similarities and difficulties are, I must say something about Hume's other real factions, those based on principle and those based on affection.

First, Hume's factions based on principle. Hume does not define the word "principle" but he obviously thinks of it as a proposition, since he distinguishes in a traditional way between what he calls abstract speculative principles and those that "beget a contrariety of conduct," namely, opposed practical principles. Speculative principles assert what is the case whereas practical principles assert what ought to be done. Among speculative principles Hume includes religious propositions such as, I suppose, the proposition that God exists; and among principles that beget a contrariety of conduct Hume includes all different, meaning opposed, political principles. Hume thinks that there are real parties or factions which are based on both kinds of principles, and it is clear that Madison agreed with him when Madison said in *Number 10* that "a zeal for different opinions concerning religion, concerning Government and many other points, as well of speculation as of practice" led to differences that have "divided mankind into parties," that is to say, into factions.[39] It should be emphasized that neither Hume nor Madison maintained that factions founded on principle—whether speculative or practical, whether religious or political—could arise only out of different economic interests. Hume explicitly distinguished between factions founded on interest and those founded on principle; and Madison, even though he failed to prevent Beard from misunderstanding him and Harold Laski from misquoting him, also distinguished between factions founded on interest and those founded on principle, using the word "opinion" instead of Hume's word "principle."[40] Had Madison been more explicit on this subject, he would have made it more obvious that he believed in a plurality of causes of faction even though he regarded economic interest as the most common and durable of these causes.

Examining Hume's distinction between factions founded on principle and those founded on interest helps us see more clearly that Madison agreed with Hume that a factional difference can arise even when the two factions do not have a difference of economic interest. It also helps us see more clearly that, unlike Hume in "Of Parties in General," Madison laid double stress on economic interest in *Number 10*. First of all, Madison focused on it rather than on other sorts of interest, for, as we shall see in a later chapter of this study—and as we can see in *Number 10* as well as in other parts of *The Federalist*—economic or property-based interests are not the only kind of interests contemplated in the philosophy of the period or in the minds of the founding fathers.[41] Second, Madison, unlike Hume, asserted flatly that the fact that people had different kinds and amounts of property was the most common and durable source of factions.

Examining what Hume says about real factions "from affection" helps us illuminate other aspects of Madison's thought on the subject.[42] When Hume first mentions this sort of faction after mentioning factions from principle and factions from interest, some readers of eighteenth-century philosophical literature might think that Hume was using the word "affection" very broadly as the equivalent of "passion" or "emotion." In that case, his three different sorts of factions would neatly correspond to the motives of reason, interest, and passion which are so often discussed as a trio in the literature of the period, a trio which we shall consider later when treating Publius's views on human motivation. If Hume were using the word "affection" in this general way, his three different sorts of factions would conveniently—for a student of the connections between the ideas of Hume and of Madison—correspond to Madison's trio of opinion, interest, and passion. But the fact is that Hume's factions from affection are *not* defined by him as factions based on passion *in general*. They are, he says, "founded on the different attachments of men towards particular families and persons whom they desire to rule over them"[43]; therefore, they are based on the particular passion of affection for, or attachment to, particular individuals or groups of individuals. Hume goes on to say that such factions are often very violent and that it may seem incomprehensible that men should "attach themselves" so strongly to persons with whom they are not acquainted, whom they may never have seen, from whom they have never received any favor, and from whom they can never hope to receive any favor. Nevertheless, he says, this sort of attachment does exist and, according to his definition, it is the foundation of a real faction, not a personal one.

I stress this because of something said by Adair. Unlike Beard, Adair deserves great praise for seeing that in one sentence of *Number 10* Madison mentions different bases of factions that seem to correspond to different bases of real parties or factions mentioned by Hume in his essay. Thus, when Madison says that "a zeal for different opinions concerning religion, concerning Government and many other points, as well of speculation as of practice" has "divided mankind into parties," Adair correctly observes that Madison owes what he says here to what Hume says about real parties from principle.[44] Immediately after saying that, Madison refers to another cause that has divided mankind into what Hume would have called real parties, namely, "an attachment to different leaders ambitiously contending for pre-eminence and power; or to persons of other descriptions whose fortunes have been interesting to the human passions," but this passage is linked by Adair with the views of Hume in a manner that I do not think is in accord with what Madison writes in *Number 10*. Adair flatly says of Madison's phrase "an attachment to different leaders ambitiously contending for pre-eminence and power": "Here is Hume's 'Personal' faction, 'founded on personal friendship or animosity among such as compose the contending parties.' "[45] In my opinion, Adair failed to see that Madison was referring here to what Hume had said about real factions founded on affection and not to what Hume had said about personal factions. Evidently Adair failed to see that Hume's factions are personal as opposed to real when those who *compose* the contending parties or factions have certain personal attitudes *toward each other;* Adair also failed to see that Hume's real factions from affection are based on "attachments" *toward persons and families whom they want to rule over them.* If members of one faction have an attachment to one leader while members of another faction have an attachment to a rival leader, then, contrary to what Adair says, the factions would be real factions from affection and not personal factions in Hume's terminology. The point at which Hume's concept of "personal factions" enters *Number 10* is when Madison remarks that mankind's propensity to fall into mutual animosities is so strong "that where no substantial occasion presents itself, the most frivolous and fanciful distinctions have been sufficient to kindle their unfriendly passions, and excite their most violent conflicts." This is the counterpart of Hume's observation that a trivial—in a sense, therefore, nonreal—difference between one color of livery and another in horse races produced the personal factions of the *Prasini* and the *Veneti* mentioned earlier in this chapter.[46]

Why, then, didn't Madison make a more explicit two-part distinction between personal and real factions and a three-part distinction among factions founded on opinion, factions founded on affection in the sense of "attachment," and factions based on *economic* interest—thereby showing not only how close he was to Hume but also how he differed from him on this subject? Adair thinks that Madison, having "no capacity for slavish imitation," compressed the greater part of Hume's essay into a single sentence of *Number 10* and that he "greatly expanded the quick sketch of the faction from 'interest' buried in the middle of the philosopher's analysis."[47] As I have already indicated, however, I think that Madison did more than "expand" Hume's views on faction from interest; he added to it significantly. When Madison called property-based interest the most common and most durable source of factions, he advocated a theory which was not in Hume's essay. But this does not mean that he subscribed to a form of economic determinism in politics or to an economic interpretation of history, as those terms are understood in the literature of Marxism.

The Absence of "Opinion" in Madison's Definition of "Faction"

Now let us turn from Madison's divergence from Hume's views and ask why Madison's own tripartite distinction among the causes of factions—differences of opinion, differences of passion, and differences of interest—is not reflected in his definition of faction. He says, we remember, that a faction is a number of citizens who are "united and actuated by some common impulse of passion, or of interest," but he does *not* say that it is a number of citizens who are united and actuated by some common impulse of *opinion.* Why?

Since Madison believed that citizens united by some common opinion about religion or government could constitute a faction, why isn't this belief of his reflected in his definition? Adair's remark that Madison did not want to be known as a slavish imitator of Hume may contain part of the answer, but I do not know that it is the whole answer. Was there something deeper, something more philosophical, involved? Let us remember that Madison explicitly deals with *motives* in his definition of "faction." He speaks of citizens being "actuated by some common *impulse* [my emphasis] of passion, or of interest." Therefore, as I have already suggested, if he had wished to insert a reference to opinion as a source of faction, he could have added to his definition of "faction" that members of it might be united and actuated by some common "impulse of opinion" which is adverse to the rights of other citizens or to the permanent and aggregate interests of the community. But he didn't make such an addition. Did he shy away on philosophical grounds from speaking of impulses of opinion, where an opinion is viewed as something formed by reason? We know that eighteenth-century philosophers disagreed about the efficacy of reason and that Hume himself denied that it alone could move men to action when he argued in his more strictly philosophical writings that it is and ought to be the slave of the passions. Was Madison under the influence of *this* Humeian view when he failed to include a reference to opinion as an impulse or motive of factious behavior? I do not think we can justifiably say so, especially when we keep in mind that Hume himself was prepared to say in his essay on factions that there are "parties from principle," where he construed a "principle" as a proposition or a belief that is formed by reason and where he said that different beliefs are capable of causing or motivating what Hume called "contrariety of conduct." Furthermore, since one of Madison's arguments for the existence of different or opposed passions among citizens is the fact that they have different or opposed opinions to which they become attached, he obviously thought that having an opinion can cause a person to have a passion. Why, then, didn't Madison's definition of "faction" reflect his view that there are factions based on opinion as well as factions based on passion and factions based on interest? I suggest—and I can do no more than suggest in the light of the scanty evidence—that he might have been moved by the idea that a *group* of citizens actuated by a common opinion or principle would not engage in factious behavior unless their common belief produced a common passion or interest which would have—if unchecked—have led them to act collectively in a manner adverse to the rights of other citizens or to the permanent and aggregate interests of the community. Madison might have thought that a group of people could share an opinion which failed to imbue all or most of them with a common zeal for their opinions or an interest in acting on them. In that case, only a group of citizens sharing a common opinion *that stimulated a common passion or interest* would, according to Madison, constitute a faction. If he held that the only kind of shared opinion which could form the basis of a faction was one which caused a common passion or a common interest, Madison might have found it sufficient to mention only the latter two sources of faction in his definition—even though he went on in *Number 10* to speak of factions founded on opposed opinions which aroused opposed passions that made men "much more disposed to vex and oppress each other."

The idea that a difference of opinion might not lead to a factional difference when men's passions or interests were not collectively aroused by that difference of opinion was explicitly adopted by Hume in his essay on parties or factions. He recognized that two groups of persons might disagree about the truth of a proposition and yet not be arrayed against each other in factions. Hume says explicitly that parties based on differences about what he called abstract speculative principles "are known only to modern times."[48] This shows that, according to Hume, premodern men divided themselves into opposed groups on the basis of a purely speculative or theoretical difference without forming factions.[49] We need not say any more to show that, according to Hume, "different opinions concerning religion"—in Madison's phrase—did not always cause factions. We may safely add that Madison agreed with this. Madison merely says in *Number 10* that "a zeal for different opinions concerning religion" and other things "have in turn divided mankind into parties" or factions; he does not say that *all* differences of opinion concerning religion have produced enough zeal to divide men into parties.

I do not want to conclude my discussion of Hume and Madison on factions without observing a difference between them which deserves special notice in the light of my earlier remark that "faction" as defined by Madison might well be regarded as an ethical term. Interestingly enough, Hume does not define the word "party," the equivalent of "faction" in his essay "Of Parties in General." He says many disparaging things about factions, just as Madison does, but he never bluntly makes a statement which is, or seems to be, as definitional as the statement by Madion which begins with the words "By a faction I understand" and ends with the words "adverse to the rights of other citizens, or to the permanent and aggregate interests of the community." By contrast, Hume says more guardedly—from a philosophical viewpoint—that "the influence of faction is directly contrary to that of laws," that "factions subvert government," and that they "beget the fiercest animosities among men of the same nation, who ought to give mutual assistance and protection to each other."[50] But, by not offering a definition which mentions the rights of other citizens or of the public good, Hume does not leave himself open to questioning from scholars such as Robert Dahl who have challenged Madison to tell them what he means in his definition of "faction" by the phrase "the rights of other citizens" and by the phrase "the permanent and aggregate interests of the community."[51]

On the Value of Reading Hume and Other Writings of Madison

In summing up the value of comparing the substantive views of Madison on faction with those of Hume, we may say that it supports the following interpretation of Madison. Like Hume, he accepted a theory according to which factional differences may be caused by three different sorts of differences among men: differences of opinion, differences of passion, and differences of interest. Moreover, comparing Madison with Hume enlarges the evidence for believing that these differences are regarded by Madison as *independent* causes of factional difference—which may therefore be said to have a plurality of causes—even though Madison, like Hume, singled out differences of interest as especially important. Such a comparison also shows that Madison singled it out in a manner which was different from that in which Hume singled it out. Madison identified differences of interest with differences based on the amount and kind of property that men have, but Hume did not in his essay on parties. Moreover, Madison called such differences the most common and durable source of factions, but Hume did not in that same essay.

In going beyond Hume in this respect, Madison became attractive to Beard, who seems to have been looking for a way to make his own method of interpreting the Constitution respectable while acknowledging its similarity with the views of thinkers in the Marxian tradition. However, had Beard read *Number 10* with Hume's essay "Of Parties in General" beside him, he might have seen how distorted an interpretation of *Number 10* he was giving. I grant that he might have seen this *without* reading that essay, but I suggest that reading it would have made it virtually impossible for him to interpret Madison as he did.

Beard might also have hesitated to interpret Madison as he did if he had attended carefully to other things written by Madison himself. In his memorandum of 1787 entitled *Vices of the Political System of the United States,* Madison used the word "factions" in a way which shows plainly that he regarded some factional differences as noneconomic in nature. "All civilized societies," he wrote, "are divided into different interests and factions, as they happen to be creditors or debtors—Rich or poor—husbandmen, merchants or manufacturers—members of different religious sects—followers of different political leaders—inhabitants of different districts—owners of different kinds of property &c &c."[52] In this passage Madison conceived factional differences so broadly as to view religious sects, groups of followers of different leaders, and even groups of inhabitants of different districts as factions. Therefore, he not only agreed with Hume in thinking that noneconomic groups can be factions, but went beyond Hume in saying that inhabitants of different districts could form opposed factions. Of course, Hume probably believed that a set of inhabitants of one district could be arrayed as a faction against a set of inhabitants of a different district who also constituted a faction, but presumably there two groups would not oppose each other merely because they lived in different places. They would oppose each other on the basis of the factors classified by Hume in "Of Parties in General"—where the factions are said to be personal or real, and if real, based on interest, principle, or affection.

Madison's long letter to Jefferson of October 24, 1787, also shows how defective Beard's interpretation of Madison was insofar as Beard concentrated almost exclusively on what Madison says about economically based factions. I grant that Madison says in this letter that in civilized society certain "distinctions are various and unavoidable," that "a distinction of property results from that very protection which a free Government gives to unequal faculties of acquiring it," and that there will be rich and poor, creditors and debtors, a landed interest, a monied interest, a mercantile interest, and a manufacturing interest. I also grant that in this letter Madison reveals his concern with economically based factions when he says that the groups of people he has just mentioned may be further "subdivided according to the different productions of different situations & soils, & according to different branches of commerce, and of manufactures." But in spite of Madison's undoubted concern with economically based factions in this letter, he shows his concern with other kinds of factions and also shows his dependence on Hume when he writes: "In addition to these natural distinctions, artificial ones will be founded, on accidental differences in political, religious or other opinions, or an attachment to the persons of leading individuals. However erroneous or ridiculous these grounds of dissention [sic] and faction, may appear to the enlightened Statesman, or the benevolent philosopher, the bulk of mankind who are neither Statesmen nor Philosophers, will continue to view them in a different light."[53]

Reading Madison's letter to Jefferson makes it even more obvious that Adair was correct in perceiving the influence on Madison of Hume's essay "Of Parties in General." In that letter, all three kinds of Hume's real factions are mentioned by Madison in the order in which Hume had mentioned them: those based on interest, those based on political or religious principle, and those based on affection conceived as an attachment to the persons of leading individuals.[54] It will be recalled in this connection that Hume's parties from affection were those "founded on the different attachments of men towards particular families and persons whom they desire to rule over them."[55] Madison's dependence on Hume is also confirmed when Madison differentiates between two kinds of distinctions that are said to underlie factions in *Number 10:* natural ones and artificial ones. Madison's "natural distinctions" are all economic in his letter to Jefferson, whereas under the heading of "artificial distinctions" Madison lists only those that Hume says are differences of principle or differences of affection. It would appear that Madison's distinction between "natural" distinctions and "artificial" distinctions was linked with Hume's treatment of distinctions based on interest as more reasonable than distinctions based on what Madison called "political, religious or other opinions," and also as more reasonable than distinctions based on what Madison called "an attachment to the persons of leading individuals." All of the differences mentioned by Madison were real for Hume, but some were more real and more material than others. Madison called distinctions based on property natural rather than artificial not because the natural ones were real and the artificial ones unreal, but because the natural ones were "the most real and most material" differences in Hume's sense.[56]

I want to conclude this appeal to other instructive writings of Madison on faction by considering two speeches that Madison made at the Philadelphia Convention—one on June 6 and one on June 26—while continuing to focus on what Madison said about the causes of faction rather than about how to control their effects, since I shall deal with the latter topic later in this study. For our present purposes his crucial statement at Philadelphia on June 6 was: "All civilized Societies would be divided into different Sects, Factions, & interests, as they happened to consist of rich & poor, debtors & creditors, the landed the manufacturing, the commercial interests, the inhabitants of this district, or that district, the followers of this political leader or that political leader, the disciples of this religious sect or that religious sect."[57] Here Madison appears to speak as though sects are not necessarily factions, but still present in what he says are the effects of his having read Hume's essay "Of Parties in General." He still mentions economic factions based on interest, religious sects, and followers of political leaders, but, as he does in his *Vices of the Political System of the United States,* he inserts a reference to inhabitants of different districts. On the whole, this passage is far less revealing of Madison's views than his letter to Jefferson of October 24, 1787.

Let us now see what Madison said about the causes of factions and allied matters in his remarks at the Convention on June 26, 1787. There too he shows that he was primarily concerned with distinctions or groups that arise "in all civilized Countries." In such countries, he says, "the people fall into different classes havg. a real or supposed difference of interests [notice the word "supposed" here]." Then Madison continues his familiar refrain that "there will be creditors & debtors, farmers, merchts. & manufacturers. There will be particularly the distinction of rich & poor." He grants that in America there were no hereditary distinctions of rank such as those which had caused "contests" in antiquity as well as in modern European states, nor the extremes of wealth and poverty to be found in the latter. Nevertheless, he continues, "in framing a system which we wish to last for ages, we shd. not lose sight of the changes which ages will produce"—changes which are exclusively economic in nature and which therefore do not reveal Madison's agreement with Hume's division of real factions into those based on principle and affection as well as those based on interest. In these remarks at Philadelphia, Madison worries that an increase in the population of the country "will of necessity increase the proportion of those who will labour under all the hardships of life, & secretly sigh for a more equal distribution of its blessings." More important for our purposes is his fear that those who secretly sigh may in time outnumber those who are not indigent, thereby taking power from the latter. "No agrarian attempts have yet been made in this Country," Madison adds, "but symptoms of a leveling spirit, as we have understood, have sufficiently appeared in . . . certain quarters to give notice of the future danger." In this speech, as reported by Madison himself, the only sort of faction that he mentions is based on economic differences and therefore it is grist for the sort of mill that Beard was grinding in 1913. Indeed, if we did not have *Number 10* itself and had only this document, Beard might well be vindicated in his monistic interpretation of Madison's theory of the origin of factions. Madison could be represented as holding that *only* economic differences of interest caused factions and that *only* the danger of "interested co-alitions to oppress the minority" was to be guarded against. No signs of the influence of Hume's pluralistic view of the causes of factions appear in this speech of June 26 as reported by Madison.[58] Moreover, in Yates's version of Madison's speech, Madison saw a great divide only between landholders on one side and traders and manufacturers on the other, thereby sharpening a certain disagreement between himself and Hume, who, as we have seen, denied that there was a difference of interest between the landed and trading part of the English nation at the time he wrote "Of Parties in General."[59] But whatever Yates attributed to Madison, we do have *Number 10* itself and we do have Madison's letter to Jefferson of October 24, 1787, both of which plainly show that Madison did not subscribe to a monistic economic theory of the causes of factions even though he singled out the various and unequal distribution of property as the most common and durable source of factions.

Madison: No Economic Interpreter of History and No Economic Determinist

In the light of the evidence offered in this chapter, we may safely conclude that Madison did not advocate a speculative philosophy of history which could be identified with that of Marx. When Madison said in *Number 10* that a landed interest, a manufacturing interest, a mercantile interest, a monied interest, and many lesser interests grow up of necessity in civilized nations, "and divide them into different classes, actuated by different sentiments and views," he was not using the word "classes" as Marx did. Marx distinguished opposing classes on the basis of what he called their relationship to the means of production, but Madison did not distinguish *his* classes in that way. Madison's class of manufacturers, his class of merchants, and his class of monied men were not differentiated from each other on the basis of their relationship to the means of production in the United States of 1787. Indeed, Madison never refers to what Marx regarded as *the* means of production at that time and place. Furthermore, it is plain that the "sentiments and views" that actuated Madison's classes did not make up what Marx would have called an ideology, meaning a totality of legal, political, religious, esthetic, and philosophic ideas. The sentiments and views to which Madison referred in *Number 10* were, as we have seen, much more limited in scope than those which constituted what Marx regarded as an ideology. It follows a fortiori that Madison did not espouse a theory of the economic interpretation of history according to which something that Marx would have called an ideology was causally determined by something economic in nature. Even if we pare down the Marxian view so that it amounts to what Beard called the theory of economic determinism in politics alone, it is obvious that the political views and sentiments which actuate a Madisonian class or faction were more limited in scope than the totality of political ideas that Marx identified with political ideology. Madison focused on factions, asserted that they could be traced to different sources or causes, and then tried to show that the most common and durable cause among these was the various and unequal distribution of property. He was, to be sure, a political scientist according to his own lights, but he was not a speculative philosopher of history in the grand manner.

As Adair has pointed out, Madison's views on faction were closer to those of Hume than to those of any other thinker—both methodologically and substantively. And although Madison laid more stress than Hume did on economic interest as a source of factions, Madison did not lay as much stress on it as Beard would have had us believe. Theory about the causes of factions becomes more and more economically oriented as we move from Hume to Madison himself and then to Madison as expounded by Beard. Therefore, it is imperative that we distinguish Madison's views on this subject from those of his unavowed master and those of his incompletely informed disciple. Madison assumed certain principles of human nature which expressed "the latent causes of faction," but nothing that he said on this score—however general—permits us to think of him as a philosopher of history on a par with Marx or Hegel as a speculator about the march of society and history.[60]

Having said this, I must add that Madison certainly made statements that could be called "theoretical," most notably the statement that the various and unequal distribution of property is the most common and durable cause of factions in civilized societies. Although the word "theory" is notoriously ambiguous, in one of its many uses it can certainly be applied to Madison's fundamental thesis about the cause of factions. Therefore, if Beard had meant to attribute nothing more than *this* "theory" to Madison when he credited him with having presented "a masterly statement of the theory of economic determinism in politics," one could not quarrel with Beard. However, the main trouble with what Beard says about Madison is that Beard identifies Madison's so-called economic determinism with a theory that Madison did *not* hold, and Beard makes this identification because he conveniently neglected certain things that Madison said. Although Adair showed this conclusively, Adair did not content himself with trying to show only this in his attack on Beard's interpretation of Madison. He also said a few other things that have drawn criticism which deserves to be considered here. In considering it, my main purpose is to clarify Adair's views, Beard's views, and ultimately Madison's views on the causes or sources of factions.

In his essay "The Tenth Federalist Revisited," Adair pointed out that in *An Economic Interpretation of the Constitution* Beard had referred to Madison's "masterly statement of the theory of economic determinism in politics," but then Adair went on "to note the ambiguous effect of Beard's book on Madison's reputation." Here is a part of what Adair wrote in a passage which has drawn some fire:

> But what of Madison himself, the "master theorist" of 1787? Perhaps the most equivocal feature of Beard's latter-day revival of Madison's fame lies in the fact that the historian's major thesis about the Constitution can be taken to imply that "theory" played little or no part in the creation of the federal Union. The Fathers, as pictured by Beard, were "practical"

men who, knowing exactly what they wanted in the way of concrete economic privileges, were willing to stage a "coup d'etat" to gain their ends.
Collectively they were exhibited as being adepts in the use of force, fraud,
and false propaganda. Beard gives no hint, however, that political theory
played any consequential role in creating the Constitution; speculation
there was in plenty in the Convention, but it was land and debt speculation, not speculative thought. Indeed, if it is possible to determine an individual's political motives by cataloguing his property, the irrelevance of
theory should be apparent. It was thus easy to deduce from Beard's study—
though he did not himself go on to make that deduction—that Madison's
"master theory" merely revealed him as a writer who was indiscreet
enough to reveal in the tenth *Federalist* the grinning death's head of economic exploitation concealed behind the decorous and misleading phrases
of the Constitution. Certainly, this was the deduction made by Vernon
Louis Parrington, Beard's most distinguished and influential disciple.[61]

Let us focus first on Adair's unguarded remark that Beard's "major thesis
about the Constitution can be taken to imply that 'theory' played little or no
part in the creation of the federal Union." It is evident from Adair's work
that the sort of theory he had in mind here was *political* theory construed as
what Madison called opinions about government. This is especially evident
when Adair writes in the paragraph quoted above: "Beard gives no hint . . .
that political theory played any consequential role in creating the Constitution." Nevertheless, it has been argued that Adair did less than justice to
Beard's respect for Madison as a theorist and philosopher. In support of this
criticism of Adair, it has been rightly said that Beard gave Madison's *Number 10* credit for having been "a masterly statement of the theory of economic
determinism in politics," that Beard said that Madison made "the most
philosophical examination of the foundations of political science . . . in the
tenth number," and that Beard referred to "the fundamental theory of political economy . . . stated by Madison." And since Adair himself recognizes
that Beard called Madison's view of the causes of factions the "master theory" of the Constitution, how, it has been asked, can Adair justifiably say that
Beard's major thesis about the Constitution can be taken to imply that *theory*
played little or no part in the creation of the federal Union?[62]

I think this criticism is based on an interpretation of Adair which is
encouraged by Adair's loose language. However, I think it can be answered
by reading Adair charitably. As we know, Adair correctly insists that Madison's *theory of the causes of factions* asserts that some factional differences
are caused by the zeal of opponents for different opinions or *theories* concerning government and some are caused by the zeal of opponents for different religious opinions or *theories,* even though most factional differences are
caused by economic differences of interest. We see, then, that Madison's
theory of the causes of factions *mentions* a zeal for different political theories,
or opinions concerning government, as one of those causes. It may be called
a second-level theory because it talks *about* the role of political theory, religious theory, and economic interest in the causation of factions. Madison's
second-level theory may also be called a pluralistic theory because it men-

tions these three distinct causes of factional differences even though it singles out economic interest as the most common and persistent cause. Adair's main (and correct) point is that Beard neglected those passages in *Number 10* where Madison followed Hume in asserting the efficacy of differences over political theory in the formation of opposing factions. That is why Adair said that Beard's major thesis about the Constitution can be taken to imply that "political theory," or what Hume called "political principles," played no consequential role in creating the Constitution. Adair based this contention on his recognition that in Beard's interpretation of Madison, differences over *political theory* played no consequential role in Madison's theory of the causation of factions. To keep matters straight, we must distinguish between Beard's obvious awareness that Madison had a *theory of the causes of factional difference* and Beard's apparent inability to recognize that differences over *political theory* could, according to Madison, cause factional differences.

It was exceedingly unfortunate, therefore, that Adair had said that Beard's major thesis about the Constitution could "be taken to imply that 'theory' played little or no part in the creation of the federal Union." Had Adair used the phrase "political theory" rather than the word "theory" in this sentence, as he does later in the passage I quoted above, he would not have been in the least vulnerable to the criticism I have been considering. I suggest, therefore, that the purely verbal difference between Adair and his critic may be resolved by pointing out that, according to Adair, Madison's pluralistic *theory* of the causes of factional differences asserted that some factional differences are caused by a zeal for different political principles or *theories,* a zeal which Madison did not uniformly regard as a "reflex" of contending economic interests. Because Beard "gives no hint" of this in his exposition of Madison's *theory* in *Number 10,* Adair rightly said that Beard underestimated the role that Madison assigned to differences over political theory in his second-level theory of the causes of factional differences. In short, Beard had undoubtedly called Madison a "theorist" of the causes of factions, but Adair was quite correct in pointing out that Beard had neglected the pluralistic character of Madison's theory of the causes of factional differences because Beard paid no attention to the passage in *Number 10* where Madison says that a zeal for different opinions or *theories* concerning government was one of the causes which had divided mankind into factions.

With this behind me, I may now reiterate that whatever kind of theory Madison advocated about the causes of factions—whether it be viewed pluralistically, as Adair viewed it, or monistically, as Beard viewed it—it was not a theory of economic determinism in politics *as that was understood in the Marxian tradition.* I also want to reiterate that it was not an economic interpretation of all history as that was understood in the Marxian tradition. For this reason, Madison was not what is sometimes called a speculative philosopher of history.

V
PSYCHOLOGY

6

The Essence of Ideal Man and
the Nature of Real Men

It is evident from what we have seen in the previous chapter that Madison's views about faction depended on a psychology or a theory of human nature, which in his day was of course a branch of philosophy. That theory is never explicitly or systematically developed in *The Federalist,* and therefore I now want to begin an effort to extract parts of it that are relevant to the main theses of Publius. It will be useful to start by examining some philosophical statements that have been made *about* Publius's psychology. It has been said, for example, that Publius espoused a theory of human nature that is not a priori but based on experience, a theory which tells us how men do behave as opposed to how men ought to behave, and a theory that is realistic or pessimistic rather than optimistic. In the present chapter I want to examine such statements so that we may better understand the nature and purpose of Publius's psychological reflections; and in the next two chapters I want to present the substantive parts of his psychology that were of most importance in political science, those parts in which he dealt with human motives. It will be difficult to separate the concerns of these three chapters completely because it will be hard to say what sort of theory of human nature Publius defended without citing and analyzing some of the substantive psychological statements that he made in *The Federalist.* Still, there is a difference between saying that his theory of human nature was empirical, descriptive, or pessimistic, and presenting the substance of his theory of motivation.

Publius's Study of Human Nature:
The Empirical Psychological Component

The authors of *The Federalist* did not regard the phrase "human nature" as synonymous with "the essence of man," and therefore they did not think of themselves as analysts of essence who did not need to engage in empirical observation of human behavior. I stress this because the phrase "the essence of man" has often been used to refer to an attribute of man which is analyzed in the definition of "man" and which is supposed to be fundamentally different from attributes that are not contained in man's essence. For example, the attribute of being rational and that of being an animal have sometimes been regarded as parts of the essence and therefore of the nature of man, whereas the attribute of being mortal has been regarded as one which is not part of his essence or nature. One way of defending this difference has been to say that although we cannot conceive of a man who is not an animal, we can conceive of one who is not mortal; and so, starting with this traditional distinction, some philosophers might well ask whether the propositions about human nature to be found in *The Federalist* were regarded by the authors as essential propositions. But *were* Hamilton, Jay, and Madison primarily concerned to reveal the essential attributes of man when they sought to characterize human nature? I think not. When Publius says that it is man's nature to be ambitious, he does not mean that ambition is an essential attribute of man. On the contrary, as we shall see later, the attributes of men that Publius singles out are usually what many philosophers call accidental rather than essential attributes. If one adopts the view that we may arrive at truths like "Every man is an animal" merely by finding out what the word "man" means or by logically analyzing the attribute of manhood rather than by observing individual men, then one may confidently say that Publius was not primarily concerned to present the essential attributes of men when he discussed human nature. And if one thinks that the essential attributes of men can be discovered merely by examining the meaning or definition of the word "man," then one will conclude that the nonessential attributes of men cannot be discovered in this a priori way. They must be discovered by experience according to such a view, and experience was what Publius appealed to when supporting most of his assertions about human nature. He was mainly interested in resting his political statements on empirically supportable truths of psychology even though he might have held that the supposedly essential proposition "Man is a rational animal" can be established merely by examining the relations between attributes, ideas, concepts, or the like. As a student of the experimental science of politics, Publius was not interested in the relations of such entities, but rather in discovering and confirming psychological propositions about men that can only be established by experience; and these propositions were not viewed by him as essential predications that were self-evident.[1] The psychological task of Publius was therefore quite different from the moral task of Jefferson in the Declaration of Independence, where Jefferson seems to have relied on some view of the essence of man when he said that certain truths about men were self-evident.

Publius's Study of Human Nature: The A Priori Moral Component

However, the fact that the authors of *The Federalist* were not—as experimental political scientists—concerned to analyze the essence of man should not obscure the fact that they were, as part-time moralists, just as committed to a rationalistic doctrine of natural law and natural rights as Jefferson was. In *The Federalist* they did not harp on these rights nor on their metaphysical and theological foundations, but if asked to defend their belief in them, they would have appealed at some point to the essence of man while using a method that may be called a priori insofar as it required no appeal to experience of man as they knew him on earth. Elsewhere[2] I have presented a detailed discussion of this dependence of American revolutionaries on Lockeian doctrines of essence, natural law, and natural rights, so here I may confine myself to saying that the authors of *The Federalist* continued to rely on the same doctrine of natural law. When they tried to unpack the God-given essence of man in order to find his duties and the rights implied by those duties, they thought of themselves as relying on what Hamilton in *Number 31* called "internal evidence" when supporting general statements about man.[3] In Chapter 3 we have seen an expression of this point of view in Hamilton's early pamphlet "A Full Vindication," where Hamilton says: "All men . . . participate in one common nature, and consequently have one common right." The same idea is expressed in Hamilton's "Farmer Refuted," where he says that the right to liberty is "conformable to the constitution of man."[4]

These early views of Hamilton, like those which he published a dozen years later in *The Federalist,* were, as I have said, Lockeian in character. In his *Essay* Locke says that (1) *the idea* of a supreme being who is infinite in power, goodness, and wisdom, whose workmanship we are, and on whom we depend; as well as (2) *the idea* of ourselves as understanding rational beings, would "if duly considered, and pursued, afford such Foundations of our Duty and Rules of Action, as might place *Morality amongst the Sciences capable of Demonstration:* wherein I doubt not, but from self-evident Propositions, by necessary Consequences, as incontestable as those in Mathematicks, the measures of right and wrong might be made out, to any one that will apply himself with the same Indifferency and Attention to the one, as he does to the other of these Sciences."[5] Notice that Locke says that merely by duly considering and pursuing two *ideas,* we may proceed to build a demonstrative science of morality; and in this same passage he goes to on tell us that "Where there is no Property, there is no injustice" is a proposition as certain as any proposition demonstrated in Euclid. I shall not examine Locke's dubious remarks about property and justice, but I do want to emphasize that Hume rejected them. Hume said that because Locke's proposition about property and injustice is based merely on a definition of "injustice," it cannot be put on a par with the Pythagorean theorem, which is really demonstrable, meaning deducible from the axioms of geometry, and not merely the result of appealing to definitions to arrive at a conclusion that Hume regarded as trivial. "That the square of the hypothenuse is equal to the square of the other two sides," Hume said, "cannot be known, let the terms be ever so exactly defined, without a train of reasoning" which ultimately proceeds from the axioms of geometry. By contrast, Hume said, to convince ourselves of the truth of the proposition "that where there is no property, there can be no injustice, it is only necessary to define the terms, and explain injustice to be a violation of property." If nobody has any property, then, by definition, there can be no injustice since there is no property to violate. By somewhat similar reasoning, Hume might have said, to convince ourselves of the truth of the proposition that if something is not a rectangle, then it is not a square, we need only define a square as a rectangle with equal sides. In this case our truth can be established without appealing to any axioms or theorems of geometry such as Euclid employed when providing the truth of Proposition 47 in Book I of his *Elements*.[6]

Nevertheless, as we have seen, Locke's notion that he could derive moral theorems in the manner of Euclid exerted a great influence on Hamilton; and we must keep this in mind lest we come to believe that the authors of *The Federalist* were more dependent than they were on the philosophy of David Hume. They may have been dependent on it in some parts of philosophy but certainly not in ethics, for Hume did not think that we could demonstrate what our duties and rights were by the use of what he called abstract reasoning. Hume dismissed the notion that one could establish the moral principles of natural law—or any moral principles—merely by due consideration of the *idea* of a supreme being whose workmanship we are, and the *idea* of ourselves as "understanding rational beings." In short, Hume dismissed the a priori Lockeian rationalism upon which the authors of *The Federalist* relied in their moral theory of duties and rights even though he undoubtedly influenced their predominantly empiricistic view of the nature of descriptive political science.

The Lockeian tendency of the authors of *The Federalist* to regard propositions of natural law about man's duties and rights as essential and a priori while regarding psychological propositions about human nature as accidental and empirical may be clarified by noting an ambiguity in the expression "law of nature" that was clearly noted by Bishop Berkeley. He wrote that "we ought to distinguish between a twofold signification of the terms *law of nature,* which words do either denote a rule or precept for the direction of the voluntary actions of reasonable agents, and in that sense they imply a duty; or else they are used to signify any general rule which we observe to obtain in the works of nature, independent of the wills of men, in which sense no duty is implied."[7] With this distinction in mind, we may say that, according to Publius, nonempirical laws of nature in the first of Berkeley's senses expressed essential and rationally establishable moral duties and rights of man, whereas laws of nature in the second of Berkeley's senses were empirical reports of the psychological attributes of man upon which Publius focused when he engaged in political science and psychology. Publius wrote far less about morals than about psychology, far less about man's moral duties and rights than about his mental traits—even though one of Publius's main purposes was to create and defend a Constitution that would protect man's moral rights. His concentration on psychology as opposed to morals showed that he had relatively little interest in portraying an ideal man. By contrast, thinkers who were mainly concerned to derive the moral laws of nature from reflection on the essence or nature of man as created by God were pre-eminently concerned with portraying an ideal man. They thought his essence had been created *by* God *and in the image of* God, and therefore they thought this ideal man unswervingly obeyed the moral laws of nature. However, man as Publius knew him was very different. For Publius the psychological laws of nature record the behavior of actual men; and Publius thought we establish these laws by recourse to experience and history. By contrast, Publius thought that the moral laws of nature tell us how actual men *ought to behave;* and Publius thought we establish *these* laws by reflecting on the God-created essence of ideal man. For the most part, Publius served as a psychological analyst who searched empirically for human motives, but if called upon to defend his moral principles, he would have transformed himself into a logical analyst of the essence of man who searched for man's duties. Such was the double life of Publius, who used Locke's rationalism when defending moral laws and Hume's empiricism when defending psychological laws.

Two Kinds of Analysis

We must not be misled, therefore, by the fact that the psychological student of human nature was also viewed in the seventeenth and eighteenth centuries as an analyst of human nature. A psychologist was thought to engage in a kind of analysis even though he did not extract man's moral duties or rights from his essence in a supposedly logical manner. We may infer this from the following remark by A. O. Lovejoy about a phase of religious thinking which preceded the period in which *The Federalist* was written:

> The religious writers . . . usually did not fail to insist that man in his original constitution and his potential supernatural destiny is an admirable creature, made in the image of God; and disquisitions on the "dignity of human nature" were not wholly lacking in conventional works of edification. But in his actual behavior, and still more in his "heart," that is, in his inner affective and appetitive makeup, the springs of action which chiefly move man in his "natural" or unregenerate state, his essential folly and depravity were exhibited as all the more glaring by contrast with what he was meant to be, conceivably might have been, and sometimes supposed himself to be.[8]

In reading this, we must keep in mind the difference between the analyst of man's heart who discovers the springs of his action and the analyst of his nature who discovers his duties. This difference rests on the difference between (1) saying that the duties of man are discovered when we logically analyze his God-created essence or original constitution and (2) saying that his springs of action are discovered when we psychologically analyze his "inner affective and appetitive makeup." The point is that in the first case we extract duties which are inside the *concept* of an ideal man who was made in the image of God, whereas in the second case we use empirical methods to discover the inner springs of individual men as they actually are. In the first case we are thought to use an a priori method because we unpack the concept of man in a rational, logical manner; in the second we are thought to use an a posteriori or empirical method because we look into the hearts of individual men. The rationalistic moralist uses logic to peer into the essence of ideal man whereas the empirical psychologist uses experience and history to uncover the springs of actual human behavior.[9] Publius, it goes without saying, was more interested in the second kind of inquiry but he would have been forced to engage in the first if required to make explicit the moral foundations of the Constitution.

Not only do we have to distinguish two different conceptions of analysis but, as we can see from what Lovejoy says, we need to distinguish between two uses of the word "natural." When Lovejoy speaks of the springs of action that chiefly move man in his " 'natural' or unregenerate state," he uses the word "natural" in a sense which is different from that which we apply to "man in his original constitution," who is also sometimes said to be in a *natural* state. The natural state which is said to be unregenerate—it is the state of a man who is not "born again"—occurs later than the natural state which is identified with his original constitution, and the later natural state of unregenerate man was the primary concern of Publius the psychologist. Therefore, the theologians about whom Lovejoy was writing would have said that unregenerate man was the primary concern of Hamilton, Jay, and Madison when they used psychological analysis to discover man's springs of action, whereas natural man in his original constitution was the focus of their attention whenever they tried to use logical analysis to extract his moral duties and rights.

Descriptive vs. Moral Judgment of Men and Their Actions

While dealing with the unregenerate actual man, Publius often made moral statements about him after describing his psychological traits. For example, after speaking of man's ambition, his rapacity, and his lust for power, Publius occasionally went on to assert something moral about man's worth; and what Publius asserted about man's worth should be distinguished from statements in the doctrine of natural law about man's duty or right to perform certain actions. On some occasions Publius would declare that man was as bad as Voltaire had said he was at the end of the following passage:

> Men in general are foolish, ungrateful, jealous, covetous of their neighbor's goods; abusing their superiority when they are strong, and tricksters when they are weak. . . . Power is commonly possessed, in States and in families, by those who have the strongest arms, the most resolute minds and the hardest hearts. From which the moralists of all ages have concluded that the human species is of little worth; and in this they have not departed widely from the truth.[10]

Although one might think that Publius's terms "rapacious" and "vindictive"—like Voltaire's terms "foolish," "ungrateful," "jealous," and "covetous of their neighbor's goods"—are moral because we often use them in sentences which are derogatory, the fact that we use them in this way does not show that they are moral terms. Moreover, the statement that a person habitually covets his neighbor's goods is not a moral statement about that person. Nor is the statement that he coveted those goods on some specific occasion. When one of the Ten Commandments orders us not to covet our neighbor's goods, it says that a mental act of a certain description ought not to be performed. Indeed, if we were given no *description* of the act as covetous, we would not know what act was being prohibited. Of course, if we should define "murder" as "homicide that one ought not to perform," then "murder" would not be a purely descriptive term but rather a moral one. But in that case the precept "One ought not commit murder" would be true by definition, which I presume it is not.[11] Something similar may be said about all of the names of proscribed and prescribed acts if the relevant proscriptive and prescriptive sentences are not to lapse into truism. These remarks make clear, I hope, why certain terms in *The Federalist* are—and must be—terms of descriptive psychology even though they denote persons or acts about which Publius might have passed moral judgments, favorable or unfavorable. Every moral generalization which asserts that a certain kind of act ought to be done, ought not to be done, or may be done contains a descriptive term which denotes the kind of act under consideration. Similarly, every moral generalization which assigns worth (or its opposite) to a certain kind of person contains a descriptive term which denotes the kind of person under consideration. And only descriptive terms were used by Publius when he engaged in empirical psychology as opposed to normative ethics or moral philosophy.

Realism and Pessimism

So far we have seen that Publius the descriptive psychologist was an experimental scientist and not a moralist bent on analyzing the essence of an ideal man. As a psychologist, he has been called a realist and even a pessimist. For example, Benjamin F. Wright tells us that "at first glance the conception of human nature stated, reiterated, and depended upon in *The Federalist* is pessimistic or, in the most usual sense of the word, realistic"[12]; Lovejoy tells us that the chief framers of the Constitution relied on what seemed to them to be "a sound and realistic theory of human nature";[13] and Beard also speaks of the realism of Publius.[14] It may be worth observing, therefore, that the term "realist" is used by commentators to suggest that a realist is one who avoids an excessively rosy or favorable picture of man. They do not bother to say that a realist is one who avoids an excessively *un*rosy or *un*favorable picture of man. And yet, since a realist is supposedly one who describes things as they are, he might be thought to avoid the extreme of rosiness on the one hand as well as that of unrosiness on the other. It would seem, then, that those who identify realism with pessimism suppose that thinkers about human nature are likely to err in the direction of optimism. Why? Probably because they think that man usually distorts reality by flattering himself; and so, while the word "realist" alone connotes nothing more than fidelity to things as they are, many commentators apply it to Publius because they think he achieved such fidelity by depicting man as worse than he was usually supposed to be. Because, it would seem, Publius supposedly pulled us back to reality by contradicting optimists, Publius is also called a pessimist. Strictly speaking, however, a pessimist is one who takes the worst view of human nature, whereas an optimist takes the best view of it. Consequently, from a logical point of view, man may not be as bad as the pessimists say he is nor as good as the optimists say he is—meaning that not *all* of man's motives are bad and not *all* of them are good.

We shall see later that this is indeed the view of Publius, but he said more about human nature that deserves our attention, since he ranked different kinds of human motives—good and bad—according to their strength; and only by attending to this ranking, as we shall in the next chapter, can we see how he used his theory of motivation to support his views in political science without limiting himself to the banal proposition that some human motives are bad and some are good. In evaluating human nature, Hume said a number of things in his essay "Of the Dignity or Meanness of Human Nature" that illuminate the views of Publius on this subject, whether or not it can be shown conclusively that the essay influenced what Publius wrote.[15] Here again we may use the history of philosophy to clarify what Publius believed even if we are unable to document the exact genealogy of his belief.

Anticipating a view of Publius, Hume argued against those who said that man is totally depraved. And in the course of his argument he exposed certain purely verbal elements of the traditional debate about the dignity or meanness of human nature while trenchantly formulating what he regarded as the real issue of the debate. That issue, he thought, had to do with the comparative strength of man's selfish and social passions as motives, and even though Hume took a position on the matter which was not—in my opinion—exactly that of Publius, examining Hume's view will help us better understand the theory of motivation employed in *The Federalist*.

In attempting to dispose of the merely verbal differences that obscured the real issue, Hume made some acute observations in the philosophy of language. When we use language to express approbation or blame, he said, we are usually more influenced "by comparison than by any fixed unalterable standard in the nature of things." To show what he meant he first pointed out that when we call an individual animal big or small, "we always form a secret comparison between that animal and others of the same species," meaning by "secret" something like "tacit" or "implicit." According to Hume, then, the sentence "Fido is big" is elliptical for the sentence "Fido is bigger than most dogs," and therefore Fido may be of the very same size as a horse which we call small because that horse is smaller than most horses.

It follows, Hume adds, that a dog of a certain size may be admired for "the greatness of its bulk" while a horse of the very same size may be admired for its smallness. Consequently, Hume confided to his reader: "When I am present . . . at any dispute, I always consider with myself whether it be a question of comparison or not that is the subject of controversy; and if it be, whether the disputants compare the same objects together, or talk of things that are widely different."[16] Hume's point is that the dispute about the dignity or meanness of human nature involves comparison, and that our assessment of human nature depends on what we compare it with.

Armed with this reflection, Hume says that when we speak of the dignity or meanness of human nature, we are likely to make a comparison between men and animals because they are "the only creatures endowed with thought that fall under our senses." And "certainly," he says without hesitation, "this comparison is favorable to mankind." He exclaims: "What a wide difference is there between these creatures!" and adds: "How exalted a notion must we entertain of the former, in comparison of the latter."[17] It is important to observe that the wide difference between the intellectual powers of man and animal about which he exclaims is an empirically describable difference between the intellectual powers of the species man and those of the species animal, whereas the exalted notion that Hume thinks we must entertain about men is the result of a moral assessment which we make after comparing men with animals. In other words, if we choose to compare men with beasts and notice certain differences between *them,* we will be led to attribute great dignity to human nature.

Consequently, Hume remarks, those who might hope to refute this favorable assessment of man by making "a new and secret comparison between man and beings of the most perfect wisdom" are, in effect, changing the subject.[18] Hume readily admits that man can form an idea of perfections that go far beyond what he has experienced in himself and that he is not limited in his conception of wisdom and virtue. Indeed, man can easily form an idea of a degree of knowledge which will be so great when compared to his own that it will make his own appear very contemptible and will also make the difference between his knowledge "and the sagacity of animals, in a manner, to disappear and vanish." Therefore, Hume argues, those who denigrate man on the basis of this secret comparison should reveal their secret by openly announcing that they are comparing him with beings of the most perfect wisdom and *not* with animals. For Hume readily admits that "man falls much more short of perfect wisdom, and even of his own ideas of perfect wisdom, than animals do of man"; and that "the latter difference is so considerable, that nothing but a comparison with the former can make it appear of little moment."[19] One of Hume's points is that a great deal of idle debate would be eliminated if people made explicit what they were comparing man with when they exalted or denigrated human nature. Consequently, he says, those who denigrate man because they are comparing him with angels would not have a *real* disagreement with those who praise him because *they* are comparing him with beasts. Their disagreement would be merely verbal.

Hume also dismisses another way of coming to a contemptible notion of the human species by means of merely verbal considerations. He observes that after comparing individuals and finding very few whom we call wise, we are likely to adopt a low view of our species in general. However, he says, in our normal use of the word "wise" we do not declare a man wise by first fixing a certain point on the scale of wisdom and then discovering that in fact very few individuals rise above that point. Rather, Hume says, what we usually do is to define a man as wise if and only if he exhibits a degree of wisdom which is attained by few. In the language of grading students, we mark on a curve and give an "A" to the few at the top of the class. From this Hume concludes "that to say there are few wise men in the world, is really to say nothing; since it is only by their scarcity that they merit that appellation." However, if it *is* to say nothing, another merely verbal argument for the inferiority of human nature is undercut.[20] So here again a tacitly comparative argument is shown to be ineffectual as a device for showing the meanness of human nature. The first argument fallaciously denigrates man by comparing him to a species to which his admirers did not compare him when they had praised him. The second argument fallaciously denigrates him by using a definition of "wise" which is bound to show that there are very few wise men, in which case it is no foundation at all on which to rest an adverse judgment of man's worth.

After exposing these secretly comparative and ineffectual arguments for the moral inferiority of man, Hume refers to a method of comparison that he respects and accepts because it does not yield conclusions about human nature that rest on silent departures from language as normally used. He says that "we often compare together the different motives or actuating principles of human nature, in order to regulate our judgment concerning it. And, indeed, this is the only kind of comparison which is worth our attention, or decides any thing in the present question. Were our selfish and vicious principles so much predominant above our social and virtuous, as is asserted by some philosophers, we ought undoubtedly to entertain a contemptible notion of human nature."[21] However, we must realize that Hume did not entertain "a contemptible notion of human nature" in his essay "Of the Dignity or Meanness of Human Nature" even though he was fully aware of man's frailty and corruptness. In that essay, Hume took a position somewhere between (1) the position of those who "insist upon the blind sides of human nature, and can discover nothing, except vanity, in which man surpasses the other animals, whom he affects so much to despise"; and (2) the position of those who "exalt our species to the skies, and represent man as a kind of human demigod, who derives his origin from heaven, and retains evident marks of his lineage and descent."[22] I stress this because I think that Publius also took a position somewhere between these two extremes, even though I suspect that Publius placed man closer to the animals and farther from the demigods than Hume did.[23] But wherever one puts Publius and Hume on the scale that extends from pessimism to optimism about man, I think one must disagree with certain views that have been advanced about Madison's evaluation of human nature. In particular, Lovejoy's views of Madison's pessimism are worth considering at some length because of Lovejoy's great erudition and analytic power; and, more important, because a consideration of his efforts to depict Madison as an extreme pessimist will provide us with an opportunity to deepen our understanding of the theory of human nature adopted in *The Federalist*.

Man as a Knave in Politics

Lovejoy, who did so much to refute the false generalizations of Carl Becker about the optimism of eighteenth-century thinkers, believed that Madison's views in *Number 10* were part of a long tradition according to which the hearts or the inward parts of individual men are depraved, corrupt, and filled with evil motives.[24] But it seems to me that Lovejoy exaggerated Madison's disparagement of man by failing to emphasize that Madison's denigration of man's motives applies primarily to man *in politics*. We know that in *Number 10* Madison spoke of faction as a dangerous vice and as a disease which caused political mischief; and we also know that for him any faction would be bad by definition because its members would be actuated by an impulse adverse to the rights of other citizens and to the permanent and aggregate interests of the community. But, while listing the latent causes of factions in *Number 10*, Madison did not explicitly attribute evil to the motives of individual men who might not be members of factions. In Madison's view, the disease of faction breaks out when men who have certain opinions, passions, or interests join with others who have the same opinions, passions, or interests to form a social group which is adverse to the rights of others and to the common good. And that is why we must stress that in *Number 10* Madison disparaged the motives of individuals acting in *political groups*. I emphasize the phrase "political groups" because I do not think that Madison held that the hearts or inward parts of all individual men are depraved, corrupt, and filled with evil motives. In *Number 10*, Madison is primarily concerned to condemn the motives of men when they participate in factions, not when they act outside of such groups. Consequently, the text of *Number 10* does not support the easy assimilation of Madison's views to the tradition which says that every man is always moved by vicious motives.[25]

This may also be seen by examining Lovejoy's formulation of a problem which was faced by the pessimistic tradition to which he thought Madison belonged, and then comparing that formulation with what Madison says in *Number 10* about his own version of the problem. According to Lovejoy, the problem was: *"How,* by means of what political device, could you bring creatures whose wills were *always* [my emphasis] moved by irrational and 'depraved' passions to behave in ways which would not be inconsistent with the 'common good.' "[26] But Madison, when addressing a similar problem, did not speak in *Number 10* about how to deal with creatures whose wills were *always* moved by irrational and depraved passions. Madison focused on citizens who were members of factions, and members of factions did not, according to Madison, constitute the whole of the community. Consequently, even though the political device recommended by Madison for dealing with factions had its origins in the method of counterpoise recommended by Lovejoy's pessimists, in Madison's hands the method was not supposed to deal with every member of society conceived as an individual whose will was moved only by irrational and depraved passions.[27] According to Lovejoy, the method of counterpoise rested on the idea "that, in framing a political constitution, you can construct a good whole out of bad parts, can make these conflicting private interests subservient to the public interest, simply by bringing all of them together upon a common political battleground where they will neutralize one another."[28] Lovejoy also says that the idea of counterpoise was illustrated in *Number 10* when Madison argued for the control of the spirit of faction by making sure, as Lovejoy puts it, "that the number and relative strength of the groups representing conflicting special interests will be such that they will effectually counterbalance one another. When they do so, no part will be able to dominate the whole, to use all the legislative and executive power of the government for its own purposes. Each faction will be unable to get a majority vote in favor of its special interest because all the other factions will be opposed to it, and thereby (Madison assumes) the 'general good,' or the nearest practicable approximation to it, will be realized." On the basis of these remarks by Lovejoy himself, it is clear that the men who have interests which must counterbalance each other in Madison's view need not constitute the whole of the community, since the community includes individuals who are not members of factions.[29] And I repeat that even those who are members of factions were not regarded by Madison as having nothing but corrupt and depraved motives.

In passing, I want to argue against Lovejoy that Madison did not subscribe to the total depravity of man when referring at the Constitutional Convention to certain views of Gouverneur Morris. I bring this particular matter up because Lovejoy points to a certain agreement between Madison and Morris about the nature of man and counterpoise in order to support the idea that Madison subscribed to an extreme form of pessimism. I do not think that any agreement which might have existed between the two friends shows what Lovejoy thinks it shows about Madison's views. On July 2, 1787, Morris spoke to the Convention on the role of the Senate and argued, among other things, that its object was "to check the precipitation, changeableness, and excesses" of the House of Representatives. "What qualities," he asked, "are necessary to constitute a check in this case? *Abilities* and *virtue,* are equally necessary in both branches. Something more then is wanted. 1. the Checking branch must have a personal interest in checking the other branch. one interest must be opposed to another interest. Vices as they exist, must be turned agst. each other." This passage is quoted by Lovejoy to show that Morris and Madison agreed about the badness of human motives and also about the need to offset the absence of "better motives" by counterbalancing bad ones.[30] But Lovejoy makes no mention of the fact that on July 11, Madison referred at the Convention to Morris as "a member who on all occasions, had inculcated So strongly, the political depravity of men, and the necessity of checking one vice and interest by opposing to them another vice & interest."[31] I call special attention to Madison's use of the adjective "political," since it suggests that he was focusing on man's motives as a member of a political group such as a faction, and not on man as such. Therefore, if he agreed with Morris, he agreed with him only to the extent of attributing depravity to man in a political situation.[32]

To lend further support to the view that Madison was not as pessimistic as Lovejoy makes him out to be, I turn to *Number 51,* which, Lovejoy thinks, expressed Madison's distrust of human nature "more sharply" than *Number 10* did. The chief passage in *Number 51* about human nature is the following:

> The great security against a gradual concentration of the several powers in the same department, consists in giving to those who administer each department, the necessary constitutional means, and personal motives, to resist encroachments of the others. The provision for defence must in this, as in all other cases, be made commensurate to the danger of attack. Ambition must be made to counteract ambition. The interest of the man must be connected with the constitutional rights of the place. It may be a reflection on human nature, that such devices should be necessary to controul the abuses of government. But what is government itself but the greatest of all reflections on human nature? If men were angels, no government would be necessary. If angels were to govern men, neither external nor internal controuls on government would be necessary. In framing a government which is to be administered by men over men, the great difficulty lies in this: You must first enable the government to controul the governed; and in the next place, oblige it to controul itself. A dependence on the people is no doubt the primary controul on the government; but experience has taught mankind the necessity of auxiliary precautions.
>
> This policy of supplying by opposite and rival interests, the defect of better motives, might be traced through the whole system of human affairs, private as well as public. We see it particularly displayed in all the subordinate distributions of power; where the constant aim is to divide and arrange the several offices in such a manner as that each may be a check on the other; that the private interest of every individual, may be a centinel over the public rights. These inventions of prudence cannot be less requisite in the distribution of the supreme powers of the state.[33]

Here Madison agrees with Hume that men are not angels, but one can fall short of being an angel without having a will which is always moved by irrational and depraved passions. And one can fall short of being an angel without becoming a beast. Why would Madison speak of *"giving"* to those who administer each of the three departments of government the "personal motives, to resist encroachments of the others" if he thought that all or most men are always moved by irrational and depraved passions—whether they are in or out of politics? When Madison says that ambition must be *made* to counteract ambition, and that the interest of the man must be *connected* with the constitutional rights of the place, Madison is not saying or implying that men always, or almost always, acted from evil motives. Rather, he seems to be saying that the branches of government should be so formed by the Constitution that the human being who happened to be president would be encouraged to have an ambition that would counteract the ambitions of human beings in the legislature. This is why Madison says that the framers of a government must *oblige* the government to control itself by encouraging its different branches to have opposing motives that will check each other. And if the framers must *oblige* them to have these mutually checking motives, they might lack such motives.

In concentrating on man's *political* rather than on his *total* depravity, Madison was closer to Hume than he was to the pessimistic tradition described by Lovejoy. Hume once wrote: "Political writers have established it as a maxim, that, in contriving any system of government, and fixing the several checks and controls of the constitution, every man ought to be supposed a *knave,* and to have no other end, in all his actions, than private interest."[34] Hume then adds the following very important comment: "It is, therefore, a just *political* maxim, *that every man must be supposed a knave;* though, at the same time, it appears somewhat strange, that a maxim should be true in *politics* which is false in *fact.*"[35] Note that Hume denies that *every* man is in fact a knave—a denial which is in accord with Hume's assessment of man in "Of the Dignity or Meanness of Human Nature." And when Hume tries to explain why every man should be supposed to be a knave *in politics,* he says that "men are generally more honest in their private than in their public capacity, and will go greater lengths to serve a party, than when their own private interest is alone concerned." Although honor serves as a great check on mankind, Hume continues, this check is in great measure removed when a man is approved by his own party if he does what serves the interest of the party.[36] This desire for the approval of others encourages knavery in men *when they take part in politics and become members of factions.* The qualification I have emphasized accords with the views of Madison, who never asserted that the motive of honor had no effect on man. Madison's point was that its effect was comparatively weak on man in politics. Therefore, like Hume, he did not assert that every man was a knave, *period,* but at most that he was a knave in politics.[37]

Hume's view on this matter was also accepted by Hamilton in 1775, when the very passage I have quoted from Hume's essay "Of the Independency of Parliament" was quoted approvingly by Hamilton in "The Farmer Refuted." In that piece we find complete agreement with some of Hume's remarks on the psychology of politics. In *The Federalist* we see similar agreement expressed by Hamilton, perhaps in more explicit form. He asks in *Number 15:* "Has it been found that bodies of men act with more rectitude or greater disinterestedness than individuals?" And he answers: "The contrary of this has been inferred by all accurate observers of the conduct of mankind." Then Hamilton proffers an explanation of this inferiority of men behaving in groups as opposed to behaving as individuals. The influence he mentions is based, he says, upon obvious reasons. "Regard to reputation," he maintains, "has a less active influence, when the infamy of a bad action is to be divided among a number, than when it is to fall singly upon one. A spirit of faction which is apt to mingle its poison in the deliberations of all bodies of men, will often hurry the persons of whom they are composed into improprieties and excesses, for which they would blush in a private capacity."[38] Here Hamilton offers only a slightly different explanation for what he and Hume accept as fact. Hume says that a man's regard for his honor will cease to be a check on him when his faction heaps approval on him for doing a knavish deed; Hamilton says that a man's regard for his reputation will be diminished as a check on him because the infamy of his knavish deed will be divided, and therefore diminished for each collaborating agent who is influenced by the poisonous spirit of faction. There are differences between the two statements, but their general import is similar. Both Hume and Hamilton believe that men will—for one or another reason—behave more knavishly while cooperating as members of a faction than they will when acting alone.[39] In this respect, Hume, Hamilton, and Madison were in agreement; and their agreement shows that all of them departed from the tradition of extreme pessimism with which Lovejoy linked Madison so closely.[40]

Concluding Remarks

In this chapter I have tried to make a number of points in preparation for a discussion of more substantive psychological questions in the next chapter, and it may be useful to collect the most important of those points here. I have argued, first of all, that although Publius believed that man's moral duties and rights are derived from his God-created nature or essence by the use of what Hume called abstract reason, Publius for the most part used what Hume called experimental reason in describing man's psychological makeup and motives. Second, I have said that the logical analysis of man's essence must be distinguished from the psychological analysis of the minds of concrete individual men. Third, I have said that the logical sort of analysis was performed on the concept of man as created by God in his own image whereas the psychological sort of analysis was performed on the motives of man as he is. Fourth, I have tried to make clear that although there is a difference between describing human actions or the whole human species and passing moral judgment, Publius engaged in both of these activities, though it must be said that he was more interested in description than in moral judgment. This brings me back to the part of the chapter in which I deal with Publius's supposed realism or pessimism.

Because I do not think that Publius presented a view of man's nature according to which all of his motives are corrupt and depraved, and because I have pointed out that he held that men have good motives as well as bad motives, I agree with E. M. Burns's sensible judgment in 1938 that Madison's view of human nature in *The Federalist* was best expressed in *Number 55:*

> As there is a degree of depravity in mankind which requires a certain degree of circumspection and distrust: So there are other qualities in human nature, which justify a certain portion of esteem and confidence. Republican government presupposes the existence of these qualities in a higher degree than any other form. Were the pictures which have been drawn by the political jealousy of some among us, faithful likenesses of the human character, the inference would be that there is not sufficient virtue among men for self-government; and that nothing less than the chains of despotism can restrain them from destroying and devouring one another.[41]

Surely this passage does not justify Lovejoy's saying that Madison subscribed in an unqualified way to Plautus's dictum that man is a wolf to man. It confirms not only the sensible statement by Burns but also the later statement by Adair that "although *The Federalist* depicts the black side of our nature, the final judgment on it is 'gray.' "[42] Of course, the band of gray between black and white is quite broad. Consequently, we may say that Hume's final judgment was also gray in his essay "Of the Dignity or Meanness of Human Nature," though Hume's gray was lighter, I believe, than that of Publius. They differed only about where to put man on the band that separated demigods or angels from beasts or knaves. And this difference put Hume and Publius themselves at different points on the band that separates extreme optimists from extreme pessimists on the subject of human nature.

Where should this recognition of grayness lead us in our effort to characterize Publius's view of human nature? Strictly speaking, to the conclusion that he adopts neither a pessimistic nor an optimistic view of man. But James P. Scanlan has wisely pointed out that although this moderate conclusion may lead us to a better understanding of Publius than the conclusion that he is a thorough pessimist, it does not afford what Scanlan calls "a functioning theory of human nature." Scanlan remarks that "to assert simply that men are both good and bad . . . explains nothing. Such a view can hardly be regarded as a theoretical source, ground, or test of political doctrines, for it has no specific implications."[43] Scanlan's view comports well with Hume's view that the experimental political scientist is not concerned to make moral statements about what is good and bad, nor about what is morally obligatory or permissible. But even if moral statements could be reduced to or translated into statements of experimental science, it is hard to see how any such translation of the statements that men have both good and bad motives could give much support to the specific political doctrines contained in the Constitution such as separation of powers, checks and balances, division of authority between state and nation, and a bicameral legislature. It is hard to see how a political scientist might defend such provisions merely by observing with Madison that there is a degree of depravity in mankind which requires a certain degree of circumspection and distrust whereas there are other qualities in human nature which justify a certain portion of esteem and confidence. A political scientist who has accepted a moral theory still needs a psychological theory about the comparative strength of different kinds of motives when he begins to construct a government which will implement his moral ideals. Such a psychological theory was one of the things that Hume called for when he sought to "compare together the different motives or actuating principles of human nature" in an effort to see which were "predominant." Saying that one motive predominated over another is different from saying that it is morally superior to another. So we are now brought to these fundamental questions: Is there in *The Federalist* a psychological theory that tells us which motives or actuating principles of human nature predominate? And if there is, what is it and how does it function in the political science of Publius?

7

Reason, Passion, and Interest

The reply to the first of the two questions raised at the end of the last chapter is that there *is* a psychological theory of human nature to be found in *The Federalist* even though it is never systematically expounded by the authors. It is primarily a theory that compares the strength of what Hume called the different motives or actuating principles of human nature. In his essay "Of the Dignity or Meanness of Human Nature" Hume compared different motives and, as we have seen, concluded that the "selfish and vicious" motives were weaker than the "social and virtuous" motives. Although he was led by this comparison to a moral judgment of human nature—and to a relatively favorable one at that—the authors of *The Federalist* were not mainly concerned to compare the actuating motives of men in order to support their less favorable moral judgment about human nature. Their primary task was to compare the strength of different motives in order to support various provisions of the Constitution and to defend those provisions against hostile criticism; their interest in psychology was therefore guided more directly by their interest in politics than by their interest in ethics. Indeed, the main point of Publius's psychology was to lend support to or to explain propositions in the science of politics. Although his theory did not assert anything explicit about the political world of constitutions, courts, and legislatures, it was offered by Publius in defense of his views about such entities. In this chapter I want to identify the main kinds of psychological motives he dealt with, namely, reason, passion, and interest; in the chapter following the present one, I want to deal in more detail with different subdivisions of these main motives in order to present Publius's view of their relative strengths; and then, after that, I want in Chapter 9 to show how this view affected his views in political science.

Publius regarded motives much as they were regarded by philosophers of the eighteenth century who tried to imitate Newtonian mechanics.[1] Publius thought that a motive could cause or produce an action in the way that a force could produce an acceleration in a body. He regarded motives as internal or mental entities whereas he thought that actions were overt and external; but, like Hume, he thought that when we say that a motive causes an action on the part of a human being, we use the word "cause" in the same sense as we use it when we say that a force causes an acceleration in a body.[2] By thinking, as Publius did, of motives as analogous to mechanical forces, we can see why he thought that some motives are stronger than others. It is also helpful in understanding him to realize that when Publius discusses human motives, he thinks he uses experimental reason to show the effects of reason as a motive. In one crucial respect, therefore, he departs from Hume's view that reason alone cannot serve as a motive of human action. The sort of reason which motivates action is, according to Publius, a combination of experimental and demonstrative reasoning, as we shall soon see.

One more preliminary observation. Although the psychological theory in *The Federalist* is primarily a theory of motivation, the authors do not provide a definition of "motive." They were more likely to use mechanical analogies to explain what they had in mind rather than to define or analyze the concept of motive. Most likely they would have accepted Dr. Johnson's identification of a motive as "that which incites the action."[3] Madison spoke for all of them when he judiciously observed in *Number 37* that "the faculties of the mind itself have never yet been distinguished and defined, with satisfactory precision, by all the efforts of the most acute and metaphysical Philosophers. Sense, perception, judgment, desire, volition, memory, imagination, are found to be separated by such delicate shades, and minute gradations, that their boundaries have eluded the most subtle investigations, and remain a pregnant source of ingenious disquisition and controversy." Madison also says in *Number 37* that *any* effort at precise definition, whether it be an effort of a metaphysical philosopher, that of a naturalist, or that of a political scientist, is bound to be plagued by obscurity. And this, he adds by way of an optical metaphor, is for three reasons: the objects dealt with are not distinct, the human faculties of those who offer definitions of them are imperfect, and words, which form "the medium through which the conceptions of men are conveyed to each other," are inadequate.[4] Here Madison is primarily concerned to warn the reader of the difficulty in discriminating and defining with sufficient certainty the provinces of the legislative, the executive, and the judiciary as well as the boundary between federal and state jurisdictions; but he felt compelled to advance a general theory of the difficulty inherent in all definition while warning his reader of the difficulty of offering definitions in the science of government.

Reason as a Motive

In spite of Madison's warning, we would do well to try to clarify how motives were viewed in *The Federalist,* and to identify them in a way that will help us better understand the theory of motivation adopted by Publius. As I have indicated, all of the motives he mentions seem to fall into three main categories that were commonly distinguished by British moralists of the eighteenth century, namely, reason, passions, and interests.[5] Whether these three classes constitute a mutually exclusive division of all human motives is debatable, but Publius sometimes writes as though he thinks that it is. It will be recalled, for example, that Madison's treatment of factions in *Number 10* depends on distinguishing opinions, passions, and interests, and that opinions were in his view formed by man through the exercise of his reason. As I have already said, Publius held that reason may cause men to act insofar as their opinions or beliefs may cause them to act. In *Number 10,* men gathered in factions are said to act mischievously, but, according to Madison and his fellow authors, reason may move a man to act in accordance with what he believes is his moral right or moral duty. In coming to believe—or in justifying his belief—that he has such a right or duty to perform a certain action, he may use two different kinds of reason that we have discussed earlier. Because Hamilton and the other authors of *The Federalist* subscribed to a rationalistic theory of morality, they held, as we have seen, that some principles of morality are self-evident and others demonstrable. Intuitive reason, they held, would certify the truth of the self-evident general moral principle that all men have a right to liberty. However, they also held that one would have to use experimental reason in establishing that Jefferson, or any other individual, was a man.[6] Then, after having established these two premises of one's argument, one could use reason in the form of logical deduction to arrive at the conclusion that Jefferson had a right to liberty. According to Publius, once this rationally derived belief about Jefferson's right was reached, he might be moved by it to struggle for his liberty. In that case, reason alone might move him in this direction even though he might also be simultaneously moved by passion or interest. This, as I have already observed, is a non-Humeian conclusion about the causal efficacy of reason which is arrived at by Publius the psychologist while supposedly using experimental reason in Hume's sense.

According to Publius, men may be even more obviously moved to act by a belief about obligation. Hamilton maintains in *Number 31* that reason of the sort that Locke called "intuitive" may certify the allegedly self-evident axiom or "primary truth"—as Hamilton called it—that "the means ought to be proportioned to the end,"[7] and Hamilton also seems to have held that the opinion that a specific means will in fact attain a specific end may be established by what Hume called experimental reason. Thus, although Hamilton held it to be demonstrable that the federal government ought to have the means essential to what he called the care of the common defense simply because the federal government was entrusted with the care of the common defense, the proposition that the raising of armies and the building of fleets would *as a matter of fact* constitute a means of caring for the common defense was probably regarded by Hamilton as certifiable by experimental reason. Under the circumstances, the proposition that the federal government ought to be empowered to raise armies and build fleets is a conclusion established by the combined use of demonstrative reason in certifying the major premise of the argument and experimental reason in certifying its minor premise. The major premise of this Hamiltonian argument about what ought to be done is moral, like the statement that all men have a right to liberty, whereas the minor premise is descriptive, like the statement that Jefferson is a man. Consequently, although it may be said that the proximate cause of a specific action is the singular moral conclusion, belief, or opinion that the action may or ought to be performed, according to Publius, a rational defense of the specific action appeals not only to a moral principle but also to a statement of fact. The motivating singular moral conclusion or belief is therefore supported by the use of what Hume called abstract reason *and* by what he called experimental reason—a combination which, as we have seen earlier, is typical of Publius's epistemological dualism. Consequently, we must not disregard the role of experimental reason in cases where Publius holds that an action has been caused by a moral belief which is a motive of reason. Publius does not say this in so many words, but it would have been hard for him to deny it.

It is important to recognize not only that *The Federalist* allows for the possibility that some human actions will be motivated or caused by rational beliefs but also that its authors regarded their own book as a reasoned defense of the proposed constitution. In *Number 1* Hamilton says that he wants to put his fellow citizens on guard against all attempts, from whatever quarter, to influence their decision about the proposed constitution "by any impressions other than those which may result from the evidence of truth." He also says in that same number: "My motives must remain in the depository of my own breast: My arguments will be open to all, and may be judged of by all." However, Hamilton's contrast between his motives and his rational arguments should not mislead us. Hamilton does not mean here that reason is not a motive that impels men to act. He merely means that in order to assess the validity of his argument, the reader need not know of any nonrational motive that he may have had in advancing that argument. Hamilton says that he will frankly acknowledge his "convictions" and freely lay before the reader "the reasons on which they are founded."[8] However, he offered those reasons in the belief or hope that they would move the reader to adopt his, Hamilton's, convictions. Reasoned argument, he thought, would produce beliefs in his readers about what ought to be done, and rational beliefs about what ought to be done, he hoped, would lead to political action.[9]

Passions and Interests as Motives

Let us now see how Publius regarded passions and interests as motives. In doing so, we must continue to bear in mind that the authors of *The Federalist* were certainly not what Madison called metaphysical philosophers, and therefore they felt little obligation to define the word "passion"; they also felt little obligation to define the words "reason," "interest," and "motive." Nevertheless, although they left these words undefined and used them as they were used in the ordinary language of their times, being well read in philosophy, they used them with awareness of what some philosophers had said about them.

Leaving aside certain niceties that will soon be introduced, we may say that Publius identified passion with what we would today call "emotion." In the language of his day, the word "affection" was sometimes used as a synonym of "passion" which denoted such things as ambition, hatred, joy, grief, and fear, but "affection" was also used more narrowly to refer to love alone.[10] Publius obviously thought that passions, emotions, or affections served as motives or causes of action; he thought that passions influence, cause, stimulate, prompt, or produce actions when human beings gratify those passions. The man who is avaricious gratifies his passion by getting hold of money, and the man who is fearful gratifies his passion by drawing away from something of which he is fearful. Passions, along with reason and interests, are also said by Publius to be "springs," meaning sources or origins, of action.

I come now to interest, which is also regarded by Publius as a motive that can produce an action. In his view, interest leads a person to do something if and only if that person thinks that doing it will be beneficial or advantageous to him.[11] This is in accord with the use of the term by several British moralists of the eighteenth century, and therefore it will be useful to inquire into the relationship between interest and passion as they were often conceived in that period. We know from our earlier discussion of Madison's views that a faction is a group of people who are united and actuated by a "common impulse of passion, *or* [my emphasis] of interest," and this phrase, as well as the context in which it appears, may be taken to suggest that an interest is not a passion.[12] Nevertheless, it would be rash to conclude on the basis of this passage, without further consideration of the ambiguous word "passion," that an interest is not in some sense a passion according to Publius. Philosophers of the eighteenth century from whom Publius learned some of his technical vocabulary often say that interests are passions, since they identify the interest of an individual with self-love, which they also call "self-interest." Since love is a passion, then, according to these moralists, self-love is a passion; and since self-love is the same as self-interest, then self-interest is a passion. Finally, when "self-interest" is shortened to "interest," interest is also regarded as a passion.[13] Shaftesbury speaks of "that Passion which is esteem'd peculiarly *interesting;* as having for its Aim the Possession of Wealth, and what we call a *Settlement* or *Fortune* in the World."[14] And Hume also regards interest as a passion in the *Treatise.*[15] However, it was Bishop Butler who provided one of the most careful and most illuminating analyses of the relationship between self-interest and passion to be found in the writings of British moralists, and he calls self-love—and therefore interest—an affection, that is to say, a passion.[16] To help clarify Publius's conception of the relationship between interest and passion, I want to digress in order to say something about Butler's views.

Bishop Butler on Passion and Interest: A Digression

Butler and his fellow moralist Hutcheson[17] distinguished between what they called the general passion of calm or cool self-interest or self-love and what they called particular passions, such as avarice, ambition, lust, revenge, anger, and joy. Butler identified the passion or affection of self-interest on the basis of at least three of its features: its special connection with the self, its generality, and its link with reason and reflection. The connection with the self is obvious, since Butler identifies self-interest with man's general desire for *his own* happiness.[18] But when Butler says that man's desire for his own happiness is *general,* he means that it is a desire to maximize man's own happiness in the long run and that it stands in contrast to what Butler calls a *particular* appetite such as the love of money—which may be gratified by appropriating a particular gold coin—or hunger—which may be gratified by eating a particular apple. The coin and the apple are said by Butler to be external things which, so to speak, particular passions pursue, whereas the object or goal pursued by self-interest is internal because that object or goal is our own happiness, enjoyment, and satisfaction, whether or not we have a "distinct particular perception" of what our own happiness is or what it consists of.[19] Because particular passions are directed toward external things themselves, these passions are not directed toward the internal pleasure or happiness that arises from external things.[20] According to Butler, our particular passion or appetite of hunger is for the food and not for the pleasure of eating the food, even though the satisfaction of our hunger by eating food gives rise to pleasure; we do not take delight in eating the apple because we love ourselves, but because we are satisfying a particular appetite for the apple. In a related vein, Hume said: "I feel a pleasure in doing good to my friend, because I love him; but do not love him for the sake of that pleasure."[21]

Concerning the link between interest and reason, Butler says that because self-love seeks external things as a means of affording happiness or pleasure to the self, self-love or interest belongs to man *as a reasonable creature.* In other words, a man who acts out of self-interest or self-love must use what Hume called experimental reason to discover what will be to his advantage, gain him happiness, or bring him pleasure, whereas a man who impulsively acts from a particular passion does not engage in such reasoning.[22] We see here what Albert O. Hirschman means when he speaks of "the wedging of interest in between the two traditional categories of human motivation," namely, reason and passion.[23] When a man acts out of self-interest, he uses reason to calculate that he will become happy by, say, gratifying his particular passion of hunger. On the other hand, while directly satisfying his hunger, he does not engage in reasoning. Therefore, Butler held that the particular affections are "quite distinct from reason."[24]

I cannot show by presenting indisputable evidence that this view of Butler, or the similar view of Hutcheson, directly influenced Publius's use of the words "interest" and "passion"; nor can I show that Publius explicitly said that interest was a species of passion broadly conceived. But I think it significant that one reader of Butler and Hutcheson, namely, Madison's teacher, John Witherspoon, said, while using "inclination" as equivalent to "affection" and "passion": "The affections cannot be better understood than by observing the difference between a calm deliberate general inclination, whether of the selfish or benevolent kind, and particular violent inclinations. Every man deliberately wishes his own happiness, but this differs considerably from a passionate attachment to particular gratifications, as a love of riches, honors, pleasures."[25] This historical bridge-passage, so to speak, lends support to the view that there was a similarity between the views of Butler and Hutcheson on the one hand and those of Madison on the other, concerning the relationship between interest and passion. It is plausible to suppose that Madison, like Butler, Hutcheson, and Witherspoon, regarded interest as a species of passion while broadly conceiving of passion as an inclination which may either be calm, deliberate, and general on the one hand or violent, nondeliberate, and particular on the other. We shall soon see, however, that the authors of *The Federalist* often used the word "passion" narrowly so as to refer only to what Butler and Hutcheson called the particular passions.

Passions and Interests as Distinguishable
Motives of Factions

The recognition that Madison sometimes used "passion" to refer only to a particular passion is in accord with, and illuminates, his statement in *Number 10* that a faction may be united by a passion *or* by an interest—a statement in which he treats the class of passions and the class of interests as mutually exclusive. It also illuminates Madison's use in *Number 10* of the phrase "the same opinions, the same passions, and the same interests," where once again passions and interests seem to be regarded as mutually exclusive. When Madison uses the word "passions" in this context, he does not use it in its broad sense as the equivalent of "affections" or "inclinations"; he obviously treats it as synonymous with what Butler, Hutcheson, and Witherspoon call "particular passions." In *Number 10,* when Madison refers to "a zeal for different opinions concerning religion" as a passion, he uses the word "passion" to refer to what Witherspoon called "particular violent inclinations," where "violent" means intense, vehement, or very strong.[26] And this narrow use of "passion" is what prevents Madison from labeling interest—conceived as the general, calm, deliberate desire for one's happiness—as a passion. Nevertheless, action from interest and action from particular passions have something important in common, which is brought out when interest is viewed as a passion in the broad sense of "passion." One who is moved by his interest in this sense is ultimately moved by a desire for happiness—a deliberate, general passion—even though he uses his reason in calculating what will bring about the satisfaction of that desire or passion. The use of reason in determining the means of achieving happiness cannot eradicate the passionate element in action determined by interest simply because one who is interested has a desire and one who has a desire has a passion in the broad sense of "passion."

However, when Madison used "interests" so as to treat the class of passions and the class of interests as mutually exclusive, he was able in *Number 10* to distinguish fairly sharply between factions based on passion and those based on interest. For a similar reason Hume was able, in his essay "Of Parties in General," to distinguish sharply between factions founded on affection and those founded on interest. When Hume defined a faction founded on affection in that essay, he said it was founded on the affection of attachment "towards *particular* [my emphasis] families and persons whom they desire to rule over them";[27] and his use of the word "particular" shows why the affection or passion of attachment itself was regarded by Hume as particular and therefore not to be identified with the general passion called "interest," upon which a different kind of faction rested in his classification. Only by recognizing that "passion" was used by Madison in *Number 10* as short for "particular passion" can we see why his definition of "faction" referred to groups whose members are actuated "by some common impulse of passion, *or* [my emphasis] of interest," and thereby enabled him to distinguish between factions based on passion and those based on interest.

The question now arises: If "interest" designates a calm, deliberate, and general passion or desire for one's own happiness, how can it be limited so as to refer on some occasions to what some commentators call "economic interest" when expounding Madison's views on faction? The answer is that men calculate or reason on certain occasions that their happiness would increase if the amount of their property were to increase, or if the special kind of property they hold were to be protected; and where such a calculation leads them to act, they act out of a concern for their own economic interest. However, when interest is viewed as the motive which impels a man to do that which is generally advantageous or beneficial to him, then it is clear that men who are moved by their interests are not always moved by *economic* interests. The qualification "economic" when applied to an interest indicates that action from interest refers to a class of actions of which only one subclass may be identified as action from economic interest. Indeed, we may form subclasses of economic interest itself, as Madison does, by distinguishing different kinds and amounts of property that one may seek to augment or protect, depending on whether one is a manufacturer, a banker, a landholder, and so on. Furthermore, some men might calculate on certain occasions that their general happiness would increase if the amount of their knowledge, rather than their property, were to increase, in which case they would have an interest in increasing their knowledge.

It is extremely important to realize that action from interest as a motive is not systematically identified in *The Federalist* with action from economic interest. Madison held that economic interest was the most common and most durable source of factions, but not that it was the only kind of human interest. When he defines "faction" so that each member of a faction may be motivated by an interest which is adverse to "the permanent and aggregate interests of the community," he indicates clearly that the latter interests are not uniformly economic. Since it is the economic interest of factions upon which Madison concentrates when he dilates on the evils of faction, and since he holds that factions are evil because they are adverse to the rights of other citizens or to the permanent and aggregate interests of the community, Madison cannot identify interest with economic interest. He regarded factious interests as mischievous either because they were adverse to the morally conceived public good or because they were "adverse to the [moral] rights of other citizens."[28]

That Madison distinguished between economic interest and interest conceived as the "ultimate happiness" of the whole community is plainly evident in a letter he wrote to James Monroe in 1786. There he speaks of a legislative measure which was being supported in the name of what he called "temporary and partial interests" as against "just & extended maxims of policy . . . which alone can effectuate the durable prosperity of the Union." He says that even if the measure should receive the approval of a majority of states or even all thirteen, the measure is not expedient or in the interest of the nation because it is not just; and then he remarks: "There is no maxim in my opinion which is more liable to be misapplied, and which therefore more needs elucidation than the current one that the interest of the majority is the political standard of right and wrong." Immediately thereafter, Madison reveals that he accepts this maxim only when the word "interest" is taken to be synonymous with "ultimate happiness." But when the word is taken in its "popular sense, as referring to immediate augmentation of property and wealth," Madison says of the maxim that "nothing can be more false." When "interest" is taken in this latter sense, he says, "it would be the interest of the majority in every community to despoil & enslave the minority of individuals; and in a federal community to make a similar sacrifice of the minority of the component States. In fact it is only reestablishing under another name and a more specious form, force as the measure of right." I think it worth noting that when "interest" is taken to be synonymous with "ultimate happiness," Madison says that "it is qualified with every necessary moral ingredient"; and this remark is crucial to his contrast between interest so conceived and economic interest. Madison's letter to Monroe also illuminates the definition of "faction" in *Number 10* because it shows clearly why, according to Madison, a faction based on economic interest alone is mischievous and evil. Such a faction is adverse not only to the moral rights of other citizens but also to a morally approved set of "permanent and aggregate interests of the community"—morally approved because it is identified with the ultimate happiness of the community. For Madison, then, a conflict between two economic interests that govern factions is a conflict between two evils, but a conflict between an economic interest and interest conceived as the ultimate happiness of the community is one between an evil and a good. No majority which is motivated by a desire for the immediate augmentation of property and wealth aims at political justice, says Madison, but, in his letter to Monroe, he explicitly says that a majority which is motivated by interest conceived as the ultimate happiness of the community does aim at political justice.[29]

If we observe the ambiguity of the word "passion" that arises from the fact that it may be used broadly so as to refer to the general, deliberate, calm passion called "interest" or "self-love" as well as to the particular passions, we find it easier to understand that certain *conflicts* between passions are quite different from others. When Publius says that the general passion of interest may be at variance with another passion, he means that a deliberate and calm passion may be at variance with a vehement particular one such as anger. By contrast, when two particular passions such as envy and love oppose each other, the conflict is different because neither envy nor love is calm or deliberate. And, of course, when two economic interests oppose each other, each of them may be calm and deliberate even though the conflict between them may generate either passionate or intellectual opposition among men who have these interests.

Clashing particular passions and clashing economic interests engaged Madison's special attention in *Number 10* when he advocated the method of counterpoise in the control of factions.[30] Here he was in agreement with his teacher Witherspoon, who called the method "overpoise." Witherspoon says that "every good form of government must be complex, so that the one principle may check the other. It is of consequence to have as much virtue among the particular members of a community as possible; but it is folly to expect that a state should be upheld by integrity in all who have a share in managing it. They must be so balanced, that when every one draws to his own interest or inclination, there may be an overpoise upon the whole."[31] Here I think that the phrase "interest or inclination" is equivalent to "interest or particular passion," in which case we may understand Witherspoon to be saying something close to what Madison implies in his definition of "faction" when he refers to a number of citizens "who are united and actuated by some common impulse of passion, or of interest." The method of counterpoise could be used to control the effects of several different kinds of factions, but, as we know, Madison concentrated on controlling the effects of those founded on economic interests which opposed each other as well as the interests of the community as a whole.

Recapitulation

In this chapter I have tried to clarify certain parts of *The Federalist* by appealing to the terminology of British philosophy in the eighteenth century. Before going on to the next chapter, I want to summarize the more important points that I have made. First of all, I have said that, according to Publius, reason can serve as a motive of action when a belief causes a person to do something that he ought to do or may do. Such a cause is, I have also said, a moral belief which the agent, when defending it properly, derives from (1) a moral principle that he defends on Lockeian rationalistic grounds and (2) a fac-

tual statement which he defends by appealing to experience. Second, I have
tried to distinguish two uses of the word "passion" that occur in *The Federalist*. One of them is a broad use which encompasses (1) the general passion or
desire for one's own happiness that is called "interest" as well as (2) so-
called particular passions such as anger, joy, greed, revenge, and love. However, on some occasions Publius uses the word "passion" to refer only to particular passions, and then he writes as though interests are *not* passions.
Third, I have tried to point out that "interest," when used broadly, is distinguished by Publius from "economic interest." Economic interest is different
from the general desire for ultimate happiness which is also called "interest"
by Madison. It is important to keep these points in mind when reading *The
Federalist*. With them in mind, we move closer to our goal of stating as best
we can the theory of motivation that underlies many of Publius's views in political science.

8

On the Strength
of Different Motives

In order to get to a point where I can formulate Publius's theory of motivation, I want to say more concretely what motives he deals with in his theory. I begin by calling attention to some important features of the motive of reason as conceived by Publius, then I present certain distinctions between the sorts of passions and interests whose strengths he compares, and after that I try to present the main generalizations that make up his theory of motivation.

Reason as a Weak Motive that Impels Few Men

The authors of *The Federalist* maintained that reason dictated the political actions that they recommended—abstract reason, which provided a justification for their moral principles, and experimental reason, which supported the means they advocated for the implementation of those principles. And while they wanted as many readers as possible to agree with them on rational grounds, they unmistakably indicated that only a small part of mankind would be likely to heed the call of reason that they issued. When speaking of "the generality of men," Hamilton or Madison often point out that man's reason is likely to be overpowered by motives of passion or interest. In *Number 6* Hamilton says that momentary passions and immediate interests have more control over human conduct than general or remote considerations of policy, utility, or justice.[1] And in *Number 22* he warns that those who have been elevated to positions of power in republics may be corruptly compensated for betraying their trust and not meeting rationally established obligations of duty.[2] In *Number 49,* after assuring us that "a reverence for the laws, would be sufficiently inculcated by the voice of an enlightened reason," Madison remarks that this voice would rarely be heard because "a nation of philosophers is as little to be expected as the philosophical race of kings wished for by Plato."[3] And when Madison speaks in *Number 55* of "very numerous

113

assemblies, of whatever characters composed," he tells us that in such assemblies "passion never fails to wrest the sceptre from reason,"[4] whereas in *Number 58* he repeats this observation when he writes that "the more numerous any assembly may be, of whatever characters composed, the greater is known to be the ascendancy of passion over reason."[5] In *Number 72,* while arguing that a president should be able to stand for reelection, Hamilton says that most men would feel much less zeal in acting from a duty (presumably dictated by reason) if they knew that the advantages of their position would have to be relinquished at a definite time than they would feel if they could entertain the hope of continuing in office by virtue of doing a good job.[6] And in *Number 75* Hamilton declares that "a man raised from the station of a private citizen to the rank of a chief magistrate, possessed of but a moderate or slender fortune, and looking forward to a period not very remote, when he may probably be obliged to return to the station from which he was taken," might be tempted to sacrifice his rationally established duty to his interest.[7] Whether Hamilton viewed the chief magistrate's duty as legal, moral, or both—and I think he regarded it as both—Hamilton thought it was established by disinterested and dispassionate reason—in other words, by a method that he thought was rarely used by the generality of men. Such candor about the relatively small number of persons who were so moved may have made some readers of *The Federalist* feel that they were persons of great intellectual distinction and great moral integrity, but Publius certainly walked a fine line when he insisted that he was presenting rational arguments to his readers and at the same time expressed doubt about the capacity of many of them to follow those arguments or to be moved by them.

While reading the authors of *The Federalist* on the comparative weakness and rarity of disinterested, dispassionate reason as a motive, we must not forget that several framers of the Constitution believed that they themselves were, as Lovejoy has pointed out, moved by reason while "constructing a scheme of government which would make for the good of the people as a whole and in the long run." The makers of the Constitution, Lovejoy remarks, found it "psychologically almost indispensable in the Convention" to assume that they—as opposed to the bulk of the people—were disinterested and dispassionate, and therefore exempt from most of the unflattering generalizations about human nature that they asserted with so much assurance. According to Lovejoy, most members of the Convention must have believed that their own arguments were not simply expressions of interest or of passion. And yet, Lovejoy adds, "all competent historians" of his own day saw that the debates at the Convention were filled with political opinions shaped by private, class, or sectional interests.[8]

Here I shall not spend time examining the causes of the framers' exemption of themselves from the unflattering generalizations about mankind to which they explicitly or tacitly subscribed. With themselves and some others in mind, they believed that a few men might rise above the passions and interests that controlled most men's actions. Furthermore, as I have pointed out in greater detail elsewhere,[9] when they cast themselves in the roles of such rational agents they—notably Hamilton—questioned the rationality of those who might dare to disagree with their allegedly self-evident pronouncements or with theorems allegedly derivable from those pronouncements. Such opponents might disagree with him, Hamilton says disdainfully in *Number 31,* because of mental defects, strong interests, passions, or prejudices. By questioning the rationality of his opponents in this way, Hamilton used his theory of self-evident truth to attack allegedly stupid members of the unruly mob as well as perversely obstinate or oversophisticated intellectuals who disagreed with him. Passion, prejudice, interest, bias, mental disorder, and ignorance are all adduced by Hamilton in order to explain why some of his opponents do not "give their own understandings fair play" and why they yield to "untoward bias" by denying, for example, the necessity of a general power of taxation in the government of the union.[10] What he has to say at these points is reminiscent of Locke's remark that a moralist can arrive at truths as incontestable as those in mathematics *if* he applies himself with "the same Indifferency and Attention" to morals as he does to mathematics.[11] For when Hamilton discovered that certain individuals disagreed with him on certain political issues, he was quick to complain of their bias, of their lack of indifference, or of their inattentiveness, thinking as he often did that he could operate in political science with an assurance approaching that of a pure mathematician. The failings that Hamilton attributed to his opponents were failings that he rarely attributed to himself, but they were certainly failings from which he thought that most of mankind suffered.

The authors of *The Federalist* regarded reason as a comparatively weak motive even though they believed that some men were moved by it in high degree, but how much strength did they attribute to the passions and interests as motives? In trying to answer this question, we must distinguish the different kinds of passions and different kinds of interests that Publius compares in his theory of motivation.[12] We must also keep in mind that although he often speaks of the passions and interests of groups such as nations, states, and factions, his concepts of these passions and interests are modeled—in a manner that is never analyzed—on his concept of an individual's passion and his concept of an individual's interest. For this reason I begin by dealing with the different kinds of passions and interests that are said to motivate the actions of an individual, then turn to those that are said to motivate the actions of groups, and finally try to formulate some basic propositions about the strength of both sorts of motives with an eye to the role these propositions play in Publius's political thinking.

The Passions and Interests of an Individual

In Publius's view, individual passions may promote social harmony or social hostility, a view which appears conspicuously in the philosophical literature that was available to him. Well before the publication of *The Federalist,* Francis Hutcheson, for example, had distinguished between *public* particular passions—particular in the sense we have already analyzed in our earlier discussion—and *selfish* particular passions. The former included love, congratulation, and compassion; the latter included ambition, covetousness, revenge, and anger.[13] And when Hutcheson used the word "public" here, he used it in a manner that was explained in Dr. Johnson's *Dictionary* as follows: "Regarding . . . the good of the community." A public passion in this sense is not a passion *of* the public but rather a passion *of* an individual which has a favorable impact on the community or public. With a related idea in mind, Publius distinguished between a class of harmonious passions that contained confidence, affection for one's family, and patriotism, and a class of hostile passions containing rage, resentment, jealousy, and avarice.[14] Here Publius's view was not unlike that of Madison's teacher Witherspoon, who distinguished between the public passions and the private or selfish passions of an individual. In the first category Witherspoon put family and domestic affection, friendship, and patriotism, whereas in the second he put love of fame, of power, and of property, doing so in the course of a discussion of what he called "our nature as it really is," which he explicitly distinguished from a discussion of "the nature of virtue."[15]

Interests of individuals, like their passions, are also subdivided by Publius into those that are hostile or antagonistic and those that are harmonious, friendly, or sociable. Like passions, such interests may be merely selfish and not antagonistic, or they may be selfish and inimical to the interests or desires of others. By contrast, there is such a thing as an individual's interest in the good of the community, and such an interest may be called public, friendly, harmonious, or sociable.[16] As in the case of an individual's public passion, an individual's public interest is distinguishable from the public's own interest in the good of the public.

There is one other subdivision of interests that I mention only briefly here, and that is the distinction between the true or real interests of an individual and those that are not. It is very difficult to say how Publius used the phrase "true interest" or its equivalent, "real interest," *as applied to an individual,* because he rarely discussed its application to any given individual in a circumstantial way. It has been said that according to Publius an individual is motivated by his own true interest when he is motivated by a desire for "permanent benefits, comprehensive benefits, and benefits which are ultimate or distant results of present action."[17] But the fact is that Publius usually speaks of a true interest and of its opposite when he is discussing the motives of groups—for example, nations—rather than those of individuals, and therefore it would be well to postpone a discussion of Publius's view of the true interests of an individual to a later point in this chapter, after we have discussed what he has to say about the true interests of a group.

The Passions and Interests of a Group

Throughout *The Federalist* Publius speaks of the motives of groups or collective bodies such as nations, states, and factions, but he never tries to give a general definition of the idea of a group motive. He speaks of a group such as a faction being united and actuated by certain impulses of passion or of interest, but he never tells us in a general way what it means to say that a group—whether it be a faction, a state, or a nation—has an interest or a passion. Despite his (understandable) failure to face the difficult philosophical question of what constitutes a group passion or a group interest, he talks constantly about group passions and group interests, and he classifies them in a manner analogous to that in which he classifies those of individuals. For example, Publius thinks that a collective body such as a nation may have hostile passions as well as harmonious or friendly passions. When speaking of the causes of hostility among nations in *Number 6*, he says that some of these causes have a general and almost constant operation upon "the collective bodies of society," identifying "the love of power or the desire of preeminence and dominion—the jealousy of power . . ." as causes of hostility among nations. After mentioning these hostile passions of groups, he lists "the attachments, enmities, interests, hopes and fears of leading individuals in the communities of which they are members,"[18] but he lists these passions of individuals primarily to show that sometimes the leaders of collective bodies have passions which they instill in those collective bodies. Therefore, he thinks, collective bodies also have attachments, enmities, interests, hopes, and fears.

If, however, one asks what Publius means by saying that a group of men has a certain passion, the closest one can come to giving an answer is that *sometimes,* according to Publius, saying that a group has a passion means that all or almost all individual members of the group have the passion. This is never said explicitly by Publius; it is merely a generalization of Madison's idea that a faction has a certain passion if and only if that passion actuates all or most individual members of the faction. Nevertheless, I hesitate to say flatly that Publius held this view of the meaning of *all* statements about group passions. For one thing, I find no passages that explicitly substantiate this interpretation of his view; for another, it seems very dubious to analyze in this way some of Publius's statements about the passions of what he calls "the collective bodies of society" in *Number 6*. Although Hamilton says there that the love of power or the desire of dominion have "a general and almost constant operation" upon nations, it would not do to say that by the statement "England has a desire of dominion" Hamilton means neither more nor less than what is meant by the statement "All or most Englishmen have a desire of dominion." Sometimes, for example, a statement such as "England has a desire of dominion" is interpreted by Publius as meaning the same as the statement "The English government has a desire of dominion," and this is very different from saying that it means the same as "All or most Englishmen have a desire for dominion." Publius never tries to define statements about the motives of collective bodies in terms of statements about the motives of the individuals who compose those bodies, and we would be wise to avoid imposing such a view on Publius.

Nevertheless, as we have seen, Publius does think that a group may have a hostile interest or a harmonious interest, just as an individual may. We know, for example, that Publius's most striking and most familiar example of a hostile group interest is that of a faction. He also held that one of the states may also be moved by an antagonistic group interest which is adverse to the interest of the national community, and that a nation may have friendly or antagonistic interests, depending on the relationship between its interests and those of the world community. By similar reasoning, we may call a group's interests selfish or public, depending on whether the group seeks its own advantage as opposed to the advantage of other rival groups or that of some larger community of which it is a part. Of course, it may seem peculiar to speak of a group's interest as selfish when one focuses on the fact that a group is not a self in the sense of a person. And yet I think we can understand what Publius intended when he said that a faction desires *its own* gain, good, or happiness rather than that of a wider community, or when he said that one of the thirteen states desires *its own* gain rather than that of the nation. Even though a faction consists of more than one self in the sense of one person, such a group may be said to be affected by *its own* interest or by self-interest, just as a nation may be said to be affected by *its* self-interest as opposed to the interest of other nations or that of mankind at large. Whether or not one thinks that the self-interest of a group must, from a certain philosophical point of view, be reduced to, or defined in terms of, the self-interest of *this* individual member of the group, and *that* individual member, and so on, one must accept the fact that Publius usually spoke of the self-interest of a group with no compunction and with no express concern about whether such a reduction could or should be carried out.

I come now to the difficult distinction that Publius draws between true group interests and those that are not true or real. As I have already indicated, Publius understandably wrote more extensively about the true interests of groups of people than he did about the true interests of individuals. When Hamilton uses the phrase "true interests" in the very first number, he speaks of the true interests of "the people of this country" viewed collectively. He says there that the decision of the people regarding the proposed Constitution may fail to be governed by what he calls "a judicious estimate of our true interests, unperplexed and unbiassed by considerations not connected with the public good," thereby indicating that he identifies the true interests of the people with the public good, and also that he thinks that an *injudicious* estimate of the people's true interests might be made because of bias on the part of someone making the estimate.

Bias, Hamilton maintains in *Number 1,* can affect the effort to discover what the people's true interests are, just as he maintains in *Number 31* that it can affect the attempt to discover the truth of a supposedly self-evident proposition. When Hamilton tries in *Number 1* to describe how bias can distort our view of what is in the people's true interest, he warns his reader that the plan created by the framers in Philadelphia "affects too many particular interests, innovates upon too many local institutions, not to involve in its discussion a variety of objects foreign to its merits, and of views, passions and prejudices little favorable to the discovery of truth." Here Hamilton looks upon any effort to discover what is in the true interest of the American people as an effort to discover real or objective truth, and therefore as an effort which may be hampered or obstructed in several different ways. When he says that the proposed Constitution "affects too many particular interests," he explains that one formidable obstacle which the new Constitution will have to encounter will be "the obvious interest of a certain class of men in every State" to resist any change that is likely to diminish the power, the profit, and the influence of the offices they hold in the state governments. Each of these individuals will therefore have a motive to distort the public's view and even his own view of how much public good would be gained by adoption of the Constitution—that motive being the fear that adoption of it would make changes in too many local institutions that happen to advance his own selfish interests.

In this passage at the very beginning of *The Federalist,* the clash between the interests of factions and the true interests of the people is foreshadowed, a clash which Hamilton thinks may lead some members of a faction to distort the true or real value of the Constitution because of their own interests. In addition, Hamilton says, there will be other men who will be moved to distort the Constitution's true or real value, namely, those of "perverted ambition" whose inordinate desire for honor or preferment also turns them aside from the proper course because they have certain "views, passions and prejudices little favorable to the discovery of truth." They will hope to aggrandize themselves by the confusions of their country, or they will flatter themselves by thinking that they will be elevated more highly by "the subdivision of the empire into several partial confederacies, than from its union under one government."[19] Hamilton warned his countrymen against the biased views held by men of particular or special interest and also against the biased views held by men subject to the passion of perverted ambition. Both kinds of men, he said, would be moved to advance distorted views about the capacity of the new Constitution to satisfy the true interests of the people. This reference to interests and passions which conflict with the true interests of the people is related, of course, to Madison's notion in *Number 10* that either factious interests or factious passions may be adverse to the permanent and aggregate interests of the whole community.

I emphasize that when Hamilton and his fellow authors speak of the true interests of a group, they regard the predicate "true" as an objective one. Truth or reality, when attributed to interests, like truth when attributed to propositions, is thought to be something external which can be discovered by a mind which is sound, well informed, and free from the influence of selfish interests or obstructive passions. Hamilton viewed it in this way when he spoke of the true interest of a nation in *Number 6,*[20] and in *Number 10* Madison speaks in the same spirit of representatives "whose wisdom may best discern the true interest of their country."[21] However, it is one thing to regard the notion of true interest as objective and another to define the notion of true interest when speaking of a community. If Publius had been pressed to define the interest of a community, I do not know whether he would have referred in his definition to the interests of the individual members of the community. In other words, I do not know whether he would have said with Bentham that the interest of the community is "the sum of the interests of the several members who compose it" and that "it is in vain to talk of the interest of the community, without understanding what is the interest of the individual."[22]

However, even though Publius did not offer this sort of definition, he would have said, I think, that when a nation acts from its true interest, it acts from an interest which is called by Publius "comprehensive" or "enlarged" as well as "permanent." For example, I think that Madison refers to nondefinitional marks of the true interest of a nation when he speaks in *Number 10* of "the permanent and aggregate interests of the community."[23] And I think he makes a similar nondefinitional comment on the true interest of a state in *Number 46* when he complains about state legislatures whose members are disposed "to sacrifice the comprehensive and permanent interest of the State, to the particular and separate views of the counties or districts in which they reside."[24] In *Number 42* Madison defends federal regulation of commerce because it will help states which export and import through other states by preventing the latter from making improper levies on the former, and thereby diminish animosity between the states. He adds in a more general vein that the "mild voice of reason, pleading the cause of an enlarged and permanent interest"[25] which transcends that of a state, will be opposed only by those who look at the true interest of the nation through the medium of passion or of narrow and *im*permanent interest. The true interest of the nation is regarded as being "out there," an entity which may be misdescribed by those who suffer from certain mental defects, from bias, or from inattentiveness even though the concept of *true* interest is left undefined. So, although it is as hard to extract Publius's definition of the true interest of a nation as it is to produce his definition of the true interest of an individual—or, for that matter, his definition of any difficult concept—passages such as those I have cited show that in his view the true interests of a nation are comprehensive and permanent by comparison to the interests that sometimes motivate smaller political bodies such as miguided states, factions, and certain individuals. Madison's identification in *Number 10* of "the permanent and aggregate interests of the community" with "the good of the whole" and "the public good" must be kept in mind even though it is difficult to show that this identification was based on a definition or on whatever sort of identity Bentham had in mind when he said that the interest of a community is the sum of the interests of the several members who compose the community conceived as a "fictitious *body,* composed of the individual persons who are considered as constituting as it were its *members.*"[26] Unlike Bentham, Publius did not approach the concept of the public interest with what Hume called a strict philosophic eye.

One cannot praise Publius's remarks on this subject for their philosophical explicitness or clarity, but there is no doubt that he believed and said that it was in the true interest of the nation to be united and to persist. Such language is consonant with Hamilton's saying to his readers at the end of *Number 1* that he proposes in a series of papers to discuss among other things *"The utility of the* UNION *to your political prosperity"* and *"The insufficiency of the present Confederation to preserve that Union."* And because Madison thought that union ought to be made more perfect and preserved, he said in *Number 10* that a wise legislator who may best discern the true interest of the country "will be least likely to sacrifice it to temporary or partial considerations."[27] A legislator who focuses on temporary considerations may arrive at a view of the nation's interests which is adverse to the permanent interests of the nation; and one who focuses on partial considerations may arrive at an account which is adverse to the aggregate interests of the nation. That is why Publius advises the people of the nation to discourage or to control the effects of forces that threaten its comprehensiveness and permanence by not electing officials who are unwise enough, ignorant enough, or venal enough to encourage those forces, whether those forces come from outside of the nation or from inside. The true interest of the nation was also regarded as enlarged and permanent, though, I repeat, not defined as such, in the Preamble to the Constitution. There it is implied that the true interest of the people of the United States is to form a more perfect union and to secure the blessings of liberty not only to themselves but to their posterity. A more perfect union would be a union more thoroughly made and therefore more comprehensive than it had been under the Articles of Confederation; and, obviously, a people who aimed to secure the blessings of liberty to posterity had permanence in mind. In his speech of June 26 before the Philadelphia Convention, Madison made clear that the founders hoped to frame a system that would "last for ages."[28]

Having devoted some attention to Publius's central but undefined idea of the true interest of a community, I think it worth devoting some to his idea of immediate interest, which is sometimes regarded as the opposite of true interest but which, strictly speaking, is not the opposite of true interest.[29] If a true interest is both permanent and enlarged, then a nontrue interest is either not permanent, not enlarged, or neither. An interest or benefit which is not permanent is usually identified by Publius with one that is immediate, and an interest or benefit that is not enlarged is usually identified by him with one that is partial. According to such terminology, an immediate interest is one which is temporally immediate—a benefit confined to the near future—and when a people is moved to satisfy an immediate interest, it seeks a benefit which will last for only a short period after the action it is moved to take. By contrast, when it is moved to satisfy a partial interest, it seeks a benefit which will not be that of the people as a whole. A partial interest for Publius is an interest which is not comprehensive in a sense which seems to involve no reference to time. A group whose actions are determined by its immediate interests may be called shortsighted, whereas a group whose actions are determined by partial or particular interests has a different kind of poor vision—one that prevents it from seeking to satisfy the interest of the whole group, however that interest is conceived. That is why I do not think that Publius *equated* immediate interest with an interest that is not true but rather with an interest that is not permanent; or perhaps it would be better to say that he contrasted immediate benefit with enduring benefit, one that lasted for much more than a brief amount of time. His underlying metaphor seems to be that of a collective body which strives to remain integrated and also to endure in time. Therefore, the wise legislator who wants to forward the true interest or advantage of that body will not only avoid being unduly influenced by the prospect of temporally immediate or short-term benefits, but will also avoid being influenced by the prospect of satisfying interests of parts of the body politic by contrast to those of the whole body politic.[30]

I said earlier that Publius does not focus very much on the true interest of individuals as opposed to that of collective bodies, but I can now elaborate on that point more effectively than I could earlier. A typical context in which Publius speaks of the interest of an individual is where Publius speaks of the self-interest of a political leader, but in such a context Publius does not linger over the difference between the true interests of a leader and those that are not true. There is little consideration in *The Federalist* of the conditions under which a leader or any other individual follows his own true interests as opposed to interests of his that are not true. Consequently, there is no tendency on the part of Publius to say that an individual's true interests are comprehensive and permanent.

As we might expect, Publius was too "realistic" to believe that each citizen was moved by the idea that it would be in his true interest to do what is in the true interest of the nation. Madison said in his letter to Jefferson of October 24, 1787, that men are not moved by the argument that their private or partial good would be increased if the permanent good of the whole were. Experience, he said, shows that such a consideration "has little effect on individuals, and perhaps still less on a collection of individuals, and least of all on a majority with the public authority in their hands."[31] Publius showed his contempt for the efficacy of a related argument when he said in *Number 10* that "we well know that neither moral nor religious motives can be relied on as an adequate control"[32] of factions whose interests run counter to the true interests of the nation. And he made a similar point in *Number 42* about groups and individuals when he said that the mild voice of reason, while pleading the cause of an enlarged and permanent interest, is "too often drowned before public bodies as well as individuals, by the clamours of an impatient avidity for immediate and immoderate gain."[33] Publius's skepticism about the strength of rational motives will become more evident when we examine what he believed about the relative strengths of the various kinds of motives we have been trying to elucidate and distinguish in this section.

The Theory of Motivation

We are now in a position to summarize certain general beliefs of Publius about the comparative strengths of the different kinds of motives we have been trying to elucidate. It is evident that, according to Publius, an individual's particular passions which are selfish or hostile are stronger motives than those which are not selfish or those which promote harmony, and also that an individual's selfish or hostile interests are stronger than those which promote harmony and are friendly. And although Publius did not say much about the strength of the true interests of an individual by comparison to those that are not true, it is safe to say that if he had attended to this question, he would have characterized the latter as stronger motives than the former. The same may be said about Publius's views concerning the corresponding motives of groups. Moreover, we can say that Publius regarded true interests and rational motives as weaker than selfish or hostile passions and interests. We can say this with confidence when speaking of Publius's views about nations, because we know that in *Number 6* Hamilton says that momentary hostile passions and immediate interests both have a greater control over a nation's conduct than "general or remote considerations of policy, utility or justice."[34] Such general or remote considerations would require an appeal to a nation's true interests and to reason, and Hamilton holds in *Number 6* that a nation's true interests and its reason are "invariably" overpowered by its antagonistic passions and its immediate interests. It is more difficult to show that Publius believed that this generalization applied without modification to individuals because, I repeat, Publius said very little about the contrast between the true interests of an individual and those of his interests that are not true. If we assume, however, that this contrast is between the "real" and the "apparent" interests of an individual, then it is very likely that Publius would have said that, as motives, the true interests and rational motives of individuals generally have less strength than their selfish and hostile passions, and also less strength than their selfish and hostile interests.

Each one of the generalizations I have mentioned so far deals either with the relative strengths of an individual's motives or with the relative strengths of a group's motives, and we may think of one motive—of an individual or of a group—as stronger than another if and only if the former, so to speak, overcomes the latter when they come into conflict. According to Publius, it would seem, one motive is stronger than another under conditions which are analogous to those under which one mechanical force is greater than another. If only two forces pull a stationary body in opposite directions along a horizontal plane against equal forces of friction, and if the body moves— that is to say, has its resultant acceleration in one of these directions—then the greater force is that which pulls the body in the direction in which the body has its resultant acceleration. And although Publius was not prepared to measure the strengths of motives in a numerical fashion, he probably believed—to continue with our mechanical metaphor—that if only two motives pull on an individual or a group in opposite directions under conditions analogous to those prevailing in our mechanical example, then the stronger motive is that which has the same direction as that in which the individual or group acts. Needless to say, such analogies with mechanics must not be pushed too far, and I do not know how Publius would have answered someone who asked whether the strength of a motive could be measured independently of an experiment in which we pit that motive against another. Publius's concept of the strength of a motive was not the clearest of concepts and I do not think that we would improve our understanding of his views by trying to say much more about that concept or its connections with mechanical ideas.

However, one of the few useful things we may say with the help of a mechanical analogy is that two motives can be compared in strength only when they are exerted on the same object. If two horses pull in opposite directions, we can see which exerts a greater force on a rock if they are both pulling on that rock and we can tell in what direction the rock accelerates. With this analogy in mind, we should observe that each of the previously formulated generalizations deals with the comparative strengths of motives that act either on an individual or on a group. One of them says, for example, that an individual will be more strongly motivated by *his* passion or *his* interest than by *his* rational motives; and another says that a nation will be more strongly motivated by *its* passion or *its* interest than by *its* rational motives. But no one of these generalizations attempts to compare the degree of motivation that an individual's self-interest exerts *on him* with the degree of motivation that his nation's self-interest exerts on *it*. If one keeps the mechanical analogy in mind, one can see that the pull of the individual's self-interest *on him* cannot be compared with the pull of the group's self-interest *on the group* just because the object which is being pulled is different in both cases.

In order to pursue these questions more concretely, let us assume that an individual citizen has an interest in not paying a tax. Let us also assume that it is in the interest of his nation that he pay the tax. These two interests are motives which, on the face of it, operate on two different things. True, the individual citizen is a constituent of the nation, but his fellow citizens are also constituents of the nation, and that is why the nation may in fact have an interest in this individual's paying his tax which is different from the interest of one, or even of more than one, of its individual citizens. Madison says in his *Memorial and Remonstrance* that "no other rule exists, by which any question which may divide a Society, can be ultimately determined, but the will of the majority"; and from this one might infer that action in accordance with the majority's will is necessarily action in the interest of the society even when the society acts against the interest of an individual or that of a minority.[35] But the interest of the society or the nation can influence an individual's action only if an individual wants to further the interests of the society or nation of which he is a constituent. It will not do to appeal to the interests of the nation in trying to influence the behavior of an individual unless that individual has some motive which will form, as it were, a bridge between him and the society, or nation, or community at large.

Such a motive, according to Hamilton, does exist in individuals, but he thinks it exists in different degrees in different kinds of individuals. In *Number 17* Hamilton writes of what he calls a "strong propensity of the human heart" that "it is a known fact in human nature that its affections are commonly weak in proportion to the distance or diffusiveness of the object."[36] Upon this principle, Hamilton says, "a man is more attached to his family than to his neighbourhood, to his neighbourhood than to the community at large."[37] And although Hamilton does not say so explicitly in *Number 17,* he seems to have believed that because *the ordinary man* is closer to himself than he is to any other "object" and because he is, in his own eyes, less "diffusive" than any other object, he is more attached to himself than he is to his family, to his neighborhood, or to the community at large. He is first in this sequence of objects which elicit his affection.

In *Number 17* Hamilton says that according to this same principle "the people of each State would be apt to feel a stronger byass [*sic*] towards their local governments than towards the government of the Union; unless the force of that principle should be destroyed by a much better administration of the latter."[38] And since Hamilton is here attributing motives to ordinary individuals, he asserts that any such individual is apt to have greater affection for, and a bias or interest in favor of, persons and governments which are closer to him and less "diffusive." Hamilton speaks in *Number 17* of "all those personal interests and familiar concerns to which the sensibility of individuals is more immediately awake"[39] when Hamilton describes the ordinary man's "esteem and reverence towards" state governments.[40] But we must keep in mind that throughout this part of *Number 17* it is the individual whose bias in favor of the local government is stronger than *his* bias in favor of the federal government. It is *the individual* who is here said to have a stronger interest in favor of one thing than *he* has in favor of another thing. Hamilton does not try to compare the strength of an individual's motives with those of the community at large, as if he were comparing the strength of a force exerted on one object with the strength of a force exerted on another. He bridges the gap between the individual's motives and those of collective bodies by making a comparative statement about the degree of esteem that ordinary men feel toward different collective bodies. He says in effect that such men will be more moved to further the interests of those collective bodies which they hold in higher esteem because such bodies are less "diffusive" and in some sense closer to them.

In referring to ordinary men when formulating Hamilton's principle, I mean to stress that Hamilton is here speaking of the strength of motives that mainly affect individuals who compose what he calls "the mass of the citizens."[41] This must be stressed because in *Number 17* Hamilton makes a very revealing and contrasting reference to speculative men. He says: "The operations of the national government . . . falling less immediately under the observation of the mass of the citizens the benefits derived from it will chiefly be perceived and attended to by speculative men. Relating to more general interests, they will be less apt to come home to the feelings of the people; and, in proportion, less likely to inspire a habitual sense of obligation and an active sentiment of attachment."[42] This passage helps us describe a conflict in which a speculative man may find himself when he has or feels a selfish *interest* in doing one thing but at the same time has a *belief* that it is in the interest of his nation that he do the opposite thing. Such a conflict is more likely to arise in the minds of speculative men because they, according to Hamilton, are more likely to perceive, in a more theoretical way than ordinary men can, the benefits that derive from a national government. But even though speculative men perceive these benefits, they are nevertheless human and therefore have selfish interests and passions which may move them, for example, not to pay their national taxes. As a result, they are men whose selfish interests may come into conflict with their *belief* that paying their taxes will advance the national interests. I emphasize that for Hamilton the speculative man's perception of, and attention to, the benefits derived from the national government is a belief, an intellectual matter. And since Hamilton believes that such men will have a "habitual sense of obligation" toward the *national* government, they are more apt to believe that *they ought* to pay their national taxes.

This leads me to formulate a generalization which goes beyond what Hamilton says about the mass of citizens because it reflects Hamilton's invidious comparison between the mass of men and speculative men. With this comparison in mind, I think we may attribute to Publius the following generalization: The self-interest of an ordinary individual is more efficacious as a motive of his action than his moral belief that he ought to do what is in the interest of his nation. On the other hand, we may also attribute to Publius another generalization, namely: The speculative man's moral belief that he ought to do what is in the interest of his nation is more efficacious as a motive of his action than his self-interest. Both of these generalizations comport well with the idea that the framers of the Constitution regarded themselves as heroic figures. Their rational moral beliefs, and especially their belief that one ought to do one's patriotic duty, they thought, were stronger motives than their self-interest in prompting their actions.

Behind this self-elevation of some of the framers there lay some ideas that may be usefully distinguished. One of them is present in the Lockeian view that a self-evident moral principle may be seen to be self-evident only by the learned few.[43] A second is the idea that the framers excelled in experimental political science. And a third is the idea that the framers were able to act in accordance with moral and political beliefs whose truth they saw through combining abstract and experimental reason. Clearly, these are three distinct marks of a man who thinks himself superior. Some men may be pure philosophers who know the allegedly self-evident principles of morality but little about the political world. Others may combine a knowledge of such self-evident principles with experience of the world and derive specific conclusions about what ought to be done *without doing it*. But a third kind of superior man knows the moral principles, has the relevant experience of the world, and manages to *do* what morality and political science together dictate.

Now I have presented and commented on what I view as the main components of Publius's theory of motivation. No doubt a careful reader of *The*

Federalist will be able to produce other generalizations about the relative strengths of motives as measured by Publius. For example, there are occasions in which he lists "prejudice" as a motive. How strong is it? In *Number 85* Hamilton says that "no partial motive, no particular interest, no pride of opinion, no temporary passion or *prejudice* [my emphasis], will justify to [a man], to his country or to his posterity" his failure to perform the duty of deciding whether Publius has defended the proposed constitution satisfactorily.[44] And there are other places, for example, *Number 31,* where Hamilton replaces Madison's trio consisting of opinions, passions, and interests, with the trio consisting of interest, passion, and prejudice.[45] Here prejudice seems to be regarded as preconceived *opinion* and therefore may be thought of as the result of using reason. Nevertheless, a complete catalogue of comparative generalizations should include Publius's estimate of the strength of this pejoratively described form of reason by comparison to that of opinion which is not preconceived. It is very likely that prejudice was thought by Publius to be more efficacious in determining the action of an individual than, so to speak, right reason, even though Publius regards prejudice as a species of opinion. In short, for Publius a bad reason is probably a stronger motive in politics than a good reason.

In spite of its incompleteness, I think the list of generalizations I have presented in this chapter constitutes the main part of Publius's theory of motivation. Some contemporary philosophers of science might not wish to dignify it by calling it a theory because it consists of a few rough generalizations that may be summed up in the observation that hostile passions, immediate interests, and partial interests play a greater part in determining human action than do friendly passions, long-term interests, group interests, and reason.[46] But even this little bit of psychological theory is enough to support some of my earlier comments on Publius's view of human nature. By recognizing that he regarded certain supposedly objectionable motives as merely stronger than others, we avoid saddling him with a view that he did not hold, namely, that the motives of all men are totally depraved. Antagonistic passions, immediate interests, and partial interests are said by him to *preponderate* in determining the actions of ordinary men, especially when they are gathered together in groups; Publius does not call them the sole determinants of human action. Furthermore, Publius does not hold that reason exerted no influence at all on men. On the contrary, he is especially concerned to insist that a rational awareness of moral duty and of the true interests of the nation was the leading motive of the framers and of those pure, noble, and virtuous men who should be elected to public office. Having said this, however, I want to repeat that Publius was not primarily a moralist. He subscribed to a rationalistic moral theory but he was mainly concerned to describe man's different motives in a way that would support his views about the political merits of the Constitution.

In the next chapter I begin to show how his theory of motivation figured in his political theorizing, but before I do so I want to remark on a paradox in Publius's psychology so far as it affected his political views. On the one hand he thought that "the mass of the citizens" felt a smaller degree of attachment to the national government than "speculative men" did, but on the other he thought that it would fall to the lot of the mass of the citizens to elect those speculative men who would rule the national government most effectively. Madison said in the Virginia Debates on the ratification of the Constitution that "the people will have virtue and intelligence to select men of virtue and wisdom. Is there no virtue among us? If there be not, we are in a wretched situation. No theoretical checks, no form of government, can render us secure."[47] With this in mind, let us now consider the philosophical foundations of Publius's ideas about how to check men of dubious virtue as well as his ideas about how to encourage good and wise men.

VI

THEORY OF ACTION
AND METAPHYSICS

9

Motive, Opportunity, and Action: The Principle of Causality at Work

One of the most important ways in which Publius uses his theory of motivation to support his political views may be seen in Madison's theory of how the effects of factions may be controlled. Because a faction for him is a group of citizens who are united and motivated by a passion or an interest which is adverse to the private rights of other citizens or to the public good, Madison wants to show how to prevent factions from acting on what he regards as morally objectionable motives. As we have seen earlier, he believes that it would be impossible to eliminate factions by removing their causes; consequently, he advises us how to control what he calls their mischievous effects. Even though he did not believe that *all* factions are based on economic interest, it will be especially useful to focus on his theory of how to control the deeds of factions founded on economic interest, since they are in his view the most common and most enduring factions. In accordance with Publius's views on the strengths of different kinds of motives, an economic faction will act oppressively when it deliberately allows its interest in property to override rational motives to behave otherwise. Either that interest will impel the faction to violate what can be rationally discerned as the private rights of other citizens or that interest will impel it to do something which runs counter to what can be rationally discerned as the public good. Therefore, a faction which acts in either way will illustrate Publius's generalization that the hostile interests of groups are stronger motives than any rational motives they may have, since discerning the private rights of other citizens or the public good would constitute a rational motive to act morally that would be overridden when a faction acted oppressively. And because Publius believes that a motive will produce an action only if the agent has an opportunity to act on that motive, the joint role of motives and opportunities in causing actions is, as we shall see in detail later, of central importance in his

131

views on how to check or control factions. For this reason, I want to discuss the interrelationship among motives, opportunities, and actions in Publius's discussion of factions, where his views on this subject are comparatively explicit. I do so not only because that interrelationship figures importantly in *Number 10,* but also because it underlies other arguments in *The Federalist* and, in general, reveals how Publius relied on a certain version of the principle of causality or universal causation.

The Motives and Opportunities of Factions

What does Madison think we should do, given the fact that we cannot eliminate the economic differences of interest that lead property-based factions to act against opposed factions, against the true interest of the whole community, or against the rights of others? How about trying to "adjust," as he puts it, these clashing interests so as to render them all subservient to the common good? When Madison raises this question in *Number 10,* he quickly dismisses the possibility of such an adjustment by an enlightened statesman who will persuade factions to refrain from acting oppressively. He dismisses this possibility by saying that enlightened statesmen will not always be at the helm and that even if they were at the helm, any adjustment they proposed would, as his theory of motivation implies, require the faction to take into view "indirect and remote considerations, which will rarely prevail over the immediate interest which one party may find in disregarding the rights of another, or the good of the whole."[1] Here we see an obvious example of Madison's view that rational ethical motives rarely prevail over motives of immediate interest. That is why, after arguing earlier in *Number 10* that it would be impossible to eliminate the differences of interest that cause economic factions to exist, and after dismissing the idea that these differences might be adjusted by enlightened statesmen, Madison concludes that relief may be found only by controlling or checking the effects or deeds of factions.[2]

Since Madison dismisses the idea that the clashing interests and passions of factions may be adjusted by enlightened statesmen, benevolent philosophers, or religious preachers, he is led to the idea of preventing the oppressive deeds of factions by "giving such an extent to [the] sphere" of a republican government "that no common interest or passion will be likely to unite a majority of the whole number in an unjust pursuit," as he says in his letter to Jefferson of October 24, 1787.[3] This letter, along with other writings of Madison outside of *The Federalist,* makes it easier to understand why he proposes a political device which he thinks will discourage groups from being united by factious motives or, failing that, eliminate the opportunities of majorities that might act oppressively. The letter shows why Madison thinks it impossible to overcome an unjust majority's ruling motive by appealing to other motives that members of such a majority might have, motives that might, in the eyes of unrealistic observers of factions, outweigh their motives for oppressing a minority.

According to Madison, there are only three such motives that might conceivably be effective under the circumstances, but they are motives which he thinks will *not* overcome the ruling motive of a faction which has become a majority. They are ineffectual because they will not serve as what are sometimes called "internal restraints" on a majority having factious motives. No one of these motives and no combination of them is strong enough, Madison says, to overcome the ruling motive of a factious majority so as to eliminate the need to control such a majority by giving what he calls an "extensive sphere" to a republic. One of these ineffectual motives we have already remarked on in an earlier chapter, namely, that of "a prudent regard to private or partial good" which would lead individual members of a faction to see that it is in the private interest of each of them *not* to act against the good of the whole community. This, Madison remarks, "ought no doubt to be sufficient of itself" to keep a majority faction from acting oppressively, but he quickly adds, as we have seen, that experience shows the pointlessness of appealing to this motive.[4] The second motive which Madison dismisses is what he calls "respect for character," meaning a respect for their own reputation on the part of members of the faction. This motive, he says, is not sufficient to keep individuals from acting unjustly. Moreover, Madison adds as he sounds a familiar Humeian theme, which is also sounded in *Number 10,* this motive "loses it efficacy in proportion to the number which is to divide the praise or the blame," meaning that it loses its efficacy when you appeal to it while trying to persuade a majority faction not to act unjustly. Madison observes that a man's reputation depends on public opinion, which is the opinion of the majority. Therefore, Madison concludes, if you want to persuade the majority from doing something by appealing to a standard of reputation which is determined by the majority itself, you can hardly expect to succeed. That majority will fix the standard by which its members' conduct is judged; consequently, appealing to that standard in order to influence members of the majority is bound to fail.[5]

The last ineffectual motive considered by Madison in his letter to Jefferson is briefly labeled "Religion," about which he bluntly remarks: "The inefficacy of this restraint on individuals is well known." After this he points out that the behavior of every popular assembly which acts on oath, "the strongest of religious ties," shows that individuals will "join without remorse in acts agst. which their consciences would revolt, if proposed to them separately in their closets." He concedes that when religion is kindled into enthusiasm, "its force like that of other passions is increased by the sympathy of a multitude," in other words, that a passionately enthusiastic religion which is shared by many people *may* have great strength as a motive.[6] However, after conceding this, he comments that "enthusiasm is only a temporary state of Religion," meaning that however successful it might be as a restraining motive, its effect in this direction will be short-lived and therefore discountable. Finally, Madison reveals his typically Lockeian distaste for religious enthusiasm by saying that while it lasts, it "will hardly be seen with pleasure at the helm. Even in its coolest state, it has been much oftener a motive to oppression than a restraint from it."[7] In short, he does not want to depend on a preaching political helmsman to counteract the motives of a faction.

Once Madison dismisses the efficacy of these three motives in counteracting a factious motive in a majority, he thinks he is left with only two ways of preventing majorities from acting oppressively. One is to prevent a majority from having a common factious motive, and the other is to put impediments in the way of any majority that should come to have such a motive—to deny it the opportunity to act oppressively. Both of these preventive measures, he thinks, will be carried out by establishing a large, well-populated republic. Before turning to his ideas on that subject, it is useful to recognize that underlying Madison's political proposal is the philosophical (and, of course, legal) theory that an agent—whether individual or collective—will perform an action if and only if the agent has both a motive and an opportunity to perform that action—a theory which is implicit in what he says in *Number 10* and elsewhere. Before applying this theory to majority factions in *Number 10,* Madison reminds us that the factions he has in mind will, by hypothesis, be acting within the framework of the popular government established by the Constitution. And since a faction may, according to his definition, be a majority or a minority of the citizens, either kind of faction will be actuated by motives which cause the deeds that Madison seeks to check or restrain. Therefore, he divides his comments so as to treat these two different cases separately. First he considers the case where the faction is less than a majority of the whole, and this, he thinks, is comparatively easy to handle. The sinister views, as he calls them, of a minority faction may be defeated by a regular vote, and, therefore, whatever such a faction may do—for example, clog the administration or convulse the society—"it will be unable to execute and mask its violence under the forms of the Constitution."[8] This reference to minority factions shows that Madison was not concerned to check the tyrannical actions of majority factions alone but rather to control the actions of *any* faction.

However, he thinks that the really hard case for an advocate of popular government to deal with is a faction that manages to become a majority, for in that case "the form of popular government . . . enables it to sacrifice to its ruling passion or interest, both the public good and the rights of other citizens."[9] Madison's point here is that the ability of the majority faction to invade the rights of others or to act against the community's true interest is created by the very form of popular government itself. Unlike a minority faction, a majority faction *is* permitted to "mask its violence under the forms of the Constitution," and that is why we have an extremely difficult problem on our hands, which Madison formulates as follows: "To secure the public good, and private rights, against the danger of such a faction, and at the same time to preserve the spirit and the form of popular government, is then the great object to which our enquiries are directed."[10] The point of this passage is to prepare us for his proposal about how to restrain the actions of a factious majority without denying its members the liberty that is characteristic of popular government as Madison conceived it. Consequently, Madison must walk a fine line.

Since, as we know, Madison does not think that the motives of the individuals who compose a factious majority can be overcome by appealing to any other motives they might have as individuals, he is forced to look elsewhere for the remedy he seeks. And that remedy consists in doing one of two things. First, form the kind of government which makes it impossible or unlikely that individuals with factious motives will form a majority. But if, unfortunately, they happen to form a majority, then we do the second thing, namely, render that majority "by their number and local situation, unable to concert and carry into effect schemes of oppression." Madison's central practical point here is that the factious impulse and the opportunity of a majority must not be allowed to coincide, to exist simultaneously. If they are allowed to coincide, Madison says, "neither moral nor religious motives can be relied on as an adequate control" of the doings of the faction, meaning that once the impulse and the opportunity coincide, the oppressive act is certainly not going to be headed off by appealing to any of the motives that he dismissed as inefficacious in his letter to Jefferson of October 24, 1787, and in other places besides *Number 10*. Madison concludes this part of his reflections in *Number 10* with an abbreviated version of what he had written to Jefferson, namely, that such rational moral and religious motives do not serve as a control on the injustice and violence of individuals, and that they lose their efficacy in proportion to the number of individuals combined in a faction, "that is, in proportion as their efficacy becomes needful."[11]

The Necessary and Sufficient Conditions for a Group's Action, for an Individual's Action, and for the Behavior of Other Objects

Before dealing more specifically with Madison's political proposals for heading off the oppressive acts of a majority faction I want to call attention to an important similarity between his theory about the two joint conditions under which a group of individuals will act and a commonly held theory about the joint conditions under which a individual will act. A man will shoot someone else, according to some philosophers and lawyers, if and only if he has both a motive for shooting the other person and the opportunity to shoot that person. Other thinkers specify three conditions rather than two because they add something which they regard as different from opportunity, namely, the ability or power to shoot the person.[12] Their point is that for a man to shoot another person, he must have a motive such as a desire for revenge; the ability to shoot that person, that is, the ability to fire a gun; and the opportunity to shoot the other person insofar as he has a gun and there is no impediment to his firing it at the other person. It follows from such a theory of individual action that we can prevent an action by doing one or all of three things: by seeing to it that an individual does not have a certain motive or that some other motive outweighs it, by seeing to it that he does not have the ability, by seeing to it that he does not have the opportunity to perform the action. Madison's theory of how to prevent the oppressive deeds of a majority is modeled on a version of this theory of how to prevent an individual human being from performing an action.

Moreover, Madison's theory and the theory of individual human action I have outlined were regarded by many philosophers whom Madison read—for example, Hume—as special cases of a more general theory about the conditions under which any object, animate or inanimate, acts (in the broadest sense of "acts"). Such philosophers held that a piece of paper will burst into flames if and only if analogous conditions are satisfied. They regarded a spark's coming into contact with a piece of paper as the counterpart of Madison's "actuating" motive or impulse; and they viewed the combination of all of the conditions which join with ignition to cause the whole piece of paper to burst into flames as the physical counterpart of what Madison called "opportunity." Madison's metaphorical use of fire when discussing factions in *Number 10* strongly suggests that he had a physical model of causation in mind when he reflected on the cause of a factious deed. Although Madison regarded a majority's motive as the counterpart of the spark and a majority's opportunity as the counterpart of the paper's being dry and surrounded by enough oxygen, Madison denied that a man who wished to prevent a factious deed could eliminate the majority's factious motive by appealing to other motives of members of the majority as he could prevent a fire by blowing out a spark which had fallen on a piece of paper. However, Madison did think that a certain kind of government could diminish the probability that men with factious motives would make up a majority. He also thought that if a factious majority were to form under such a government, it would very likely be denied the opportunity to carry out its motives in action. Keeping such a physical illustration in mind may improve our understanding of Madison's views on the defects of what he calls pure democracy and the advantages of representative democracy, which he calls a republic. In any event, we would do well to observe the similarity between Madison's theory of how to prevent individuals from performing certain actions and a theory of how to prevent an inanimate object from behaving in a certain way. That similarity underscores the extent to which the science of politics as conceived by Publius relied on conceptions of the causes of action and behavior that were current in the eighteenth century. With this similarity in mind, I shall now examine some of Madison's reflections on pure democracy and republican government.

The Defects of Pure Democracy:
The Structure of Madison's Argument

Madison believed that a pure democracy would not be likely to prevent a majority from developing a factious motive or from having an opportunity to act on such a motive. A "pure Democracy" is defined by Madison as "a Society, consisting of a small number of citizens, who assemble and administer the Government in person." In a pure democracy, he says, "a common passion or interest will, in almost every case, be felt by a majority of the whole."[13] So, he holds, a pure democracy will certainly not prevent a majority of the people from having the same factious motive; on the contrary, it will do just the opposite. Furthermore, it will also provide ample opportunity for a factious majority to oppress the minority. For these reasons, a majority in a pure democracy may be compared to a dry piece of paper which is surrounded by oxygen and which is touched by a spark in the hands of a factious leader. That spark, or bit of fire, will quickly spread to every part of the paper—every individual in the majority—thereby forming a factious majority which will then inflict damage on the minority. There is little or nothing in the society to stop the factional fire from spreading through the majority and little or nothing to keep the inflamed majority from acting in a manner which will be harmful to the minority.

This may be seen by reflecting on Madison's definition of a pure democracy. It has two fundamental features which are expressed in two propositions: a pure democracy consists of a small number of citizens, and the citizens of a pure democracy assemble and administer the government in person. From the first proposition that a pure democracy consists of a small number of citizens, it follows, according to Madison, that there will probably be very few distinct factional interests in a pure democracy, since a small group of citizens is not likely to exhibit a great variety of such interests. It follows in turn from the scarcity of the factional interests that a majority of the citizens will stand a good chance of being members of the same faction. Since there will not be many economic causes for a majority to espouse, there will be a good chance that it will converge on one. The fact that a democracy consists of a small number of citizens also implies that any majority, and therefore any factious majority, will be composed of a small number of citizens, since any majority of a small body will itself be small. On the other hand, from the second proposition about a pure democracy—that all of the citizens of a pure democracy assemble and administer the government in person—we may infer with the help of some other propositions that a small-numbered factious majority of all of the citizens will live in a small territory. How else could all the citizens administer the government in person in the period of which Madison was speaking? Summing up, we may say that the small population of a pure democracy—its first fundamental feature—makes it very likely that a pure democracy will contain a small-numbered majority which has a factious *motive*. And the fact that the citizens of a pure democracy must assemble and administer the government in person—the second fundamental feature of a pure democracy—makes it likely that a factious majority in a pure democracy will have an *opportunity* to "concert and execute their plans of oppression."[14] Finally, according to Madison, if a small-numbered majority has both a factious motive and an opportunity to act, it will in all likelihood invade the rights of others or act against the common good, as it has in past pure democracies, those "spectacles of turbulence and contention' which have always "been found incompatible with personal security, or the rights of property."[15]

When we view the defects that Madison saw in a pure democracy in terms of our metaphorical fire, we may see more clearly—as I have said earlier—why a factious motive (spark) will have an easy time running through a small-numbered majority (a small piece of paper). The metaphorical fire also helps us see more clearly why the fact that every citizen lives close to every other in a pure democracy will make it easy for factional flames to spread through a majority which will then execute its plans of oppression without impediment. One sees that Madison was influenced by an analogy of this kind when he spoke of "factious leaders" who "may kindle a flame within their particular States, but will be unable to spread a general conflagration through the other States" of a federal union.[16] Why will they be unable to spread a general conflagration of this kind? Because, Madison says, the federal union will be a representative government and not a pure democracy; so let us examine why Madison thought that a republican or representative popular government would eliminate factiously motivated majorities as well as their opportunities, thereby controlling or checking the effects of faction while preserving the spirit and form of popular government.

The Advantages of a Republic:
The Structure of Madison's Argument

In *Number 10* Madison introduces his discussion of the advantages of a republic by saying that he understands by a republic "a Government in which the scheme of representation takes place."[17] In *Number 39* Madison writes more fully about republics. He says: "We may define a republic to be, or at least may bestow that name on, a government which derives all its powers directly or indirectly from the great body of the people; and is administered by persons holding their offices during pleasure, for a limited period, or during good behaviour."[18] I do not know why he first says that we may "define" a republic in this way and then draws back to say that at least we "may bestow that name" on the form of government he describes as republican in *Number 14*. Perhaps he was expressing his general hesitancy about offering definitions; perhaps he was indicating that he did not care whether the word "republic" was ordinarily used in the manner reflected in his definition. In *Number 10* he reveals a similar indifference to whether a certain attribute is or is not *by definition* possessed by the form of government he had in mind. Even though he says in *Number 10* that he *means* by a republic a government in which "the scheme of representation takes place," he goes on to specify *two* attributes of republics which distinguish them from pure democracies and which, he says, are of fundamental importance in contributing to the elimination of, or to diminishing the likelihood of, factious deeds in a republic. The first of these attributes—the attribute of delegating the government to a small number of citizens elected by the rest—is an immediate consequence of what Madison *means* by a republic, an immediate consequence of the "scheme of representation" that takes place in such a government. The second attribute—which is not as obvious a consequence of the definition of a republic—Madison expresses by saying that a republic, by comparison to a pure democracy, "may be" extended over a greater number of citizens *and* a greater sphere of country. It is this second attribute which, in Madison's view, is principally responsible for rendering "factious combinations less to be dreaded" in republics than in pure democracies,[19] and therefore I want to concentrate on it before considering why Madison thinks that by exploiting this feature of a republic we can diminish the danger that majorities will act oppressively in a republic as opposed to a pure democracy.

When trying to understand the second attribute of a Madisonian republic we should bear in mind its conjunctive nature and the fact that it is repeatedly said by Madison to be an attribute that a republic *may* possess. If a republican government is administered by representatives or delegates of the people, then, according to Madison, the government *may be* extended over a great number of citizens *and* a greater sphere of country than a pure democracy. The citizens of a pure democracy, he says, are necessarily few in number and confined to one spot, but the citizens of a republic elect other people to run the government for them and that is why the number of citizens *may be* larger and the territory they inhabit *may be* larger than both must be in a democracy. Because a republican government has this double possibility, the chances are that factions will not form in it and that if they form, they will not act in ways that Madison deplored.

Why does Madison say so often that a republic *may be*—not *must be*—extended over a great number of citizens and a great sphere of country? Why does he say in *Number 14,* for example, "that in a democracy, the people meet and exercise the government in person; in a republic they assemble and administer it by their representatives and agents. A democracy *consequently* [my emphasis] will be confined to a small spot. A republic *may be* [my emphasis] extended over a large region"?[20] I think that Madison asserted that a republic may be extended over a large region because he wished, for one thing, to deny the view of Montesquieu "on the *necessity* [my emphasis] of a contracted territory for a republican government," as Hamilton stated the Frenchman's view in *Number 9*.[21] In *Number 14* Madison himself criticized the "artifice of some celebrated authors" who held that a republic *"can never* [my emphasis] be established but among a small number of people, living within a small compass of territory."[22] Here Madison took Montesquieu and others to be asserting not only that a republic necessarily extends over a small territory but also that it necessarily contains only a small population; and that is one reason why Madison asserted that a republic *may be* established in a large territory and *may be* occupied by a large number of people.

I should add, however, that although Madison thought that a republic's territory and its population *may be* expanded beyond that of a pure democracy, he did not recommend exploiting that possibility without qualification.

His doctrine about the size of a republic, he said in his letter to Jefferson of October 24, 1787, "can only hold within a sphere of a mean extent," an extent that was large but not too large. Madison went on: "As in too small a sphere oppressive combinations may be too easily formed agst. the weaker party; so in too extensive a one, a defensive concert may be rendered too difficult against the oppression of those entrusted with the administration."[23] Madison gave an additional reason for not wanting too extensive a republic in *Number 14,* where he began by pointing out that a pure democracy has a limit—"that distance from the central point, which will just permit the most remote citizens to assemble as often as their public functions demand; and will include no greater number than can join in those functions"—and where he then pointed out that a republic also has a natural limit, namely, "that distance from the center, which will barely allow the representatives of the people to meet as often as may be necessary for the administration of public affairs."[24] Clearly Madison wanted the republic to extend over a large territory but not over a boundless one. Once again we see Madison walking a fine line. He wanted to prevent majorities from acting tyrannically against minorities of the people but he did not want to check them so much that they would be denied the opportunity to defend themselves against a tyrannical administration.

Although I have called special attention to passages in *The Federalist* where Madison limits himself to saying that a republic's territory and population may be extended beyond that of a pure democracy, there is a passage in his letter to Jefferson of October 24, 1787, where he says that he will "prove in contradiction to the concurrent opinions of theoretical writers, that [the republican] form of Government, in order to effect its purposes, must operate not within a small but an extensive sphere."[25] Since the word "must" rather than "may" appears in this passage, I want to square its appearance there with what I have been saying about Madison's emphasis on the possibility rather than the necessity of an extended and well-populated republic. The point is that Madison's emphasis on *possibility* occurs when he is thinking about a republic as by definition representative and therefore administered by delegates elected by a group of people which does not *need* to be small in number or live in a small place. However, when Madison writes in his letter to Jefferson about a majority in such a republic and considers the ways in which it can be prevented from acting oppressively, he first refers to three ways in which he thinks it could conceivably be prevented from doing so by mentioning three possible restraints in the form of counteracting motives. Then, after rejecting all three of these ways of preventing majority factions from acting oppressively, he is left, he thinks, with only one possibility—that of making the republic spacious and populous; and that is why he there concludes that the republic *"must* [my emphasis] operate not within a small but an extensive sphere." In so concluding, he does not fall into inconsistency with what he says elsewhere about the *possibility* of a republic's being large and populous. While reflecting on the fundamental features of a republic and arguing against Montesquieu, he concludes that a republic *may* be extended and *may* be populous; while reflecting on what he regards as the only possible ways of preventing a republican majority from acting oppressively, he says, after eliminating all but one of those ways, that the remaining way—making the republic extensive and populous—is *necessary* as a means of preventing a republican majority from acting oppressively. What is possible in one context therefore becomes necessary in another, and without inconsistency.

Since Madison thought that a republic was better than a pure democracy at controlling factions because, unlike a pure democracy, a republic may extend over a large territory *and* may contain a large number of citizens, I want to say something about another passage, this time in *Number 10,* which should not mislead us about what feature of a large republic is uppermost in Madison's mind. After telling us there that majority factions in a pure democracy have the opportunity to act oppressively in their small territories, Madison writes:

> Extend the sphere [i.e., territory], and you take in a greater variety of parties and interests; you make it less probable that a majority of the whole will have a common motive to invade the rights of other citizens; or if such a common motive exists, it will be more difficult for all who feel it to discover their own strength, and to act in unison with each other. Besides other impediments, it may be remarked, that where there is a consciousness of unjust or dishonorable purposes, communication is always checked by distrust, in proportion to the number whose concurrence is necessary.[26]

If read literally, this passage seems to make a republic's *largeness of territory* the sole cause of the elimination of majorities ruled by factious motives *and* of the elimination of their opportunities to act. The point is that, when read out of context, the passage seems to tell us that merely by extending the geographical sphere of a popular government we will accomplish all the things that diminish the likelihood that factious majorities will exist as well as the likelihood that they will have opportunities to act. However, upon reading other things written by Madison, and even upon reading *Number 10* alone, we can see that he did not think that expansion of territory would of itself create the advantages that republics have over pure democracies. He did not mean, for example, that if you merely expanded the territory in which a *small* group of people lived under a republican government, you would realize the possibilities of republican government that he thought would prevent factious behavior.

Obviously, he did not think that a small group would, merely by moving into a large space, produce that variety of parties and interests which would in turn diminish the likelihood that factious majorities would form and act oppressively in a republic. When Madison wrote in *Number 10,* "Extend the sphere, and you take in a greater variety of parties and interests," he had already written of "the greater number of citizens *and* [my emphasis] extent of territory which may be brought within the compass of Republican, than of

Democratic Government," and already said that "it is this circumstance principally which renders factious combinations less to be dreaded in the former, than in the latter." When Madison wrote those words and soon thereafter recommended the virtues of extending the sphere, he was thinking of the proposed republic of the United States, which he regarded as both spacious and populous, as is evident from what he says in *Number 51* about how to protect minorities from oppressive majorities. The sort of extension he favors, he says in that number, "will be exemplified in the federal republic of the United States," where "the society itself will be broken into so many parts, interests and classes of citizens, that the rights of individuals or of the minority, will be in little danger from interested combinations of the majority." The degree of security attained in this way, Madison adds, "may be presumed to depend on the extent of country *and* [my emphasis] number of people comprehended under the same government."[27] Therefore, I conclude, when he spoke in *Number 10* of extending the sphere, he was referring to an extension of territory which would be *accompanied by* taking in a greater variety of parties and interests as a result of taking in a greater number of people. He meant that the larger republic of the United States would be more effective in controlling the effects of faction than any of the smaller republics he identified with the individual states because the United States would simultaneously make actual the two important possibilities of a republican government—that of permitting a greater population and a larger territory than a pure democracy permitted—and do so, as he says in his famous letter to Jefferson on this subject, "within a sphere of a mean extent."

Once we recognize that in Madison's view the proposed federal republic would realize both of these possibilities, we may ask whether Madison believed that in such a republic a *large citizenry* would do nothing but prevent the formation of small factiously motivated majorities whereas a *large territory* would do nothing but prevent such majorities from having opportunities to act oppressively. I do not think that he split things up in this neat way. He held that not only a large territory but also a large citizenry would contribute to denying a majority *the opportunity* to act oppressively. I grant that he says in *Number 10* that the greater variety of parties and interests in a republic will "make it less probable" that a majority will develop a common factious motive, thereby allowing some readers to think that a large citizenry—the source of this greater variety of interests—would *do nothing but* diminish the probability that a majority would have a factious *motive*. But, by using the language of probability here, he allows for the possibility that a majority *might* develop a factious motive in that republic despite the variety of parties and interests created by the largeness of its citizenry. He reveals his belief in this possibility when he says immediately afterwards that "if such a common motive exists [in a majority faction], it will be more difficult [in a republic and therefore in a majority with lots of people] for all who feel it to discover their own strength, and to act in unison with each other." In the light of this statement, we may ask: What feature of a republic makes it difficult for this factious majority, which "feels" a common motive, to discover its own strength?

In other words, what makes it difficult for a majority, all of whose members have or feel a certain factious motive, *to know* that they constitute a majority? Is it, according to Madison, the size of the territory, the size of the population, or both? I think both. Obviously, the size of the territory would, in Madison's mind, contribute to that difficulty in a country of the kind that Madison knew in 1787. He meant that people who live in distant parts of a *large country* with poor means of transportation and communication would have difficulty in discovering that they constituted a majority faction. But it would seem that the *large number of citizens* who made up a factious majority of a republic's large population also contributed, in Madison's view, to the difficulty that such a majority might have in coming to know its own strength or size. Because a group of persons who "feel" a common interest might want to know that they constitute a majority before taking oppressive action, the largeness of their number would, like the largeness of the country, put an obstacle in the way of their learning whether they did constitute a majority and therefore put an obstacle in the way of their acting oppressively. Consequently, the largeness of a factious majority's number may, like the largeness of the territory in which it resides, prevent it from acting oppressively.

To add further evidence for this—if further evidence should be required—I want to requote another statement from the passage in *Number 10* that begins with the words "Extend the sphere" and ends with a reference to other "impediments" that will block action on the part of a factious majority. Madison says "that where there is a consciousness of unjust or dishonorable purposes [on the part of a factious majority], communication is always checked by distrust, in proportion to the number whose concurrence is necessary."[28] Here again he reveals his belief that *the opportunity* of a factious majority to act may be obstructed by its large numbers because those large numbers will make members of the faction afraid to reveal their unjust motives to each other. Collective action on their part will be impeded by their knowing that they are all men with unjust purposes and hence not to be trusted. This impediment to communication among knaves will increase in strength as the number of knaves in a factious majority becomes larger, thereby diminishing the opportunity of that majority to act oppressively. In the passage of *Number 10* which begins with words "Extend the sphere" we can see, therefore, how the largeness of a republic's population may deny a majority faction the opportunity to act by way of certain psychological mechanisms which are only cursorily described by Madison but which reveal his considerable insight into group psychology. He saw that the largeness of a factious majority might produce a certain kind of ignorance *and* a certain kind of knowledge that would impede action, and that such ignorance and such knowledge were directly responsible for the impediments he thought would be put in the way of factions by a large and populous republic.

I think that Madison's insight into the psychology of factions is worth stressing in the light of what I said earlier about his reference to inefficacious motives, motives that he thinks will not stop majority factions from acting oppressively. Although Madison thinks it is pointless to appeal to certain motives of the men who compose factious majorities in trying to persuade them not to act oppressively—and for this reason thinks that they must be located in a republic that will prevent them from acting oppressively because it is spatially large and contains lots of people—we must not infer from this that Madison believed that the whole job of restraining factious majorities would, as a matter of brute, unexplainable fact, be carried out by big populations and wide open spaces. Madison believed that there was a psychological mechanism which underlay the fact that large numbers and large territories would inhibit action on the part of majority factions. In other words, Madison relied on a psychology of group behavior which he thought would explain the effectiveness of the republican remedy of large populations and large territories. When he urged that men living in republics with lots of people would be less likely to perform factious deeds, he was presupposing something about how men's minds worked even though he did not recommend appealing to the psychological motives he dismissed in his letter to Jefferson of October 24, 1787. That is why he said that men of factious inclinations who live in a big country with lots of other people would have difficulty in discovering that they all had common inclinations. And that is why he said that these same men, having dishonorable inclinations, would hesitate to confess that they had those inclinations to lots of other men who also had them.

It should, however, be kept in mind that Madison looked with disfavor on *all* factions, whether national in scale or not. His large citizenry living in a large territory was therefore a remedy which he thought would not only control national factions but also those that might be located in individual states. This becomes more understandable if we take into account the context in which Madison summarized his views on factions to Jefferson on October 24, 1787, and when he discoursed on the same subject in his *Vices of the Political System of the United States,* written in April of 1787. In both of those places Madison complained about the mutability of the laws of the individual states, and in the letter to Jefferson he made very clear that he was disappointed in the Constitution because it failed to give the national legislature a veto on the laws of the states. In other words, when he first cited the advantage of a republic of many people living in a large territory, he thought that the people of such a republic would be represented by a legislature having such a veto. This would have given legal teeth to his theory of how to control the effects of local factions, teeth which he could not portray or celebrate in the picture he painted in *Number 10* because his fellow framers did not agree with him. Several passages in that number take on extra significance when we think of Madison's suppressed desire for a national legislative veto, especially the passage that reads: "The influence of factious leaders may kindle a flame within their particular States, but will be unable to spread a general conflagration through the other States."[29] In Madison's view the individual states were small republics in which factions were more likely to arise than in the large republic he identified with the union. Therefore, Madison thought, a flame kindled in a small republic might be more easily prevented from turning into a general conflagration that would spread throughout the large republic of the United States if the large republic's legislature could veto laws passed by small republics which had fallen under the influence of factious leaders. If the national legislature had such a veto, it would be even easier to understand why Madison wrote in *Number 10:* "It clearly appears, that the same advantage, which a Republic has over a Democracy, in controling the effects of faction . . . is enjoyed by the Union over the States composing it."[30] A national legislature with the power to veto laws passed by state legislatures would have made it even easier for a large and populous republic to deny a factious majority the opportunity to act.

The Motives and Opportunities of Representative Bodies

So far I have concentrated on Madison's ideas about the effects of a large population and a large territory in preventing factious majorities of *the whole people* from acting oppressively in a republic, but now I want to comment on a section of *Number 10* in which Madison praises a large and well-populated republican government for its salutary effect on *the body of representatives* that the people elect. In this section Madison never uses the words "motive" and "opportunity," but the concepts expressed by them are nevertheless at work. Madison begins with his well-known observation that the chief effect of a representative government is to delegate government to a small number of elected officials who will refine and enlarge public views by passing them through the medium of a body of citizens who are the antithesis of a faction. These elected officials, he thinks, will be wise men who discern the true interest of the country, who are patriotic, who love justice, and who will be least likely to sacrifice the true interest of their country to temporary or partial considerations. However, Madison adds, if men of factious tempers, of local prejudices, or of sinister designs should try to win office as representatives of the people, the very largeness of the population of an extended republic will deny them the opportunity to engage in "the vicious arts"[31] that will get them elected so that they can betray the interests of the people. Because representatives must be scrutinized by a greater number of citizens in order to be elected in a well-populated republic, those who have treacherous motives will stand a poorer chance of being elected. In addition, Madison supports his view that large republics will elect representatives with superior motives by means of an argument which uses arithmetic and which I have analyzed in detail in Chapter 4, above. Here I wish to stress that even though Madison does not explicitly use the words "motive" and "opportunity" when discussing the character of representative bodies in a large and populous republic, the concepts expressed by those words were in his mind.

Madison's idea that a republican government will deprive corrupt representatives of the opportunity to carry out schemes of oppression is evident in *Number 63* when he says that even if indirectly elected senators were to be impelled by corrupt motives, the system of government provided for in the

Constitution would deny them the opportunity to act corruptly. It is hard to exaggerate the extent to which Madison and his fellow authors employed the concepts of motive and opportunity. Madison thought that the federal republic formed by the Constitution created obstacles that would deny tyrannically minded governmental authorities from acting tyrannically; and he thought that it created obstacles—though different ones—which would prevent one oppressively minded part of the people from acting oppressively against another part of the people. Underlying his political points in these instances there was always the more general philosophical principle that an act will be performed if and only if an individual or a group has both the motive and the opportunity to perform it. I now want to show how this principle, which is so central in *The Federalist,* rests on an even more general principle, that of causality or of universal causation.

Motive, Opportunity, and the Principle of Causality

The principle in question may be regarded as a corollary of the principle of causality. If we assume that an action is performed just in case it has a cause, we must realize that that cause is what is sometime called "the whole cause." In other words, the action will occur if and only if the agent performing it has been stimulated in a certain way while in a certain state or condition. The stimulant or precipitant in the case of a majority faction is its ruling motive, and the state or condition in which it is may be summed up by saying that it has the opportunity to act on that motive. Therefore, the motive and the opportunity *taken together* constitute the whole cause of factious behavior for Madison. That is why he believed that by eliminating this whole cause one could, in advance, prevent the mischievous action, which is to say, control the effects of faction. Like Hume, however, he was aware that although human acts have whole causes which bring them into existence, we cannot always state these whole causes because of the complexity of human behavior. Moreover, Madison saw that an event would be prevented even if only part of its whole cause were eliminated. Therefore, even if a majority were to have a factious motive, it would not act oppressively if it lacked the opportunity to act; conversely, if it had the opportunity, it would not act oppressively if it lacked the motive. That is why Madison recommended that the impulse and the opportunity of a faction not be suffered to coincide if one wished to keep it from acting. The conjunction of impulse and opportunity was, in his view, like the conjunction of a spark and the other conditions which, together with that spark, lead to fire. Such a conjunction leads to fire and fire would not break out in its absence.

The principle of causality, which underlay Madison's practical advice in *Number 10,* was never formulated explicitly by him in *The Federalist,* but Hamilton *tried* to formulate that principle when he said in *Number 31* that there are self-evident maxims in ethics and politics such as "there cannot be an effect without a cause."[32] I emphasize the word "tried" because Hamilton's formulation of the principle of causality leaves something to be desired. Years before *The Federalist* appeared, Hume had criticized the sort of formulation offered by Hamilton as "frivolous" when Hume said that the very idea of an effect contains that of a cause, and for that reason renders Hamilton's version of the principle of causality truistic. Obviously, Hume argued, there cannot be an effect without a cause, since an effect is by definition brought about by a cause. On the other hand, Hume says, we cannot defend the belief that every object which begins to exist—that is, every event—has a cause by appealing to Hamilton's truistic maxim any more than we can show that every man is married by pointing out that every husband must have a wife.[33] Hume held that the principle of causality when properly stated is neither intuitively nor demonstratively certain. Nevertheless, he was guided by it in his discussion of human behavior because he sought the causes of human behavior, just as all the authors of *The Federalist* did. Madison, as we know, presented what he regarded as the causes of factions and concluded that because it would be unwise or impossible to eliminate these causes, we should try to control the effects, that is to say, the oppressive deeds of factions. But we should bear in mind that his proposal about how to control their effects issued in statements about what would prevent those deeds from occurring, that is to say, statements about what would cause them not to occur.

I mention Hamilton's departure from Hume's formulation of the principle of causality merely to show once again how wobbly a Humeian Hamilton was. He may have admired Hume as a "solid" and "ingenious" thinker but he did not always fully understand his views or their implications. For this reason, Hamilton's version of the principle of causality in *Number 31* shows how doubtful it is to trace too much of his philosophy to Hume. On the other hand, although Madison, like Hamilton, said a good deal about the causes of certain political phenomena, he does not state any version of the general principle of causality in *The Federalist*. Madison appears to have accepted some form of metaphysical determinism, but, unlike some Marxists, he was wise enough not to try to deduce from it the doctrine of economic determinism or, for that matter, any substantive proposition in political science. Hume's proposition that "every object, which begins to exist, must owe its existence to a cause" does not logically imply Madison's proposition that the various and unequal distribution of property is the most common and durable cause of factions. Nor does the proposition which says that the action of a group is caused by its having both a motive and an opportunity logically imply Madison's proposition that a factious majority will be caused *not* to act oppressively by locating it in a republic as opposed to a pure democracy. Madison's arguments for the main causal theses in *Number 10* show that although he sought the causes of certain political phenomena, he did not try to defend these two theses by deducing them from the principle of causality or anything like it. His method in *Number 10* was therefore very different from Hamilton's method in certain parts of *Number 31,* where Hamilton appears to hold that the federal government's power to tax can be deduced by means of an argument which assumes the allegedly self-evident principle that the means ought to be proportioned to the end. Madison was guided by a belief in the principle of causality but in *The Federalist* he did not defend that belief on dubious grounds nor did he try to use it fallaciously.

In concluding this chapter I remind the reader that in *Number 10* Madison proposes a method of *preventing* factious deeds because they are morally objectionable. There is no doubt that Madison used moral notions when he defined factions, moral notions which he never defined or analyzed in *The Federalist*. I have already indicated that the notion of the public good is identified with "the permanent and aggregate interests of the community" in *Number 10* and that Publius contrasted those interests with interests that are neither partial nor temporary; but a philosopher or political scientist who seeks much more light on this moral topic or on that of private rights will be disappointed when studying *The Federalist*. Publius seems to have assumed that his readers had sufficient understanding of private rights and the public good to know why he was so anxious to prevent majorities from being actuated by factious impulses or, failing that, to deny them the opportunity to act on them.

10

Combining and Separating Motives and Opportunities

Although Publius's discussion of the dangers of majority factions contains what is probably his best-known application of the concepts of motive and opportunity, this discussion was only one of many contexts in which he used these concepts. In *Number 10* they are used in order to show how to prevent actions which are deemed to be objectionable; but sometimes, when Jay, for example, discusses the advantages of one national government over thirteen separate state governments and over three or four separate confederacies, he uses the concepts of motive and opportunity in order to show how to produce national actions of which he approves. Sometimes such a combination is thought by Jay to lead directly to national action in the interest of the American people, and sometimes it is thought to lead indirectly to the true advantage of the American people by producing national action which will deter collective bodies with questionable motives—for example, certain states or confederacies, certain foreign nations, and all factions—from combining their motives with opportunities to act against the interest of the American people. I begin this chapter with a discussion of both of these ways of using the notions of motive and opportunity in the earliest numbers of *The Federalist*. Next I try to show that Hamilton seems to have agreed with Madison in thinking that factions cannot be eliminated from civilized society and therefore should be denied the opportunity to give their motives free rein by acting oppressively. After that, I show how the ideas of combining and dividing motives and opportunities are connected with three fundamental political ideas of those who framed the Constitution: the idea of separation of powers, the idea of a federal union composed of states, and the idea of checks and balances. Then I comment on a fundamental difference between Madison's method of preventing majorities from developing factious motives or from acting oppressively and what may be called constitutional methods which are proposed in *The Federalist* for preventing actions deemed to be objectionable. And, finally, I deal with Madison's failure to label slaveholders as a faction in *Number 10*.

In emphasizing that Publius sometimes used the concepts of motive and opportunity while trying to *encourage* action, I try to make clear that *The Federalist* was not dedicated to defending a government which serves only as a watchman over private rights because its power is separated into powers and jurisdictions that check and balance each other merely for the sake of preventing tyrannical invasion of those rights. Exclusive concentration on *Number 10*'s argument for preventing the motives and the opportunities of factious majorities from coinciding should not lead us to think that this was the only way in which the concepts of motive and opportunity were used by Publius. Not *every* motive was to be prevented from issuing in action, only those of which Publius disapproved. Moreover, some motives of which Publius approved were to be helped to realize themselves, so to speak, by providing them with appropriate opportunities. The method of counterpoise, which might lead to deadlock on the part of a government when all of its branches managed to check each other into equilibrium, was not the only method used in *The Federalist*. Counterpoise was a device for preventing supposedly objectionable motives from issuing in oppressive actions by putting impediments in their way, but Publius did not spend all of his time trying to defend impediments to action. How could he, when he wanted an energetic, united national government to act? With this in mind, let us look at Jay's argument for such a government, an argument which favors the combining of motives and opportunities.

Combining the Motives and Opportunities
of a United America

For the most part, Jay argues, one nation can give another nation a just cause or a just reason for making war on the first either when the first violates a treaty with the second or when it engages in direct violence against the second. Jay begins his argument in *Number 3* by concentrating on violations of treaties and points out that a disunited America, having treaties with five maritime nations, might easily give just cause for war to five nations which were in a position to attack it. In such a situation, Jay held, "it is of high importance to the peace of America, that she observe the laws of nations towards all these Powers";[1] and this, he goes on to say, "will be more perfectly and punctually done" by one national government than by thirteen states or by three or four confederacies.[2] According to Jay, a national government will perform the action of peacekeeping better than thirteen states or three or four confederacies because it will have the motive and the opportunity to do so. To show that the national government will have the motive, Jay points out that as soon as an efficient national government is established, "the best men in the country will not only consent to serve, but also will generally be appointed to manage it," since the national government "will have the widest field for choice, and never experience that want of proper persons, which is not uncommon in some of the States."[3] This chance to pick leaders from a large pool makes it likely, Jay continues, that the administration, political counsels, and judicial decisions of the national government "will be more wise, systematical and judicious, than those of individual States, and consequently more satisfactory with respect to other nations, as well as more *safe* with respect to us."[4] By putting men with such motives in charge, a national government will take foreign affairs out of the hands of the states. While "the prospect of present loss or advantage, may often tempt the governing party in one or two States to swerve from good faith and justice," in a united America, "those temptations not reaching the other States, and consequently having little or no influence on the national government, the temptation will be fruitless, and good faith and justice be preserved."[5] Here Jay is merely arguing in a general way that the leaders of the national government will have motives which are superior to those of the leaders of state governments.

A later passage in *Number 3* makes use of both the concept of motive and that of opportunity. Jay says that even if the governing party of a state should resist temptations that would lead to aggressive actions against other nations, such temptations ordinarily result from circumstances peculiar to the state and therefore may be shared or applauded by a great number of the state's inhabitants. Consequently, "the governing party [of the state] may not always be able if willing to prevent the injustice meditated, or to punish the aggressors."[6] In other words, the governing party may be denied the opportunity to act on good motives because of local circumstances. By contrast, Jay says, "the national Government, not being affected by those local circumstances, will neither be induced to commit the wrong themselves, nor want power or inclination to prevent, or punish its commission by others."[7] According to Jay, a national government would not have the motive to commit wrong, but it would have a combination of the power *and* the inclination or motive to prevent or punish actions that might get us into war—a combination which the governing party of a state might not have. Here Jay used the word "power" in *Number 3* much as Madison used the word "opportunity" in *Number 10*. For these reasons Jay held that a united national government would tend to keep the American people out of war because such a government had motives and opportunities which individual states were not likely to have. Individual states might well violate treaties with other nations, thereby creating a danger of war which would not be eliminated by the governing parties in such states nor, of course, by a local citizenry having short-sighted and partial motives.

It will be recalled that, according to Jay, another danger to America might arise because just causes for war might be given by Americans to other nations through American use of direct violence. Speaking of the dangers that might be created by direct violence on the part of Americans, Jay says that "one good national government affords vastly more security against dangers of that sort, than can be derived" from thirteen separate states.[8] Such violence, he says, is "more frequently caused by the passions and interests of a part than of the whole, of one or two States than of the Union."[9] Individual states, he says, had by their improper conduct provoked wars with Indians, but even the feeble national government under the Articles of Confederation had rarely done so. Border states, he also says, "under the impulse of sudden irritation, and a quick sense of apparent interest or injury, will be most likely by direct violence, to excite war"[10] with Spanish and British territories near such states. However, Jay continues, the dangers that might be created by states motivated in this way would be lessened by "a national Government, whose wisdom and prudence will not be diminished by the passions which actuate the parties immediately interested."[11] By virtue of its wisdom and prudence, Jay thinks, the national government will have motives which are more rational than those of the states. Furthermore, Jay remarks as he concludes *Number 3,* the national government will have it in its "power" to settle amicably whatever incidents might tend toward hostilities.[12] Along with its power, it will have motives that are "more temperate and cool"; it "will be more in capacity to act advisedly than the offending State"; it will not be affected by the pride that may affect states as well as individual men who get into difficulties with Indians or with foreigners near the borders.[13] In short, an efficient national government will have the motives on the one hand and the power or opportunity on the other to keep America not only from violating treaties but also from engaging in direct and unlawful violence that will invite aggression on the part of other nations.

It is very important to observe, therefore, that when Jay uses the concepts of motive and opportunity in showing that a national government will act in a salutary way, he does not say that the impulse and opportunity of the national government should *not* be allowed to coincide; on the contrary, he *wants them* to coincide. Plainly, then, the theory that an action is performed if and only if a motive and an opportunity coincide is a neutral theory as employed in *The Federalist.* It is invoked by Publius not only in arguments intended to show how objectionable actions may or will be prevented but also in those intended to show how approved actions may or will be performed. The national government is treated with great respect by comparison with individual states or confederacies made up of a small number of states. According to Publius, states are not inherently bad—as factions are—but states can easily be motivated by partial interests or immediate passions which lead them to act against reason and the true interests of the people. When that happens, their impulses and their opportunities to act on them must not be suffered to coincide, and the collective body which can prevent them from coinciding is a national government which has enough power to act on its supposedly wise, prudent, cool, temperate motives.

I have been concentrating up to now on showing why Publius thinks that a united America will avoid giving just cause to other nations for making war on it. However, Jay points out in *Number 4* that if the American people wish to make themselves safe against the use of foreign force, they must not only refrain from giving just causes of war to other nations but must also put themselves and continue themselves in a situation "as not to *invite* hostility."[14] Jay observes that even if they do not give just cause for war to other nations and do not provoke it by violating treaties or engaging in direct violence, they may invite hostility simply by virtue of being in certain economic circumstances. America, Jay observes, is a rival of France and Britain in the fisheries; it is their rival and that of other European nations in navigation; it competes with several nations in the trade with China and India. And because it is an economic rival of many nations, "jealousies and uneasinesses" may lead those nations not to regard its "advancement in union, in power and consequence by land and by sea, with an eye of indifference and composure." These circumstances, Jay points out, may create what he calls "inducements to war" in other nations, "and . . . whenever such inducements may find fit time and opportunity for operation, pretences to colour and justify them will not be wanting."[15] What should America do in that case? Put itself in a position where it has a national government, he replies, which is efficient and well administered, which will regulate trade prudently, organize and discipline a militia, manage America's resources and finances discreetly, reestablish its credit, and let the people be free, contented, and united. In that case, those who might not look at America "with an eye of indifference and composure" will see it differently: "they will be much more disposed to cultivate [America's] friendship, than provoke [America's] resentment."[16] Therefore, if a foreign power seems to be combining its hostile economic motives with an opportunity to put them into operation, America should give it pause by uniting. A united America will cause a potential adversary to think twice before attacking, and the potential adversary's second thought will prompt it to avoid making war on America.

In sum, *Number 3* and *Number 4* depict a national government which *combines* its superior motives and its opportunities so as to perform actions which promote the good of the American people. When indirectly promoting that good, the national government will prevent the objectionable motives of an *American state* and its opportunities from combining so as to provoke foreign nations into war with America; the national government will act similarly when preventing the objectionable motives of a *foreign nation* and its opportunities from combining so as to make war on America. In both cases the national government will prevent the action of another agent by *dividing* what I have called the whole cause of such an action. However, a national government which has *only* a motive to do such dividing, and therefore no opportunity to act on that motive, will not succeed in either of these jobs. That is why the national government must have *both* a motive and an opportunity to separate the motives and opportunities of provocative American states and menacing foreign nations if it is to accomplish one of its most important goals, the prevention of wars which are not in the true interests of the American people. That is why the allegedly superior leaders of the national government must be given certain opportunities or powers which will permit them to implement their superior motives. It should be clear, however, that when Jay says that an efficient national government will be led by "the best men in the country," and hence by men of superior motives, he does not mean that those motives will *always* be working in the minds of those good men, any more than Madison means that the motives of members of factions will always be at work in their minds. Jay means that such men will *tend* to be moved by impulses of a patriotic and rational kind. They are not men of "factious tempers" in Madison's phrase but men of rational, patriotic tempers. They are men of wisdom, but men of wisdom are not always moved by wise impulses. Because the superior administrator of government was supposed to have a tendency to choose wisely and patriotically, the efficient, energetic government which he administered was also supposed to have a tendency to choose wisely and patriotically.

In *Number 5* Jay argues similarly that three or four separate confederacies, like thirteen separate states, will not serve the interests of the American people as well as one national government. Each confederacy would have partial interests and, like nations which border each other, would be involved in disputes or war or live in constant apprehension of them. According to Jay, the fact that two confederacies border on each other will not only cause envy and jealousy to motivate them but it will also provide them with opportunities for belligerency if—as is likely—one confederacy should become stronger than the others. Unlike the union produced by one national government, a simple alliance between such confederacies, he adds, would not produce "that combination and union of wills, of arms, and of resources, which would be necessary to put and keep them in a formidable state of defence against foreign enemies."[17] In this passage Jay sums up one of the most important advantages of an America united under one government in terms that underscore the importance of the notions of motive and opportunity in Publius's argument. A united nation which has a will that unites the wills of its member states will have superior motives and it will have arms and resources that will afford it the opportunity to act in defense of the nation.

In *Number 6* Hamilton provides us with more examples of how the ideas of motive and opportunity are used in *The Federalist* to defend union. Wholly disunited states or states which are united in partial confederacies would, he says, have frequent and violent contests with each other. The motives for the actions of such states or confederacies would ultimately derive from the fact that "men are ambitious, vindictive and rapacious"; and the fact that such states or confederacies would be "unconnected sovereignties, situated in the same neighbourhood," would provide the opportunity for these violent contests.[18] In *Number 7* Hamilton adds that the "inducements" or motives that disunited but neighboring states would have to make war on each other are "precisely the same inducements, which have, at different times, deluged in blood all the nations in the world."[19] These inducements, he continues, are particularly illustrated in the motives which lead nations to engage in territorial disputes, in commercial competition, in disputes about apportionment of the public debt, and so on. A disunited America, Hamilton concludes, would provide the opportunity which would render the parts of America "a prey to the artifices and machinations of powers equally the enemies of them all. *Divide et impera* must be the motto of every nation, that either hates, or fears us."[20] In response, America must unite so as not to be ruled by enemies, for an enemy who divides it out of motives of hatred or fear will have an excellent opportunity to rule it.

Hamilton on Separating the Motives
and Opportunities of Factions

The idea that a united America would act in the true interests of the American people by separating the motives and opportunities of hostile groups is further illustrated in *Number 9,* where Hamilton declares that a firm union would bring liberty as well as peace by serving "as a barrier against domestic faction and insurrection."[21] In this number Hamilton says a few things which anticipate what Madison has to say about faction in *Number 10,* but Hamilton is not nearly as systematic as Madison in his treatment of the subject. In *Number 9* Hamilton tries to turn the tables on critics who had attacked the "ENLARGEMENT of the ORBIT" within which the American systems of government were made to revolve by a Constitution which called for the consolidation of several smaller states into one "great confederacy."[22] Hamilton tries to rebut these critics by arguing that even Montesquieu, the hero of those who favored "a contracted territory for a republican government,"[23] favored "a CONFEDERATE REPUBLIC as the expedient for extending the sphere of popular government and reconciling the advantages of monarchy with those of republicanism."[24] In Hamilton's words, this union, or this extension of the sphere of popular government, will serve "as a barrier against domestic faction and insurrection," "suppress faction and . . . guard the internal tranquillity of States, [so] as to increase their external force and security," and "repress domestic faction and insurrection."[25]

When relying on Montesquieu in order to establish this point, Hamilton presents some translated quotations from the *Spirit of the Laws,* in which Montesquieu says that in a confederate republic several smaller states agree to become members of an assemblage of societies which is capable of increasing "by means of new associations" until the assembled societies "arrive to such a degree of power as to be able to provide for the security of the united body." The form of this extended society, Montesquieu says, "prevents all manner of inconveniences" by erasing, in effect, opportunities that might combine with the motives of objectionable agents to produce objectionable actions. If a single member of the confederate republic should be motivated to usurp the supreme authority of the confederate republic, says Montesquieu, that member would not be likely to have equal authority and credit in all the states, because if it were to have too much influence over one of the other states, it would alarm the rest. And if it were to subdue one part of the confederate republic, Montesquieu says, the part that remained free would then overpower the would-be usurper before it could "be settled" in its usurpation. We may say, therefore, that Montesquieu's confederation of states is a mechanism which will prevent the motive and the opportunity of a would-be usurper from coinciding, and thereby prevent an act of usurpation.

Hamilton seems to think that factions are in Montesquieu's mind when the latter says: "Should a popular insurrection happen, in one of the confederate States, the others are able to quell it. Should abuses creep into one part, they are reformed by those that remain sound. The State may be destroyed on one side, and not on the other; the confederacy may be dissolved, and the confederates preserve their sovereignty."[26] Presumably the imagined insurrection to which Montesquieu refers is, according to Hamilton, brought about by a faction within the state in which that insurrection occurs. Nevertheless, it is not very easy to see why Hamilton thinks that Montestquieu's remarks as quoted by Hamilton in *Number 9* illustrate the tendency of the union to repress domestic faction as well as insurrection.[27] Hamilton does not define "faction" in *Number 9,* but what Hamilton says there about faction is compatible with Madison's idea in *Number 10* that a barrier against faction will prevent the ruling motive of a faction from combining with an opportunity to express itself in action. Hamilton did not disagree with Madison's view in *Number 10* that factions may be checked or controlled but not eradicated in civilized nations.

Some readers of *Number 9* who come upon Hamilton's remark that the union has a tendency to "suppress faction" and "repress domestic faction" might think otherwise, but I think their reading of Hamilton would rest on an incorrect interpretation of his words "suppress" and "repress." Hamilton used them in order to convey the idea of preventing factious passions and interests *from issuing in action,* and not to convey the idea of exterminating factions. This is evident in what Hamilton says about faction in other numbers. In *Number 15* he refers to "a spirit of faction which is apt to mingle its poison in the deliberations of *all* [my emphasis] bodies of men," so it seems unlikely that he thought that factions could be destroyed by political devices even though the "solid and ingenious" Hume had said in "Of Parties in General" that this could be done—albeit with difficulty.[28] In *Number 21* Hamilton says, in order to show the advantages of a union, that "a successful faction may erect a tyranny" in one of the states which the union would keep from spreading to other states, but he does not mean that the union would be able to eradicate factions altogether. When the deeds of a tyrannical faction are prevented from spreading, the faction itself is not thereby destroyed.[29] In *Number 22* Hamilton says that "greater scope" will be given to "domestic faction"[30] by requiring unanimity rather than a majority in the votes of public bodies, but in that same number there is no suggestion that factions would be destroyed if majority rule were to be followed. In *Number 27* Hamilton says that "a turbulent faction" in a state may suppose itself able to contend with friends of the government in that state, "but it can hardly be so infatuated as to imagine itself a match for the combined efforts of the Union."[31] Yet, whatever its degree of turbulence or infatuation, the faction of which Hamilton speaks here may continue to *exist.* In *Number 59* Hamilton allows that a strong faction in each of certain states may influence the rulers of those states even while a union exists, so once again Hamilton does not seem to say that the union will obliterate factions.[32] In *Number 61* "a predominant faction in a single State" is said by Hamilton to be capable of existing in a union,[33] and in *Number 65* Hamilton says that factions and "their animosities, partialities, influence and interest" can exist in a nation governed by the proposed Constitution.[34] In the latter number Hamilton asks us not to forget "that the demon of faction will at certain seasons extend his sceptre over all numerous bodies of men,"[35] and in *Number 71* Hamilton refers to the "ill-humors" that may prevail "in a predominant faction in the legislative body" of the proposed government.[36] I need not say any more to show that Hamilton never contemplated the total extirpation of factions in a civilized nation. That is why I think that when Hamilton spoke of *suppressing* or *repressing* factions in *Number 9,* he meant preventing them from *expressing* their passions or interests in action. In other words, he thought that they could be denied the opportunity to act on their common interests or passions—the motives that make them a faction—which is what Madison says more explicitly in *Number 10.*

It does not follow that Hamilton and Madison advocated exactly the same method of preventing factiously motivated groups from acting in accordance with their motives, since an object which is stimulated to act in a certain way can be prevented from acting in that way by the use of different methods. An ignited piece of paper may be prevented from burning up either by smothering it or by pouring water on it, and something analogous may be said of ignited factions which have not yet acted. When Hamilton speaks in *Number 9* about the enlargement of the orbit created by consolidating the American states into a confederate republic, he does not spell out the effects of enlargement upon factions as carefully as Madison does in *Number 10.* Nevertheless, ever since John Quincy Adams said that *Number 9* and *Number 10* were "rival dissertations upon Faction and its remedy," some commentators have distinguished between the Hamiltonian and Madison methods of dealing with factions. For example, Professor Alpheus Thomas Mason thinks that Hamilton "elaborated his remedy for factions" in *Numbers 70, 71, 76,* and *78,* a remedy which, according to Mason, contrasts more sharply with Madison's remedy in *Numbers 10* and *51* than Hamilton's remedy in *Number 9* does.[37] In my opinion, however, what Hamilton says about factions in *Number 9* does not contrast sharply with what Madison says in *Number 10,* chiefly because of 9's lack of specificity; and for a related reason I do not think that *70, 71, 76,* and *78* present much that "rivals" what Madison says about factions in *Number 10.*

It is true that in *Number 70* we find Hamilton saying that energy in the executive is essential "to the security of liberty against the enterprises and assaults of ambition, of *faction* [my emphasis] and of anarchy." It is also true that *70* is the notorious number in which Hamilton seems to express approval of Roman dictators who employed their absolute power "against the intrigues of ambitious individuals, who aspired to the tyranny, and the seditions of whole classes of the community, whose conduct threatened the existence of all government."[38] Therefore, it is fair to say that an energetic executive, according to Hamilton, will serve in some way as a barrier against the "assaults," and therefore against the objectionable deeds, of factions. However, in *Number 70,* as in the other numbers cited by Alpheus Thomas Mason, Hamilton is not primarily concerned to say in general terms what the remedy of faction is, and that is my main reason for denying that in *70, 71, 76,* or *78* he presents us with anything that could be called a theory about the control of factions which stands in sharp contrast to that of Madison in *Number 10.* I grant that some of the views expressed in those numbers and in *Number 9* diverge from certain views of Madison about factions, but the statement of John Quincy Adams and Alpheus Thomas Mason that there are "rival dissertations upon Faction and its remedy" in *The Federalist* seems to me to go too far. Madison's *Number 10* and *Number 51* together constitute a dissertation on factions, but I find no rival dissertation by Hamilton in *The Federalist.* Such a rival of Madison's *Number 10* would have to show in a systematic way—if it were to comport with Mason's interpretation of Hamilton—how an energetic executive and a judiciary with indefinite tenure would prevent factions from acting,[39] but Hamilton's unsystematic remarks on the roles of these branches of government in blocking factions hardly bear comparison with Madison's intricately fashioned view of how to deny factions the opportunity to act.

How, according to Hamilton, would the executive or the judiciary prevent a faction's ruling motives from leading it to act against private rights or the public good? He certainly does not tell us with any specificity in *Number 70* how an energetic executive will secure the right of liberty against the assaults of faction; nor does he tell us with specificity in *Number 78* how he thought the federal judiciary—upon which Mason says he placed perhaps even greater reliance—would provide a safeguard against factions.[40] As a matter of fact, the main point of *Number 78* about the judiciary is that it will be the least dangerous of the three branches of government to political rights, not that it will exercise the most effective restraint upon the invasion of those rights. The judiciary, Hamilton says in *Number 78,* has no influence on the sword or the purse—as the executive and the legislature, respectively, have—and therefore "can take no active resolution whatever." Hamilton goes on to say that the federal judiciary "may truly be said to have neither Force nor Will, but merely judgment; and must ultimately depend upon the aid of the executive arm even for the efficacy of its judgments."[41] For this reason the judiciary could hardly, in Hamilton's view, exert a direct effect in blocking the deeds of a faction. On the contrary, Hamilton says in *Number 78* that if the judiciary "should be disposed to exercise WILL instead of JUDGMENT" by going beyond its job of declaring the sense of the law, it would, as a consequence, substitute its pleasure for that of the legislative body—something it should not do.[42] The only way in which the judiciary might block a faction is by blocking a legislative faction which had passed a law that was incompatible with the Constitution, but this blocking of a legislative faction was not described by Hamilton in *Number 78* as something which would diminish the likelihood that a factious majority of *the people* would act against private rights and the true interests of the nation. I grant that judicial blocking of a legislative faction might, under certain circumstances, curb a faction of the people which the legislative faction represents, but Hamilton does not spell this out in a form that would permit us to say that he advocated a theory of factions which was as full and systematic as that advocated by Madison in *Number 10* or in a part of *Number 51*.

At the Philadelphia Convention Hamilton expressed some reservations about Madison's views on factions, reservations which Hamilton set down in notes on Madison's speech of June 6. There Hamilton considers Madison's "two principles upon which republics ought to be constructed": one, "that they have such an extent as to render combinations on the ground of interest difficult"; the other, that there be a "process of election calculated to refine the representation of the People." What Hamilton says about the first principle is of most concern to us while comparing the views of Hamilton and Madison on factions. Hamilton allows that "there is truth in both these principles but they do not conclude so strongly as [Madison] supposes." Hamilton's very truncated comments about the first principle do not indicate that he thought that factions—"combinations on the ground of interest"—could be eradicated. Rather, the general tendency of his comments seems to be that Madison's extended republic would not succeed in making it as difficult as Madison thought it would for factions to act oppressively. Moreover, there is no suggestion in these notes as to what methods Hamilton would use in dealing with factions.[43]

Separation of Powers, Federalism, Checks and Balances: Their Connections with Publius's Theory of Action

Now that we see that Publius does not always recommend that motives and opportunities be separated or that both be totally eliminated in order to prevent action, and that he sometimes urges that the wise and cool motives of some agents be combined with opportunities or powers to implement those motives, especially in order to check the acts of certain states, certain nations, and *all* factions, we may clarify certain passages in Madison's *Number 51* with Publius's neutral and therefore double-edged theory of action in mind. In Chapter 6 above I quoted a passage from *Number 51* while disputing the view that Madison was an extreme pessimist about man's motives, but now I want to consider the same passage in the light of my expansion of Publius's elliptically expressed theory, an expansion according to which *the whole cause* of an action is not usually a motive by itself but rather a combination of a motive and a power or an opportunity. While approaching this passage from *Number 51* in this way, however, we must keep in mind a point of Hume's that I emphasized in my earlier discussion of the passage, namely, that we may come to different assessments of man's motives, depending on what comparison we make. If we compare men with demigods or angels, we will assess their motives less favorably than if we compare men with beasts.

In *Number 51* Madison chose to compare men with angels and arrived at certain related views about the dangers posed by ruler to the ruled, about the separation of powers, about a federal republic, and about checks and balances.

In one passage in *Number 51* which I have quoted in an earlier chapter, Madison says that "if men were angels, no government would be necessary,"[44] thereby repeating something close to Hamilton's statement in *Number 15* that government has been instituted "because the passions of men will not conform to the dictates of reason and justice, without constraint."[45] Madison also says in *Number 51* that "if angels were to govern men, neither external nor internal controuls on government would be necessary."[46] Therefore, Madison begins with the assumption that, *in any government,* the motives of the governed as well as those of the governors are not angelic. However, Madison holds, in any government some of the natural rights—and, in that sense, powers—which the people have are surrendered to the governors;[47] and here Madison echoes Jay's statement in *Number 2* that the people must cede some of their natural rights to any government in order to vest it with the powers it needs for governing.[48] Consequently, governors with nonangelic motives pose a threat to the governed, a threat which must be taken especially seriously in a popular government. In such a government the people will understandably fear that the governors may become oppressive usurpers who will abridge natural rights which are inalienable and which have not been ceded to them; the people will also fear that the governors may abuse those rights which have been ceded to them. Therefore, Madison reasons, the people will wish to check such nonangelic motives of governors and will try to deny the governors the opportunity to act on such motives. Clearly, the governors are here viewed by Madison with a fear that resembles his fear of members of a faction in *Number 10*. I say "resembles" because a faction is *by definition* actuated by unjust motives which are adverse to private rights and the public good, whereas, according to Madison, the governors of a popular government are not unjust by definition. Still, he seems sufficiently suspicious of them to suppose with Hume that they are knaves, and therefore to treat them as though they would act oppressively if given the opportunity. In spite of the praise that Madison heaps on the motives of the good governors when he is defending their administration of a united national government, he does not think their motives are so good as to need no checking at all. When he compares their motives to those of the governors of individual states or to those of members of factions, he judges them very favorably; but, naturally, when he compares their motives to those of angels, his judgment is different and he concludes that they should be checked.

When in *Number 51* Madison describes the ways in which the Constitution tries to deny nonangelic rulers the opportunity to oppress the people, he begins by describing how these rulers' nonangelic motives may be checked to some degree in "a single republic," one which is not federal or divided into states. According to Madison, an ideal single republic which contains separate legislative, judicial, and executive branches will deny rulers who are supposed to have tyrannical motives the opportunity to act on such motives because, in such a single republic, one department will not have the opportunity to make the laws, to interpret them, and to enforce them. But this is not the only point at which the notions of motive and opportunity enter Madison's argument while he confines himself to describing the separation of powers in an ideal single republic. They also enter his argument when he tries to show how "the interior structure" of such a government may be so contrived that its three departments "may, by their mutual relations, be the means of keeping each other in their proper places."[49] In other words, although Madison believes that a government with three separate departments will put an impediment in the way of a potential tyrant, Madison wants to show how these three separate departments will *remain* three separate departments if they have appropriate motives and opportunities.

Madison begins to explain how the separation of powers will be *maintained* when he says—while diverging from Hamilton's metaphorical statement in *Number 78* that the judiciary lacks a will—that "each department should have a will of its own; and consequently should be so constituted, that the members of each should have as little agency as possible in the appointment of the members of the others."[50] Madison admits that this principle cannot be adhered to rigorously because that would require the people themselves to make all appointments "through channels, having no communication whatever with one another." But what does he have in mind when he says that the legislative, the judicial, and the executive branches of government should each have wills of their own? To say that an agent should have a will of its own is to say at least that it should have the faculty or ability to choose what to do; but it is also to say that the agent's will should not be under the control of another agent's will. What Madison meant when he said that each branch of government should have a will of its own becomes clearer when he says that members of each branch of government should not depend on members of other branches for the emoluments connected with their offices, remarking that if the executive magistrate or the judges were "not independent of the legislature in this particular, their independence in every other would be merely nominal."[51] Madison meant that no branch of the government should be the slave of or dictated to by any other branch of the government. And this implies that the choices of a given branch should not, for example, be the results of coercion, intimidation, or bribery by some other branch. Why does he urge this? Because he fears that if two branches of government were to be under the domination of a third, the whole system of separation of powers would collapse and tyranny would follow, as he says in *Number 47*. He fears "the accumulation of all powers legislative, executive and judiciary in the same hands, whether of one, a few or many, and whether hereditary, self appointed or elective."[52]

Because Madison wants to prevent tyranny by preventing any one branch of government from imposing its will on the wills of the other two, he is led, as we have seen in Chapter 6, to advocate what has been called the method of counterpoise. The great security against a concentration of power in one department, he says, "consists in giving to those who administer each department, the necessary constitutional means, and personal motives, to resist encroachments of the others." I emphasize that Madison speaks here of giving constitutional means *and* personal motives to those who administer each department, which amounts to giving them opportunities as well as motives for resisting encroachments. And I emphasize it lest we neglect the connection between the concept of opportunity and "constitutional means" when we describe Madison's method in *Number 51* for *keeping* the separate powers separate. Hamilton asked in *Number 33:* "What is the ability to do a thing but the power of employing the *means* necessary to its execution?" and the concept of ability, as we have seen, was often thought by Publius to be the same as the concept of opportunity or as contained in it.[53]

The need to give an endangered department both the opportunity and the motive to resist encroachment is consonant with the military metaphor that Madison uses throughout this passage. "The provision for defence must in this, as in all other cases," he says, "be made commensurate to the danger of attack." Obviously, he views the three branches of government as potential enemies who must be provided with weapons that they know how to use as well as motives that will lead them to use those weapons without impediment if and when they must be used. It is misleading, therefore, to focus exclusively on Madison's statement that "ambition must be made to counteract ambition," because that seems to imply that the potential adversaries need be supplied only with motives. In the statement just after that, Madison makes it clear that each branch must be given more than a motive, for he writes: "The interest of the man must be connected with the constitutional rights of the place," meaning that the man's interest and his constitutional rights in the sense of legal powers or opportunities must coincide or combine if he is to resist attacks. It is also misleading, for a similar reason, to focus exclusively on Madison's summary of counterpoise as the "policy of supplying by opposite and rival interests, the defect [i.e., absence] of better motives"[54] if that is construed as a case of pitting only motives against motives. Madison was led to speak in this way because he assumed that the reader would understand that the opposite and rival interests of which he spoke were the interests of men who held governmental office in one department and therefore in some sense *had* the legal powers, means, and opportunities to engage in appropriate resistance when attacked by similarly endowed men who held governmental office in another department.

Once we recognize that the Madisonian version of counterpoise takes place between agents who have both motives and opportunities to resist encroachments upon each other, we can see once again that Publius was not always trying—as he did in *Number 10*—to keep the motives and opportunities of agents from coinciding. Publius did not hold the absurd view that *every* individual or collective body should always be *prevented* from acting. Sometimes he proposed combining or conjoining a motive and an opportunity of a political agent so as directly to produce approved governmental action by that agent, particularly when he describes how an energetic national government would act by comparison to a state or a confederacy or a faction. And when he described how the separation of powers would be maintained, he assigned to each department of government a combination of motive and opportunity which would lead each department to resist the encroachments of the other two. In the course of such resistance, one department would combine a motive and an opportunity in order to divide a motive and an opportunity of another department. And even while not *actively* resisting, the first department will *show* that it will, if provoked, actively resist encroachment by another department. Merely by giving the impression that it will combine a motive and an opportunity to resist encroachment, it will, Madison thinks, probably deter another department from encroaching on it. And so long as the departments keep from encroaching on each other, the whole system in which governing departments are separate will prevent the governors—who hold office in the system—from oppressing the people, that is to say, deny them the opportunity to act on tyrannical motives.

We must now observe that whereas separation of powers, according to Madison, exploits the concepts of motive and of opportunity in a "single" republic, America is said by Madison in *Number 51* to be doubly protected against tyranny and usurpation because, under the Constitution, it will be a "compound republic." By this Madison means that the power surrendered by the people to governors will be divided into what is surrendered to the state governments and what is surrendered to the national government, which in turn separate their received powers into three departments. "Hence," Madison says, "a double security arises to the rights of the people. The different governments [state and national] will controul each other; at the same time that each will be controuled by itself [insofar as its powers are separate]."[55] All of this control involves checking the feared oppressive actions of those who govern the people. The federal government and the state governments will check and balance each other while each kind of government will in turn be divided so that their executive, legislative, and judiciary departments will also check and balance each other. And this double system of checking and balancing that goes on in the interior of a compound republic is supposed to serve, as I have indicated, as a course of insuperable or almost insuperable obstacles which presumably knavish rulers will have to overcome in order to carry out knavish tricks on the people.

Any reader of *Number 51* will see that Madison's view of how a federal republic guards the people against oppression by their rulers is similar in a certain respect—though not in all respects, as we shall soon see—to what Madison says about controlling factions in *Number 10*. To emphasize this similarity, Madison follows his summary in *Number 51* of how the mechanisms of a compound republic will prevent rulers from oppressing the people with a reformulation of part of what he has said about factious majorities in *Number 10*. Whereas the mechanisms of a compound republic guard the society against its rulers, he says in *Number 51,* the existence of different interests in such a republic will guard one part of the society against the injustice of another part by making it "very improbable, if not impracticable," for a factious majority to invade the rights of individuals or of the minority.[56] He also says once again that the existence of a lot of interests—and therefore of factions—will be encouraged by having a lot of people living in a spacious republic. This, Madison goes on to say, "must particularly recommend a proper federal system to all the sincere and considerate friends of republican government." Because factious majorities are more likely to be oppressive "in exact proportion as the territory of the union may be formed into more circumscribed confederacies or states," a 'republic which contains such circumscribed confederacies or states will afford less security for the rights of every class of citizens. Consequently, he continues, "the stability and independence of some member of the government, the only other security, must be proportionally increased." What Madison is driving at here is that if a "proper federal system" which discourages the division of the republic into more circumscribed confederacies and states is not adopted, then the resulting republic, in which factious majorities can easily act, will degenerate to the point where "some power altogether independent of the people would soon be called for by the voice of the very factions whose misrule had proved the necessity of it."[57]

Madison's defense of this prediction proceeds as follows. He says that the whole purpose of establishing government and civil society is the establishment of justice, which, he adds, has always been and always will be pursued. Moreover, he says, it will be pursued until it is obtained or until liberty is lost in the pursuit. Imagine, Madison continues, that men live in a republic in which a majority or stronger faction can "readily," that is to say, without impediment, unite and oppress the minority or weaker faction. In such a society, Madison says, anarchy reigns, just as it reigns in a state of nature where the weaker *individual* is not secured against the violence of the stronger. Therefore, just as in a state of nature even the stronger individuals are moved by *the uncertainty* of their condition to submit to a government which may protect the weak as well as themselves, so in a republic which contains stronger *factions* which can readily unite and oppress weaker *factions,* the more powerful factions will be gradually induced by this same uncertainty to seek a government which will protect the weaker as well as the stronger factions.

What would be sought after in such a government would, Madison says, be "some power altogether independent of the people" and in that case the pursuit of justice would certainly end in the loss of liberty.[58] For Madison says earlier in *Number 51* that it is possible (though obviously not desirable from his point of view) to provide against the evil of factious majorities by "creating a will in the community independent of the majority, that is, of the society itself," and that this method prevails in all governments having a hereditary or self-appointed authority.[59] He regards this method as a precarious security, however, since a power which is independent of the society may as well espouse the unjust views of the majority as the just interests of the minority; it may even be turned against both factions. Consequently, any republican government which does not, through a "proper federal system," permit an expansion of its territory and population will, Madison predicts, encourage the destruction of republican liberty. This prediction is followed in *Number 51* by a declaration that in the extended republic of the United States, with the great variety of interests which it embraces, "a coalition of a majority of the whole society could seldom take place on any other principles than those of justice and the general good."[60]

Notice, however, that this declaration does not follow from Madison's assumption that an extended and well-populated republic would very probably prevent factious majorities from forming or from acting. To say that such a republic would very probably accomplish this result is not to imply that it would very probably encourage the formation of majorities based on the principles of justice and the general good. This optimistic note is, as it were, slipped in by Madison because it enables him to say that in an extended republic there will be less danger to a minor party "from the will of the major party" and consequently less pretext to provide for the security of a minor party by introducing into the government a will which is not dependent on the major party, "or in other words, a will independent of the society itself."[61] Here Madison seems to argue that because a large republic with a large population will be *unlikely* to produce *factious* majorities, it will be *likely* to produce majorities founded on the principles of justice and the general good. But this is a *non sequitur*. Even if one were to grant that in a large republic with a large population majorities will be less likely to have factious motives and to act oppressively, it does not follow that in such a republic majorities will be more likely to share or to act on the morally attractive motives mentioned by Madison.

In order to make this point as clear as I can, I must refer yet another time to Madison's view that factious majorities are united and actuated by some impulse of passion or of interest which is adverse to the rights of other citizens—hence opposed to justice—or adverse to the permanent and aggregate interests of the community—hence opposed to the general good. Consequently, what Madison says at the end of *Number 51* is that if we put the impediments of a large federal republic in the way of factious majorities, "a coalition of a majority of the whole society could seldom take place on any other principles than those of justice and the general good." But why should this shift to the opposite extreme occur? Why should a large federal republic, simply by virtue of diminishing the likelihood that an *im*moral majority will form, make it *very likely* that a *moral* majority—if I may use that expression—will form? One may grant that whatever diminishes the probability that an immoral majority will form increases to some extent the probability that a moral majority will form. But it does not follow from this that the probability of such a moral majority's forming will be very high. Madison does not seem to reckon on the possibility that a majority in an extended and populous federal republic will fall somewhere between a wicked faction and a blessed coalition. This becomes evident when we see what he says in the penultimate sentence of *Number 51*. Proceeding from his optimistic view regarding the emergence of a moral majority, he says: "It is no less certain than it is important, notwithstanding the contrary opinions which have been entertained, that the larger the society, provided it lie within a practicable sphere, *the more duly capable it will be of self government* [my emphasis]."⁶² Of course, if we have eliminated or diminished the likelihood of factious majorities by instituting a large federal republic, such a republic will be more duly capable of self-government because we have—by hypothesis—gotten rid of things that would probably block self-government. But a society which is *more duly capable* of self-government is not the same as a society in which the majority very probably acts in accordance with the principles of justice and the general good. A society may become *more capable* of self-government when it rids itself of factious majorities, because ridding itself of factious majorities makes it more probable that nonfactious majorities will form. But being *more capable* of self-government in this sense or respect does not imply that a majority of the society will share the motives dictated by the principles of justice and the general good. At best, a society which is more capable of self-government in this sense will create an opportunity or some chance for a moral majority to form, but *some chance* for that to form is not necessarily *a very good chance*. The concluding sentences of *Number 51* are therefore very puzzling. Indeed, when Madison implies that because a majority in an extended republic could seldom be actuated by any principles other than those of justice and the common good, there would be "less danger to a minor from the will of the major party," one wonders whether he has forgotten his definition of "party"—which he regards as synonymous with "faction." One might well wonder in this way if one should interpret Madison to be saying here that a moral majority is a party or a faction.

According to this interpretation of Madison, a minority party or faction need not fear a majority party or faction which subscribes to principles of justice and the general good, but such an interpretation would lead Madison to a contradiction since it would have him saying that a majority party or faction is motivated in a manner which is incompatible with his definition of "faction" in *Number 10*. It might be more charitable to interpret Madison as saying what we attributed to him earlier, namely, that in an extended republic there would be a small chance that a majority would be factious and therefore a big chance that it would be "moral," but such charity would take Madison out of the frying pan of contradiction and into the fire I described when I spoke earlier of his *non sequitur*. Madison, in short, is faced with a dilemma, both horns of which lead him into logical trouble in *Number 51*.

Two Ways of Denying Opportunity: Constitutional and Nonconstitutional

While considering the denial of opportunity in *The Federalist* we should note that there is a difference between the sort of obstacle that Madison advises us to put in the way of governors by separating the three branches of government and the sort of obstacle that he advises us to put in the way of a faction by preventing it from becoming a majority or from acting oppressively. The first sort of obstacle is legal insofar as the separation of powers is incorporated in the Constitution itself, whereas Madison's recommendation that the republic of the United States embrace a large territory and a large population is not expressly incorporated in the Constitution.[63] As we have seen in an earlier chapter, Madison had argued unsuccessfully at Philadelphia for "a constitutional negative on the laws of the States . . . [in order] to secure individuals agst. encroachments on their rights," and his argument for this negative or veto was supported by the "immoderate digression" in his letter to Jefferson of October 24, 1787, the digression in which he discussed the method of controlling factions by constructing a large and well-populated republic. As I have indicated earlier, the power of a national legislature to veto laws of the states would have given constitutional powers to the national government of the spacious and well-populated federal republic for which Madison argued in *Number 10* and *Number 51*. Had Madison been able to persuade the Convention to grant the national legislature this power to veto laws passed by states, then, he thought, a legal obstacle which was not put in the way of factions *would have* been put in their way by the Constitution. As the editors of Madison's *Papers* point out, he believed that the virus of faction was most rampant at the state level and that it would not be effectively controlled unless the national legislature were given the power to veto state laws.[64]

In his letter to Jefferson of October 24, 1787, Madison begins his argument for an extensive republican government as a safeguard against factions by saying: "It may be asked how private rights will be more secure under the Guardianship of the General Government than under the State Governments, since they are both founded on the republican principle which refers the ultimate decision to the will of the majority, and are distinguished rather by the extent within which they will operate, than by any material difference in their structure. A full discussion of this question would, if I mistake not, unfold the true principles of Republican Government. . . ."[65] I need not repeat certain points in the digression that follows this statement since I have already discussed them. However, I do wish to make clear what the main link is between Madison's desire to give the national legislature a veto over laws passed by the states and his belief that an extensive republic will deny factions the opportunity to become majorities and to act oppressively. The link is that states are small republics in which factions are more likely to arise than they are in large republics. Therefore, states will be more likely than the nation to pass laws that are favored by majority factions within the states, and for this reason states will be more likely to pass laws that invade the private rights of their own citizens. "The General Government," Madison goes on to say, "would hold a pretty even balance between the parties [i.e., factions] of particular States, and be at the same time sufficiently restrained by its dependence on the community, from betraying its general interests."[66]

Since Madison failed to persuade the Convention to give the national legislature a veto over laws passed by the states, he did not persuade it to create what he regarded as a legal or constitutional device which would prevent majority factions in the states from pushing through legislation that would be motivated by their factious impulses. That is why what he said in *Number 10* and *Number 51* about controlling the effects of factions contains proposals that concentrate so heavily on geography and population. It is fair to say, therefore, that although the doctrine of separation of powers rests on the idea that encroachment by one department on another may be resisted if and only if the department encroached upon has both the motive and the *legal* opportunity to resist when it counteracts the motive and the *legal* opportunity of the encroaching department, the Madisonian formula in *The Federalist* for controlling the unjust behavior of a majority by denying it an opportunity to form and act does not advocate the use of legal or constitutional impediments. Of course, one might say that recommending that a large and well-populated republic be formed was tantamount to recommending that the American republic be a federal union of the thirteen states and that this in itself was a recommendation of a legal or constitutional sort. Nevertheless, it is obvious that what Madison recommended in *Number 10* and *Number 51* for controlling the effects of factions was not a constitutional or legal remedy by comparison to the remedy which was created by the formation of a federal union.

Tyranny, Slavery, and Irony

Although I have devoted this chapter to comparing the use that Publius makes of the ideas of motive and opportunity when discussing factions and his use of these same ideas when discussing other matters, I want to emphasize once again a significant difference between Madison's view of the deeds that unchecked majority factions may perform and other deeds that may be prevented or performed by manipulating motives and opportunities. The deeds of unchecked majority factions are *by definition* morally wrong in Madison's eyes, whereas—to take a different kind of example—the national government's prevention of the states' provoking war is described by Publius as a likely causal consequence of the government's motives and opportunities without much moral fanfare about the value of avoiding war. To be sure, he thinks that such prevention will redound to what he calls the political prosperity of the people, but he does not spend as much time moralizing about the evils of war as he does when he is condemning factions. On the other hand, when Madison advises us how to control factions by denying them opportunities, he thinks he is telling us how to prevent tyranny, virtually the worst sin in his book. That is why his discussion of the maintenance of separate powers by the use of checks and balances is also morally fervid. On the face of it, he is merely using the concepts of motive and opportunity to show how illegal encroachment can be prevented, but the fundamental aim of preventing such illegal encroachment is to prevent usurpation of power, and therefore tyranny, on the part of the government. That is why Madison's discussions of how to control factions and political usurpers involve the most dramatic and conspicuous use of the concepts of motive and opportunity.

Madison's discussions of how to control factions and political usurpers were so dramatic and so conspicuous as to make *Number 10*'s silence on slavery equally dramatic and conspicuous. As David F. Epstein has pointed out, Madison did not discuss slavery in *Number 10* whereas that subject had figured prominently in the discussion of factions which appeared in Madison's speech to the Convention on June 6, 1787.[67] There Madison said that the mere distinction of color had been made "in the most enlightened period of time, a ground of the most oppressive dominion ever exercised by man over man," and his notes on his own speech indicate that he thought the unjust laws which permitted slavery were in place because of "the real or supposed interest of the major number"—the slaveholders—acting as a factious majority. The lesson we are to draw, said Madison as he summarized his discussion of slavery and other legally enshrined injustices, was "that where a majority are united by a common sentiment and have an opportunity, the rights of the minor party become insecure."[68] In his reference to slavery Madison seemed to be saying that the major party was constituted by the slaveholders and the minor party by the oppressed slaves, and also that "in a Republican Govt. the Majority if united have always an opportunity" to make the rights of a minor party such as that of the slaves insecure. Immediately after saying this, Madison proposes his famous remedy of enlarging the sphere, and so it would seem reasonable to infer that while making his speech he regarded that remedy as one which would prevent the oppressive dominion of slavery.

By contrast, *Number 10,* appearing in a book which defended the Constitution that countenanced the existence of slaves when euphemistically and shamefacedly referred to as "person[s] held to service, or labor," does not use the word "slavery" for what Madison had earlier called the most oppressive dominion exercised by man over man. And what is more, Madison's definition of "faction" seems calculated to prevent his readers from calling the slaveholders an oppressive faction. Why? Because, as Epstein has pointed out, that definition not only requires a faction to be a number of "citizens," it also requires those who have their private rights invaded by a faction to be "citizens." And since the slaves were not citizens, they could not be the objects of factional oppression, though they could be regarded as members of the community whose permanent and aggregate interests might be adversely affected by slaveholders.[69] I repeat, however, that the slaveholders and slaves are never mentioned in *Number 10* when Madison illustrates the idea of factional difference. The slaveholders were not *said* to be a faction on the score of having an impulse adverse to the rights of the slaves *or* on the score of having an impulse adverse to the public good. They could not, by Madison's definition of faction, be said to be tyrannical. Therefore, one irony of *Number 10* (and of *Number 51*) was that the author of them could not condemn or even mention the tyranny involved in what he himself had called the most oppressive dominion ever exercised by man over man.

If any reader should think that Madison was not deliberate in using the word "citizens" in his definition of the word "faction," that reader should consult *Number 43*. There Madison says that a "minority of CITIZENS may become a majority of PERSONS" when he is discussing "illicit combinations for purposes of violence," combinations which may be checked by the superintending power of the national government as described in Article IV, Section 4 of the Constitution. His point seems to be that sometimes a minority faction may become a majority faction by adding to its ranks "alien residents," "adventurers," or "those whom the Constitution of the State has not admitted to the rights of suffrage." The latter three sorts of individuals are not citizens but they are persons, and Madison shows by a peculiarly oblique turn of phrase that even nonpersons may associate themselves with a majority faction when he says: "I take no notice of an unhappy species of population abounding in some of the States, who during the calm of regular government are sunk below the level of men; but who in the tempestuous scenes of civil violence may emerge into the human character, and give a superiority of strength to any party with which they may associate themselves."[70]

In this passage we may note another irony that is connected with Madison's definition of "faction" in *Number 10*. As we have seen, that definition makes it impossible to say that slaveholders constitute a faction on the score of tyrannizing over slaves, simply because the latter are not citizens. However, in *Number 43* Madison virtually says that a "minor party," that is to say, a minority faction, may become a majority faction through the addition of slaves to its ranks. By virtually saying so, he virtually alters the definition of "faction" he gives in *Number 10*. For, according to *Number 43,* the majority of "persons" into which a minority of "citizens" is transformed by adding slaves has every feature of a faction as defined in *Number 10* except that of being composed exclusively of citizens. So what we have is the following situation. In *Number 10* Madison could not call the slaveholders an unjust or oppressive faction because he could not call the slaves citizens, but in *Number 43* he is virtually forced to give the name "faction" to a group of individuals some of whom are slaveholders and some of whom are slaves when that group is an illicit combination for purposes of violence. Therefore, we may say that the slaves function differently at different places in Madison's system. When they are oppressed, that fact is not sufficient to turn their masters into a faction by the logical standards of *Number 10,* but when they join their masters they may turn the resulting group of masters *and* slaves into a virtual faction.[71]

In calling attention to this feature of Madison's thinking, I do not wish to deny his sympathy for the slaves or his awareness that they were the objects of tyranny. Unfortunately for him, they were also regarded as property when the Constitution was drafted and therefore he was faced with a supposed conflict of natural rights. This is obvious in the Virginia Debates on the adoption of the Constitution, where George Mason had described Section 9 of Article I of the Constitution as a "fatal section" because it allowed the importation of slaves for twenty years after 1788. "As much as I value a union of all the states," he said, "I would not admit the Southern States into the Union unless they agree to the discontinuance of this disgraceful trade, because it would bring weakness, and not strength, to the Union." Mason added that even though this "infamous traffic" be allowed to continue, slave-holders would have no security for the property in slaves they held already because there is no clause in the Constitution to secure it. Moreover, he said, Article V expressly prevented any amendment of the objectionable section of the Constitution before 1808, so that it permitted the continuance of the slave trade for twenty years. In short, Mason had two objections which he summed up by saying that "they have done what they ought not to have done, and have left undone what they ought to have done."

I have summarized Mason's remarks mainly to prepare the way for Madison's comments on the issues raised by Mason. About the disgracefulness of the slave trade Madison had only this to say: "I should conceive this clause to be impolitic, if it were one of those things which could be excluded without encountering greater evils. The Southern States would not have entered into the Union of America without the temporary permission of that trade; and if they were excluded from the Union, the consequences might be dreadful to them and to us." There is no talk in Madison's speech about the oppressive dominion of man over man. Indeed, he quickly leaves the part of Mason's speech in which Mason accuses the framers of doing what they ought not to have done, and spends much more time on what Mason had to say about the insecurity of property in slaves. Madison takes pains to point out that Congress cannot lay such a tax on slaves as would amount to manumission and that another clause of the Constitution secures the property held in slaves. He also points out that Article IV, Section 2, clause 3 says that "no person held to service or labor in one State under the laws thereof, escaping into another, shall, in consequence of any law or regulation therein, be discharged from such service or labor, but shall be delivered up on claim of the party to whom such service or labor may be due." In effect, then, Madison denies Mason's claim that "they . . . have left undone what they ought to have done," pointing out that "this clause was expressly inserted, to enable owners of slaves to reclaim them."[72]

When one reads these remarks of Madison, one is first of all struck by the fact that he is more concerned to show that the right to property in slaves is not threatened by the Constitution than he is to attack an oppressive tyranny over slaves. And, second, one is struck by the fact that he is moved in this direction not so much because he regarded the natural right to property as prior to the natural right to liberty but because he was worried that the Union might fall apart if the right to property in slaves was not protected by the Constitution. In any case, it is obvious that Madison was, for various reasons considered in this chapter, not disposed to brand the slaveholders as a faction whose motives and opportunities would or should be separated by a large and populous republic. On this subject Madison was more concerned with the permanent and aggregate interests of the American Union than he was with the natural rights of man.

VII
ETHICS

11

The Nonnaturalistic Ethics
of Natural Rights

Any reader who has had the patience to read this far knows that I have been anxious to distinguish several different kinds of beliefs or propositions to which Publius subscribed; and if such a reader has enough patience to finish reading this book, he or she will see that I try later on to delineate the structure of what may be called the total body of Publius's beliefs. Before I make that effort, however, I want to consider an attempt by the distinguished political scientist Robert A. Dahl to treat some of Madison's views in a manner that reveals the influence of a method of philosophizing that was highly popular when Dahl published his book in 1956, a method associated with the use of formal logic and the sharp differentiation of empirical statements, definitional truths, and value statements. In his illuminating and valuable study,[1] Dahl analyzes what he calls "the 'Madisonian' theory of democracy." Although he is critical of Madison's views, Dahl presents a comprehensive and comprehensible interpretation of them, and for this reason I will find it useful to examine what Dahl has to say even though I have some reservations about it from a philosophical and from a historical point of view. Dahl thinks that Madison, though lucid, logical, and orderly in his thinking, "did not always articulate his assumptions as to fact, definition, or value," and therefore Dahl finds it necessary to supply what seems to him to constitute these assumptions. Some of Dahl's readers may become wary when he remarks that he is concerned with Madison's "style of argument" rather than with "a perfect reproduction of Madison's words,"[2] but a scholarly student of Madison's words should not be prevented by the seemingly disarming nature of this remark from carefully examining what Dahl has to say about Madison's views, especially those in ethics.

Dahl uses a somewhat formal deductive approach while expounding and criticizing a fundamental part of *The Federalist,* and about this one cannot complain so long as the empirical statements, the definitions, and the value statements attributed to Madison faithfully represent Madison's thinking, so long as Dahl's deductions are validly made, and so long as the comments by Dahl strike one as philosophically illuminating. I want to begin, however, by pointing out that what Dahl calls *"Hypothesis 1"* does not faithfully represent Madison's thinking. Dahl admits that the language of this hypothesis is "more modern" than Madison's, but he maintains that it captures Madison's ideas as expressed in his *Vices of the Political System of the United States* and in his letter to Jefferson of October 24, 1787.[3] *Hypothesis 1* is called a "hypothesis" by Dahl because it is, according to him, an empirical statement of fact as opposed to a definition or a value statement. It reads as follows:

> *Hypothesis 1:* If unrestrained by external checks, any given individual or group of individuals will tyrannize over others.

As I have indicated in earlier remarks on Madison's view of human nature, I do not think that this proposition is asserted, implied, or assumed by Madison.[4] But since Dahl thinks his interpretation of Madison is supported by what Madison says in his *Vices of the Political System of the United States,* I want to quote the last paragraph of that document:

> An auxiliary desideratum for the melioration of the Republican form is such a process of elections as will most certainly extract from the mass of Society the purest and noblest characters which it contains; such as will at once feel most strongly the proper motives to pursue the end of their appointment, and be most capable to devise the proper means of attaining it.[5]

In my opinion, this statement, as well as others made by Madison, shows that he thought that there are individuals whose purity and nobility make them counterexamples to the generalization that Dahl attributes to Madison in *Hypothesis 1*. In Madison's view, not every individual who is not restrained by external checks will tyrannize over other individuals if only because Madison thinks that these pure and noble characters will have "the proper motives to pursue the end of their appointment," which implies that they will not have to be prevented by external checks from tyrannizing over others.

What about Dahl's contention in *Hypothesis 1* that, according to Madison, every *group* which is not restrained by external checks will act tyrannically? I think it is obvious on the basis of Madison's discussion of factions in *Number 10* that he does not accept this part of Dahl's *Hypothesis 1* either. If he had accepted it, he would have been committed to the view that *every* group of individuals constitutes a faction, and he certainly did not believe that. Since Madison singles out factions and certain classes of rulers as special groups of citizens who would or might act tyrannically if not denied the opportunity to do so, I cannot help concluding that Dahl departs from Madison's views by attributing *Hypothesis 1* to the father of the Constitution. Dahl supports his attribution of this hypothesis to Madison by referring to the latter's speech at the Philadelphia Convention on June 6, but reading that speech makes me even more confident in asserting that Madison did not try to defend as strong a statement as *Hypothesis 1*. What he does try to defend in that speech is the more limited assertion that "in all cases where a majority are united by a common interest or passion, the rights of the minority are in danger." True, after saying that, he tries to show that certain internal "restraints" of the kind that he also discusses in *Vices of the Political System of the United States* and in his letter to Jefferson of October 24, 1787, will not be effective in checking a factious majority's deeds. So Madison says: "The lesson we are to draw from the whole [of the evidence he purports to give earlier in the speech] is that where a majority are united by a common sentiment and have an opportunity, the rights of the minor party become insecure. In a Republican Govt. the Majority if united have always an opportunity." There follows a statement by Madison that "the only remedy"—presumably what Dahl would call an "external check"—is "to enlarge the sphere" of a republic in a manner we have discussed sufficiently in earlier parts of this study.[6]

The crucial thing to observe is that Dahl overgeneralizes in *Hypothesis 1* when he offers that as an assumption which Madison tacitly makes. In the speech of June 6 and elsewhere, Madison limits himself to saying that where a *majority* is united by a common interest or passion and also has an opportunity—as it always will, he adds, in a republican government—the minority is in danger. And in *Number 10* he goes further and allows that a *minority* may be a faction insofar as *it* is actuated by an impulse of passion or of interest which is adverse to the rights of other citizens or to the permanent and aggregate interests of the community. Consequently, the most that we can extract from these passages of Madison is that *some* groups of citizens, namely, those that constitute minority or majority factions, will engage in tyrannical acts if their impulses are not checked by an external restraint of the sort that is provided by a large and well-populated republic. In sum, when we examine the sources on which Dahl himself relies, we can see that Dahl's *Hypothesis 1* is un-Madisonian on two counts. Madison does not hold that *every* individual who is unrestrained by external checks will tyrannize over others, and he does not hold that *every* group which is unrestrained by external checks will tyrannize over others. As we have seen earlier, Madison may agree with Hume that it is a just political maxim that every man must be *supposed* a knave even though it is false to say that every man *is* a knave, but Dahl's *Hypothesis 1* is not offered with that Humeian qualification. It flat-footedly attributes a belief to Madison that I do not think is Madison's; indeed, it was rejected by Madison in some of his statements about human nature.

Having shown that Dahl's *Hypothesis 1* is not an expression of Madison's ideas, let me now consider two corollaries of *Hypothesis 1* that Dahl distinguishes, namely:

> *Hypothesis 3:* If unrestrained by external checks, a minority of individuals will tyrannize over a majority of individuals.
> *Hypothesis 4:* If unrestrained by external checks, a majority of individuals will tyrannize over a minority of individuals.[7]

Do these statements represent what Madison believes? I do not think so, and for a reason that is related to the inadequacy of *Hypothesis 1:* overgeneralization. Madison does not hold that *every* majority or *every* minority will act tyrannically if it is not restrained by external checks. Dahl's *Hypothesis 3* and his *Hypothesis 4* leave out the important qualification that the majority or the minority in Madison's mind is a factious one which is united by a common passion or interest that is adverse to private rights or the public good; therefore, I cannot accept Dahl's *Hypothesis 3* and *Hypothesis 4* as Madisonian.

At this point I had better say something about that difficult phrase "external checks." Dahl introduces it in his *Hypothesis 1* and therefore defines the phrase as follows:

> *Definition 1:* An "external check" for an individual consists of the application of rewards and penalties, or the expectation that they will be applied, by some source other than the given individual himself.[8]

Madison's reason for urging an *external* check on factious majorities has been discussed at sufficient length in Chapter 9, above, but I want to emphasize here that Madison thought that he had proposed an external check on factious *minorities* when he said in *Number 10* that the actions of such a minority would be prevented by a majority vote. It will be recalled that he said in *Number 10* that the sinister views of a factious minority would be defeated by what he called a regular vote, adding that such a minority would be unable to execute and mask its violence under the forms of the Constitution.[9] This is all he says on the subject in *Number 10,* but it is clear that he thought the vote of a majority was an external check on a minority faction since it was not internal, as were the motives he dismisses as inefficacious in *Vices of the Political System of the United States,* in his speech of June 6 to the Convention, and in his letter to Jefferson of October 24, 1787.

Whether Madison was correct in his view of how to check a factious minority or majority is, of course, another matter. We should observe, however, that if we regard the majority's constitutional power as an external restraint on a factious minority, we must, if we use Dahl's *Definition 1,* think of that minority as expecting some penalty if it were, in its actions, to flout the vote of the majority, and that such an expectation would serve as the direct restraint. We should also observe that Madison's recipe for checking a factious majority by creating a large and populous federal republic works by way of similar expectations that come about as the consequences of erecting such a republic. In Chapter 9 I have said as much as I think the text permits us to say about the psychological mechanisms whereby such a republic, according to Madison, would check the deeds of a factious majority. Dahl represents Madison as holding that the existence of a large and populous republic will prevent members of factious majorities from acting factiously by making them see that they will suffer pain that will originate outside of themselves, unlike the pain which would be created if they were to disregard the three motives that Madison dismisses as inefficacious in his letter to Jefferson of October 24, 1787.

I now turn to another effort by Dahl to improve Madison's argument, his effort to clarify Madison's view of tyranny. The word "tyrannize," as we have seen, appears in Dahl's *Hypotheses 1, 3,* and *4,* and therefore Dahl feels obliged to offer his *Definition 2,* which reads as follows: " 'Tyranny' is every severe deprivation of a natural right."[10] About this definition he makes a number of comments that lead him to formulate the statement he calls *"Hypothesis 2,"* which I shall present after I consider Dahl's comment on what he takes to be an inadequate definition of "tyranny" by Madison. Dahl criticizes Madison for saying in *Number 47* that "the accumulation of all powers legislative, executive and judiciary in the same hands, whether of one, a few or many, and whether hereditary, self appointed, or elective, may justly be pronounced the very definition of tyranny."[11] Dahl maintains that Madison was here giving his strict definition of "tyranny," but it seems to me that Dahl leans too heavily and too literally on Madison's use of the word "definition" in the passage. I do not think that Madison believed that the word "tyranny" was synonymous with "the accumulation of all powers legislative, executive and judiciary in the same hands, whether of one, a few or many, and whether hereditary, self appointed, or elective." Neither did Jefferson—whom Madison quotes in *Number 48* as saying in his *Notes on the State of Virginia* that the concentrating of the legislative, executive, and judiciary powers "in the same hands is precisely the definition of despotic government."[12] I think that all that Madison meant to say in connecting the accumulation of powers in the same hands with tyranny is that such an accumulation of power would "lead" to tyranny. In other words, Madison held that the link between the accumulation of powers and tyranny is causal rather than definitional, which is just the point that Dahl thinks he generously makes for Madison when he formulates the following subargument, whose major premise is the *Hypothesis 2* that I mentioned earlier.

> *Hypothesis 2:* The accumulation of all powers, legislative, executive, and judiciary in the same hands [causally] implies the elimination of external checks (empirical generalization).
>
> The elimination of external checks produces tyranny (from *Hypothesis 1*).
>
> Therefore the accumulation of all powers in the same hands [causally] implies tyranny.[13]

As I have previously indicated, I think that presenting this bit of reasoning as a gift to Madison is a case of bringing coals to Newcastle. Any reader who thinks otherwise should recall that in *Number 37* Madison expresses his doubt about our ability to define *any* terms accurately, especially terms of political science.[14] We should also recall that in *Number 48* Madison says that the founders of the republics of the American states "seem never to have recollected the danger from legislative usurpations; which by assembling all power in the same hands, must *lead* [my emphasis] to the same tyranny as is threatened by executive usurpations."[15] The word "lead" is obviously used here in a causal sense, and in a summary statement in *Number 48* about the effects of assembling all power in the same hands, Madison remarks: "I have appealed to our own experience for the truth of what I advance on this subject. Were it necesary to verify this experience by particular proofs, they might be multiplied without end."[16] For these reasons, I cannot agree with Dahl's remark that "Madison's explicit definition [of 'tyranny'] is unnecessarily arbitrary." If Dahl had more generously recognized Madison's "very definition of tyranny" for what it really was in Madison's mind, namely, a statement about something that would as a matter of fact produce tyranny, Dahl would have seen that it was not intended as a definition at all and therefore could not be condemned as an "arbitrary" definition. Dahl would also have seen that his remark that Madison's "explicit definition is unnecessarily . . . argumentative"[17] was questionable. Madison *intended* to be argumentative in his remark about the accumulation of powers insofar as he thought he was asserting something that he thought was supportable by empirical evidence. He was reporting what he regarded as only one way in which tyranny would come about when he spoke of the assembling of all three powers of government, legislative, executive, and judiciary, in the same hands as "the very definition of tyranny." Those hands would bring about tyranny by one causal route, whereas a factious majority might, as we have seen, bring it about by another causal route. Because Dahl rightly or wrongly—and I believe wrongly—thinks that Madison made a mistake by defining "tyranny" as "the accumulation of all powers, legislative, executive, and judiciary, in the same hands," Dahl is led, as we have seen, to formulate a definition of "tyranny" which he thinks would be congenial to "the whole cast of Madison's thought . . . [and] helpful to the logic of his argument,"[18] namely, " 'Tyranny' is every severe deprivation of a natural right."[19]

Now that I have said enough about Madison's allegedly faulty definition of "tyranny," I want to consider what Dahl has to say about the definition which he thinks Madison would have been better advised to use in his theory, a definition which also provides problems according to Dahl, but problems of a different kind. The point is that Dahl finds fault with this alternative definition even though he proffers it in the interest of improving Madison's argument. And every serious student of *The Federalist* should take Dahl's uneasiness into account while trying to understand certain fundamental ideas in that work. For even though Dahl's alternative definition is not one that we find in Madison's writings, Dahl is justified not only in offering *some* definition of "tyranny" to fill a gap in Madison's theory, but also in registering his difficulties with the term "natural rights" in the definition he injects into Madison's theory. Dahl complains that these natural rights are not clearly specified, that there was no perfect agreement among Madison's contemporaries as to which rights were natural rights, and that "the absence of an agreed definition of natural rights is one of the central difficulties of the Madisonian theory."[20] Here, of course, we must distinguish between the question whether Madison or the other authors of *The Federalist* were in agreement about *examples* of the concept of natural rights and the question whether they agreed about how to *define* the term "natural rights." In other words, we must distinguish between the question whether the authors of *The Federalist* failed to agree on what logicians call the extension or denotation of the term "natural rights" and the question whether they failed to agree about how to analyze or define the intension or connotation of the term. The authors of *The Federalist* never address the second question even though the concept of natural rights played a fundamental role in their political thought.

It would seem, however, that in *Number 10* Madison regarded "the rights of property" as natural and that in the same number he called "an equal division of property" one of those "improper or wicked" projects which factious leaders might encourage as they incited their followers to invade the natural rights of others.[21] There is also reason to believe that the three unalienable rights mentioned in the Declaration—those of life, liberty, and the pursuit of happiness—were regarded by Publius as examples of natural rights, though I should add that, under the influence of thinkers such as Burlamaqui, he may have regarded these three natural rights as "primitive" while he regarded property as an "adventitious" natural right.[22] However, it is one thing to give examples of natural rights and another to give what Dahl calls an explicit definition of the concept of natural right. Dahl seeks an explicit definition of "natural rights"—and an "operational" definition at that—because he thinks a reader of Madison would be helped by such a definition in determining what groups are factions by virtue of invading natural rights and also in determining whether a republic is or is not tyrannical. Dahl points to the unsatisfactory consequence of the absence of such a definition on Madison's belief, as formulated by Dahl, that "the goal that ought to be attained, at least in the United States, is a non-tyrannical republic."[23] To round out the set of basic propositions and definitions that Dahl presents, therefore, I should add Dahl's formulation of Madison's definition of a republic, which is based on what Madison says in *Number 39:*

> *Definition 3:* A republic is a government which (a) derives all of its powers directly or indirectly from the great body of the people and (b) is administered by persons holding their office during pleasure, for a limited period, or during good behavior.[24]

Now that I have presented Dahl's *Hypotheses 1, 2, 3,* and *4,* his *Definitions 1, 2,* and *3,* and what he calls the Madisonian ethical axiom or postulate that a nontyrannical republic "ought to be attained, at least in the United States," I want to recapitulate what I have said about his effort to present the basis of "the Madisonian system." I call it "the basis" because he says that the remainder of the system "consists of predictive statements, definitions, and inferences derived from what has been given" in these four hypotheses, three definitions, and one ethical statement.[25] I have disputed on textual grounds Dahl's attribution of *Hypotheses 1, 3,* and *4* to Madison and, therefore, if I am correct, *Hypothesis 2* is the only statement of the three that is left standing when we test Dahl's version of the basis of Madison's theory against what Madison says. I have agreed, however, with Dahl about the failure of Madison to provide an explicit "operational" definition of "natural rights" or of what he calls "private rights." Madison fails to provide such a definition when he is discussing tyrannical governments and when he is discussing tyrannical factions.

I might add in passing, however, that Dahl's definition of tyranny as every severe "deprivation" of a natural right may not put us in the best position to find a Madisonian solution to the problem. If we understand "deprivation" to refer to the taking away of something, it follows that tyranny, according to Dahl's definition, involves taking away a natural right. I suggest that the word "invade" or "violate" would be a better one to use—as Dahl occasionally recognizes[26]—insofar as it expresses the idea of preventing a person from doing what he *may* do while it permits us to say that the person whose natural right is invaded or violated continues to *have* the right even while it is being invaded or violated. In a similar spirit, I suggest that we replace Dahl's word "attained" by an expression such as "guarded effectively" in the very brief "excursion into ethical theory" that Dahl makes when he tries to show how Madison probably deduced the statement "The goal that ought to be attained, at least in the United States, is a non-tyrannical republic." Dahl's excursion proceeds as follows: "(1) Natural rights ought to be attained (axiom); (2) attainment of natural rights is non-tyranny (from Definition 2); (3) a republic is a necessary although not a sufficient condition for non-tyranny"; therefore, the goal that ought to be attained is a nontyrannical republic, which was to be proven.[27] This argument is better expressed as follows. We ought to live in a society in which natural rights are guarded effectively (axiom). A society in which natural rights are guarded effectively is identical with a society in which there is no tyranny (by a definition of "tyranny" which is a revised version of Dahl's *Definition 2* and by a few other obvious steps). Therefore, we ought to live in a society in which there is no tyranny. But every society in which there is no tyranny is a society which has a republican government. Therefore, we ought to live in a society which has a nontyrannical republican government.

Since I am not primarily concerned in this study to defend Madison's philosophical views, but rather to understand them, I want to say that Dahl's demand for an "operational" definition of the term "natural right" was, first of all, anachronistic. That it was anachronistic might not have been of great concern to Dahl, for Dahl treats Madison's theory of republican government almost as if it had been advanced in 1956 and therefore subject to the same strictures as Dahl would have leveled against a contemporary of his who had advanced the same theory. Nevertheless, it is not likely that Madison—if he had been confronted by Dahl in a conversation across the centuries—would have felt the force of Dahl's request for a definition of "natural rights" that would give it "operational meaning." Indeed, he might have asked Dahl to explain what he had in mind when he used the phrase "operational meaning."[28] On the other hand, were Dahl to have asked Madison in that imaginary conversation for a definition of the term "natural rights," without requiring that it be "operational," Madison might have sent him to books on natural law in which Dahl would have found a set of views that I shall try to state as clearly and as succinctly as I can.

According to this set of views, as I have pointed out earlier, God, the creator of man, gave him a certain nature or essence when God gave him life, reason, and a desire for his own happiness. Therefore, these three attributes are contained in the essence of man as created by God. The argument continues as follows. Since God is an omnipotent, wise, and beneficent creator, he would not have given man an essence which contained these three attributes if he had not thought that man *should* preserve his life, perfect his reason, and pursue happiness, for God does nothing in vain. And if God thought that these are man's natural duties because they are derivable from attributes contained in man's nature or essence as God created it, then man has these duties and three corresponding natural rights simply because the duty to perform an action implies the right to perform that action. To be sure, there might have been debate among theorists about which attributes are contained in the essence of man, but whichever they were, they were deemed to underlie certain duties which imply corresponding natural rights. A natural right, therefore, might have been defined by Madison as one that was derived from a natural duty, and a natural duty, he might have said, was derived from the essence or nature of man as created by God.[29]

Now we may ask: Would Dahl have been satisfied by this definition of "natural right"? I doubt it. Why? Because, I suspect, Dahl would not have found this definition "operational." He shows his distaste for the sort of definition of "natural right" that I have been presenting on behalf of Madison when he says that he wishes to avoid a discussion of the concept of natural right and its utility in political theory because such a discussion would "take us very far afield into a voluminous and almost endless subject."[30] On the other hand, Dahl uses the phrase "natural right" in the definition of "tyranny" that he gives, as it were, to Madison, and he declares that "it is self-evident" that this definition "would be entirely empty unless natural rights could somehow be defined."[31] Consequently, Dahl is in a peculiar predicament which he fully appreciates. He wants to be fair and helpful to Madison, so he formulates a definition of "tyranny" which contains the phrase "natural right." But Dahl is unwilling to accept that phrase as undefined in his exposition of Madison's views and also seems unwilling to accept what he, Dahl, would have regarded as a nonoperational definition linking the idea of natural right with that of God. In short, Dahl demands "operational definitions" for terms like "tyranny" and "natural rights," but he has trouble in finding or providing such definitions while trying to be faithful to Madison's intent. The irony is that Dahl defines "tyranny" for Madison in order to make explicit Madison's dependence on the concept of natural rights, but when Dahl tries to define that concept operationally in accordance with his own philosophy, he fails.

Inevitably we are led to wonder how Dahl understands the phrase "operational definition," as well we might. We are never explicitly told by Dahl how he understands it, so we must try to infer what he has in mind by look-ing at some of his examples, whether he regards them as correct "operational definitions" or not. The following, Dahl suggests, is an example of an opera-tional definition of "natural right," but one that is unacceptable to Dahl for reasons that I shall soon state: A natural right is "the right of every individ-ual to do what he wishes to do."[32] Let us proceed on Dahl's apparent assump-tion that, according to this definition, there is exactly one natural right that every individual has, namely, *the* right to do what he wishes to do. Why does Dahl reject this supposedly operational definition? Because, in conjunction with Dahl's definition of "tyranny" and what he observes about governments, it would force him to say that *every* government is tyrannical. According to Dahl, every government prevents some individuals, for example, criminals, from doing as they wish; and Dahl does not think that every government is tyrannical. Dahl is foiled, therefore, in this one attempt to define "natural right" operationally, but he does not try to present any other operational defi-nition of it. Apparently because he is unable to formulate an operational defi-nition of "natural right" which is superior to this one that he rejects, Dahl gives up the effort to present an operational definition of "natural right" and with it the effort to provide us and Madison with an operational method for discovering whether we are in a state of tyranny when that is defined as one in which natural rights are violated or invaded.

Instead, Dahl considers an approach in which a government will be said to act tyrannically if and only if it restrains certain "kinds of behavior" with-out requiring any attention to whether it is violating something called natural rights. The question naturally arises: *What* kinds of behavior? Dahl con-siders the possibility of specifying them indirectly by first saying what kinds of behavior a *non*tyrannical government will restrain. He supposes, for ex-ample, that a nontyrannical government will restrain those and only those kinds of behavior that "every individual (or every adult) in the community believes to be undesirable."[33] In that case a government would be called tyr-annical—or not nontyrannical—if it should restrain even one kind of behavior that is not unanimously condemned by the community. Dahl quickly dis-misses this conception of a tyrannical government as absurd because it would render a government tyrannical if it punished murder and *one* murderer be-lieved that it was undesirable to punish murder. Dahl then considers the pos-sibility that a *majority's belief* should determine what sort of government is or is not tyrannical, and properly rejects this as un-Madisonian because of Madison's belief that a majority could be tyrannical and therefore have be-liefs that would lead to its calling the wrong governments tyrannical or non-tyrannical. Finally, Dahl turns to what he calls "the only remaining possibil-ity," which is that some specified group in the community, "not defined as the majority, but not necessarily always in opposition to it, would be empowered to decide" whether a government is tyrannical or not.[34]

This last method of determining "operationally" whether a government is tyrannical is also rejected by Dahl as un-Madisonian, but for a reason that I do *not* think is Madisonian. Dahl refers to his *Hypothesis 1,* which has it that *every* man will act tyrannically if unchecked, in which case no man would be fit, by Madison's standards, to be a member of the body which has the last say on whether a government is tyrannical. But Madison does not rule out the idea that some men will be able to decide what behavior is or is not tyrannical. They are the pure and noble characters who, he thinks, can be extracted "from the mass of the Society" by a process of elections. They "will at once feel most strongly the proper motives to pursue the end of their appointment, and be most capable to devise the proper means of attaining it."[35] They are counterexamples to Dahl's *Hypothesis 1* because they are the citizens of *Number 10* "whose wisdom may best discern the true interest of their country, and whose patriotism and love of justice, will be least likely to sacrifice it to temporary or partial considerations."[36] The point to keep in mind is that Madison thinks that such people exist, and therefore Dahl cannot rule out the possibility that they exist merely by appealing to the un-Madisonian *Hypothesis 1*. I realize, of course, that some political scientist might persist in a search for "operational definitions" by asking for a litmus test on the basis of which a community would be able to spot these sterling characters, but if *such* a test had to be made by polling the beliefs of members of the community, the same question would arise all over again. Who is to be the custodian who will decide who the custodian is to be? And so on indefinitely. The whole enterprise of defining "tyranny" operationally by appealing to *the beliefs* of a selected body of citizens is bound to lead to this difficulty.

Notice, however, that although a "definition" of the "meaning" of the word "tyrannical" which refers to the beliefs of these pure, noble, patriotic, and wise men would be "operational" by Dahl's standards—because Dahl thinks that beliefs about what is desirable are examinable by what he regards as the method of empirical science—I do not think that Madison would have agreed that a statement about such beliefs constituted "the meaning" of various statements in the theory of natural law that he accepted. Such beliefs of pure, noble, patriotic, and wise men were attitudes toward moral propositions regarded as abstract entities, but Madison seems to have held that those moral propositions were as different from the believing attitudes of wise men as the binomial theorem was from Newton's believing attitude toward the binomial theorem. We might, according to Madison, view the beliefs of pure, noble, patriotic, and wise men as guides to what is true in the doctrine of natural law, just as we might view the beliefs of Newton as guides to what is true in mathematics. But, Madison seems to have held, propositions about natural rights can no more be reduced to or identified with those beliefs than propositions about numbers can be reduced to or identified with the beliefs of mathematicians. For this reason, Dahl's efforts at extracting the "operational meaning" of Madison's statements about natural rights and tyranny by discovering what someone believes was bound to be un-Madisonian.

In considering Dahl's unsuccessful attempt at defining "tyranny" operationally for Madison, we must distinguish two strains in eighteenth-century American thought. One is the idea that there is such a thing as objective justice which may be discovered by anyone who is not demented or influenced by either passion or interest which is partial or immediate. This is connected with the idea that no man's opinion should be dictated to him by another man since a man's opinion depends only on the evidence contemplated by a man's own mind—an idea which is so central in Madison's *Memorial and Remonstrance against Religious Assessments* of 1785 and in Jefferson's *Bill for Establishing Religious Freedom* of 1779.[37] According to this view, no man can do another man's thinking for him as he tries to establish the truth on any subject, whether it be a subject of science, religion, or morality. Therefore, the beliefs of no man or set of men about justice or tyranny can be used as the basis for determining what these words "mean." In short, when a man says that a government is tyrannical, he does not *mean* that some person, or more than one person, *believes* that the government has acted in a certain way. And this is, I think, the fundamental reason why the effort to define the meaning of "tyranny" operationally by referring to the beliefs of people— whatever their number, supposed virtue, or intelligence—is not Madisonian. The second strain of eighteenth-century thought that we must keep in mind, however, is the idea that the people could be swayed by passion or interest in a manner that would cloud their judgment, and consequently their wise, noble, patriotic, and intelligent governors would, at least on some occasions, be better able than the people to discover what was morally just.

According to this second strain, the people would be well advised to rely—at least sometimes—on their elected governors as rational seers of moral truth, truth which could be corroborated by the people themselves when they were not under the influence of passion or bias. However, because Madison believed that he was speaking about objective moral reality and not about beliefs when he used the word "tyrannical," we can see why he would have spurned the kind of operationalism that identifies the meaning of this word by referring to the beliefs of *any* citizens about what was desirable or undesirable. He would not have defined "tyrannical" by referring to the beliefs of a minority, to the beliefs of a majority, to the beliefs of the whole community, or even to his own beliefs about what was desirable or undesirable. Madison did not think that when he declared something to be a natural right, or that a society was just, or that a faction or government was acting tyrannically, he meant something that could be analyzed or defined by referring to beliefs conceived as psychological attitudes. And that is why we cannot, while being faithful to Madison's intent, define the word "tyranny" in a manner that Dahl proposed and was understandably forced to abandon.

Certainly we are not offered such a definition in *The Federalist* and, what is more, we are not presented with any definition of "tyrannical" that shows it to be an empirical term. The terms "tyranny" and "natural rights" are not, as used by Publius, terms in what Hume called experimental science. They are moral or ethical terms. Therefore, it is not surprising that a twentieth-century operationalist like Dahl finds it difficult to apply his operationalism to "natural rights" and "tyranny," as construed by Madison, since experimental science is the only domain in which operationalism has any chance of being able to operate and Madison shows no signs of having regarded ethics as an experimental science.

Just as the terms "natural rights" and "tyranny" are moral for Madison, so the term "faction" is. This is made especially clear by contrasting Madison's definition of factions with what Hume has to say about them. Although Madison owed a great deal to Hume on this subject, I have noted earlier that Hume, unlike Madison, does not *define* factions in a way that makes them necessarily blameworthy. In "Of Parties in General" Hume says that the founders of sects and factions ought to be detested and hated "because the influence of faction is directly contrary to that of laws,"[38] but he is not thinking of moral laws here and he never defines "faction" as Madison was later to define it in what seems like a deviation from Madison's wariness in *The Federalist* about defining *any* terms. Factions, according to Hume, oppose other factions, but according to Madison's definition, they not only oppose other factions but they are impelled to violate private moral rights or oppose the public good. One passage in Hume which shows that he did not think that the motives of a faction are by definition objectionable appears in his essay "Of the First Principles of Government." In that essay he says that "when a faction is formed upon a point of right or principle, there is no occasion where men discover [i.e., reveal] a greater obstinacy, and a more determined sense of justice and equity," even though he also says in the same essay that when men *act* in a faction, they are apt "to neglect all the ties of honour and morality, in order to serve their party."[39] Moreover, in Hume's essay "Of the Parties of Great Britain," we find yet another statement which reveals an attitude toward factions that is less condemnatory than the one expressed by Madison in *Number 10*. While speaking of the Court party and the Country party, Hume says in a note:

> These words have become of general use, and therefore I shall employ them without intending to express by them an universal blame of the one party, or approbation of the other. The Court party may no doubt, on some occasions, consult best the interest of the country, and the Country party oppose it. In like manner, the *Roman* parties were denominated Optimates and Populares; and Cicero, like a true party man, defines the Optimates to be such as, in all their public conduct, regulated themselves by the sentiments of the best and worthiest Romans; *pro Sextio*. The term of Country party may afford a favourable definition or etymology of the same kind; but it would be folly to draw any argument from that head, and I have no regard to it in employing these terms.[40]

I have taken this opportunity to contrast Hume's view of faction with that of Madison in order to emphasize that Madison does not limit himself to using empirical or experimental terms when he tries to tell us how to prevent governments and factions from acting tyrannically. As a framer and defender of the Constitution, Madison used ethical terms such as "justice," "private rights," "tyranny," and "faction" at critical points in his argument. Therefore, the "science of politics" as he conceived it was not what it would have been if he had strictly followed the classification of the sciences presented in Hume's *Enquiry Concerning Human Understanding.* As I have pointed out in Chapter 2, above, Hume held in that work that politics was an experimental science which treats of "general facts, . . . where the qualities, causes and effects of a whole species of objects are enquired into," whereas in the same work he said that "morals and criticism are not so properly objects of the understanding as of taste and sentiment."[41] So far as I know, however, Madison does not think that the ethical term "adverse to the rights of other citizens" can be shown to be synonymous with some term of experimental science, and for this reason his term "faction" is not experimental. And because "faction," like "tyranny," is not an experimental term for Madison, no one can give an operational definition of "faction" that is Madisonian. *The Federalist* was primarily a work in descriptive political science, but two of its most fundamental terms do not seem to have been regarded by Madison as experimental or empirical in character.

This is a convenient place at which to remark on a phrase in Madison's definition of "faction" which is not treated at any length by Dahl, the phrase "permanent and aggregate interests of the community." Although Dahl complains at great length about the fact that tyranny of majority factions is never provided with an operational definition that is Madisonian, he never complains at any length about the absence of an operational definition of the term "the permanent and aggregate interests of the community." He merely says: "As to the 'permanent and aggregate interests of the community,' so far as I am aware no political group has ever admitted to being hostile to these."[42] Nevertheless, there is an important difference between the term "natural right" and the term "permanent and aggregate interests of the community" which should not go unnoticed. The latter term *seems* to be empirical even if it should be as difficult to provide an operational definition for it as it is to provide a similar definition for the term "natural rights." Therefore, when Madison says that the community's permanent and aggregate interests have been adversely affected, he *intends* to make a statement which can be tested empirically even though he never provides us with anything resembling a litmus test by means of which we can decide whether or not a group is united by some common impulse of passion or interest which is "adverse . . . to the permanent and aggregate interests of the community." When Madison speaks of a faction's being united and actuated by this sort of impulse of passion or interest, he intends to say that the impulse motivating the faction is adverse to something like the public's happiness, and this, it would appear, may be established by experimental methods—even according to Madison. By contrast, as we have seen, showing that a faction's impulse or passion is adverse to the natural rights of other citizens is not a purely empirical matter for Madison. Therefore, according to Madison, there is an epistemological gulf between testing the statement that all individuals have certain natural rights—especially unalienable rights—and testing the statement that the public is in a happy condition. If so, he was bound to hold that there was a similar epistemological gulf between testing the statement that certain natural rights have been adversely affected and testing the statement that the community has been made unhappy or that its permanent and aggregate interests have been adversely affected. Testing the first sort of statement would ultimately force him to refer to certain duties, imposed by God, which imply these rights; the second sort of statement would not. The public interest, whether defined or not, is discovered empirically; private rights are not. I say this with full awareness that Publius and Jefferson think that every people has a natural *right* to pursue happiness. But whether a people is pursuing happiness and whether it achieves happiness is quite a different question from whether every people has a right to do so. The former is a question of fact for Publius, the latter is not; for him the former is answered by appealing to empirical evidence, whereas the latter is not.

This distinction of Publius is compatible with accepting the objectivity of statements about private rights and of those about the permanent and aggregate interests of the community. When he says in *Number 31* that certain primary truths "contain an internal evidence, which antecedent to all reflection or combination commands the assent of the mind," he thinks he is speaking of some objective reality which is mirrored in those truths and the truths that follow from them.[43] Insofar as these truths are in the doctrine of natural law, he thinks they refer to duties and rights that are ultimately established by appealing to "internal evidence." On the other hand, according to Publius, when we say that something promotes the permanent and aggregate interests of the community, we also say something about an objective reality which is established by external evidence—that is to say, experimentally.

This confidence in the objectivity of both kinds of statements is the basis of what may be called Publius's elitism in epistemology. He thought that some people would be better able than others to perceive the truth of self-evident propositions concerning duties and rights. He says in *Number 31* that when someone's mind does not assent to a primary truth, it must be because of "some defect or disorder in the organs of perception, or from the influence of some strong interest, or passion, or prejudice."[44] However, he also thought that some citizens would be better able than others to discern "the true interest of their country" and that "it may well happen that the public voice pronounced by the representatives of the people, will be more consonant to the public good, than if pronounced by the people themselves convened for the purpose."[45] In short, some individuals are better able than others at discerning objective natural rights and duties, and some individuals are better able than others at discerning the permanent and aggregate interests of the community. This is Publius's view even though he followed Locke in thinking that natural rights and duties are discerned in accordance with mathematical canons of abstract rationalism whereas he also held that the public good, happiness, or interest is discerned empirically. All, he thought, were objectively discernible, though by different means and in spite of the fact that none of them could be given operational definitions of the kind that Professor Dahl was so anxious to have.

However, I do not think that Professor Dahl could have been very surprised to find that Madison provides us with no operational definition of the term "natural right," with no operational definition of the term "tyranny," and therefore with no operational definition of the term "faction." Nor should Dahl have been surprised to find that he himself could not provide such operational definitions for those terms while remaining faithful to Madison's intent. But then, as I have suggested earlier, Dahl does not provide us with an operational definition of the term "operational definition." What, then, shall we say about his very lucid effort to formulate Madison's views and to criticize them? First, that his rendition of Madison's views in what Dahl takes to be the basis of Madison's system is not strictly in accord with what Madison believes about human nature as it is. And, second, that Dahl's unsuccessful generous attempt to provide "operational meaning" by way of definitions for Madison's two closely related terms "private rights" and "tyranny" is not in accord with what Madison thought about natural rights. Madison's concept of natural rights was not what twentieth-century philosophers would call—in an ironical twist of terminology—a naturalistic concept, that is to say, a concept which can be defined in the descriptive science of human nature. Those who think that *Madison's* notions of private or natural rights can be so defined are bound to be stymied by some of the things that Madison says about these rights, especially about the right to religious freedom. Therefore, all of Madison's admirers who are operationalists should realize that they cannot turn him into an ally on the subject of natural rights. We see once again that *The Federalist,* hard headed, Humeian, and realistic as it tried to be in political technology, appealed to Lockeian principles of natural law, which are not empirical by the standards of twentieth-century operationalists.

VIII

A SUMMARY VIEW

12

A Philosophical Map
of *The Federalist*

Since my chief purpose in this study has been to call attention to the role of philosophy in *The Federalist*, I want to gather together in this chapter the main propositions to which I have called attention with this purpose in mind. I want not only to restate some of those propositions in order to highlight them, but I want to organize them in a way that will show their connections with each other in order to portray in a systematic way the body of beliefs to which Publius appealed—sometimes explicitly, sometimes tacitly—in his attempt to defend the Constitution of the United States. His defense, when viewed logically, concluded with a statement that the Constitution ought to be adopted or ratified—a statement in normative or substantive moral philosophy which went beyond recommending the signing of a piece of paper, since the ratification of the Constitution involved the acceptance of a moral statement about an entire mode of government. And since Publius accepted the responsibility of giving arguments in support of this statement, I shall begin this survey with some comments on the role of moral philosophy in his argument.

The Role of Normative Moral
Philosophy in Publius's Argument

In order to understand the role of moral philosophy or ethics in Publius's argument, we must distinguish different tasks that have been associated with that discipline. It has been said by some commentators on the history of ethics that moral philosophers have been mainly concerned with trying to say what we mean to say of an action when we say that we have a right or a duty to do it, and what we mean to say of governments, for example, when we say that they are good or bad. But if we adopt this view of the task of moral philosophy as definitional or analytical, then it is obvious that the authors of *The Federalist* were neither moral philosophers nor followers of moral philosophers whose definitions or analyses of moral concepts they explicitly adopted in *The Federalist*. Publius often refers to the natural or moral rights of men but never tries to define the notion of natural rights. He says in *Number 51* that justice is *the* end of government and of civil society, but never tries to define "justice." He also says in *Number 62* that a good government will accomplish *the* object of government, which is the happiness of the people, but he makes little effort to go beyond that to say what the term "good government" means. Nor, I might say in passing, does he—in this case Madison, the author of both numbers—acknowledge any inconsistency in saying that justice and happiness are each of them *the* end of government. With charity, therefore, we had better think of them as the two ends of government in Madison's view. For him, a good government ought to establish justice and promote the welfare or happiness of the people as a whole—a very important proposition in the normative ethics of Publius.[1] However, it would be as incorrect to say that Publius was a systematic normative moralist as it would be to say that he was a systematic analyst of moral concepts or terms. Because he was a well-read politician, he was influenced by systematic moralists and by analysts of moral ideas. He was also influenced by theorists of ethical knowledge who tried to say how we know that ethical beliefs are true. But this does not mean that Publius was a full-fledged moral philosopher. It means that throughout *The Federalist* he shows signs of having thought seriously about the analytic and epistemological aspects of moral philosophy in ways that deserve attention, and that by trying to extract and clarify his views on these matters we can illuminate the fundamental beliefs expressed in *The Federalist*.

Before considering other aspects of the document I want to remind the reader of some other substantive moral principles on which Publius relied. I have noted his Lockeian idea that some of the people's natural rights ought to be ceded to government in order to vest it with requisite powers, as well as his idea that certain natural rights are unalienable and inviolable. And I have often called attention to his fear that governments and factious majorities would act tyrannically and wrongly violate the natural rights of individuals. In addition, I have remarked on the fact that Publius makes certain substantive moral statements which do not expressly concern natural rights but rather the goodness of government. Like many moral philosophers whom he read, he was aware that a distinction must be made between these two kinds of statements. This is especially evident in his view that a faction could have impulses of passion or of interest which were adverse to the natural rights of other citizens *or* to the permanent and aggregate interests of the community, the former being what he called "private rights" and the latter being what he called "the public good."[2]

Publius's Theory of Ethical Knowledge
and His Theory of Experimental Knowledge

I have also tried to illuminate the philosophical framework of *The Federalist* by calling attention to certain parts of Publius's theory of ethical knowledge.

I have, for example, pointed out that the moral statements in which Publius said that all men had certain natural rights were supported either by his saying that they were self-evident truths or by his saying that they were deducible from such truths. I have also pointed out that when Publius said that the permanent and aggregate interests of the community were satisfied, he made a moral statement that was empirical for him because it was equivalent to stating that the people had attained some degree of happiness. To be sure, the authors of *The Federalist,* like Jefferson, accepted the statement that the people have a natural right to pursue happiness, and this statement was for them self-evident. But they distinguished between saying that the people have a right to pursue happiness and saying that they have attained happiness, and they thought that they would not lapse into any inconsistency by holding the former statement to be self-evident and therefore established merely by examining ideas while holding that the latter statement could be established only by observation. With this in mind, I have maintained that some moral statements made by Publius were allegedly established by the rationalistic techniques described by Locke when he said that morality could be a demonstrative science, whereas other moral statements made by Publius were tested by the use of empirical or experimental science. I now wish to summarize what I have said about Publius's general theory of experimental knowledge.

Although Publius regarded the principles of natural law as undeniable axioms or theorems in a demonstrative science, we have seen that he did not usually regard the truths of the science of politics nor those in what we would today call psychology in this way. He held that the vast majority of political truths, whether general or singular in logical form, are tested by "experience" or "history." These terms were usually regarded as synonymous by Publius. It is true that he occasionally limited history to what might be called "historical experience" when he had experience about the distant past in mind, and sometimes he limited the word "experience" to his own experience or the experiences of his contemporaries. But any difference between Publius's use of the word "history" and his use of the word "experience" is philosophically negligible when we compare Publius's view of truths that are tested by experience of the past or of the present with his view of moral principles. When Publius said that we can test a political or psychological statement by the use of "reason," he usually did not mean what Locke called "intuitive reason" or the faculty of perceiving the truth of self-evident propositions. Nor did Publius have in mind what Locke and Hume called demonstrative reasoning, which they thought was used in logically deducing theorems from self-evident axioms. In those rare instances when Hamilton ventured to say that a political truth could be demonstrated, he did so with some hesitation, as we have seen in Chapter 3. Generally speaking, he and the other authors of *The Federalist* did not try to use demonstrative reasoning when defending their political and psychological beliefs, precisely because they held that politics and psychology were experimental sciences. They therefore used what they and Hume regarded as experimental reasoning.

Most of Publius's statements about human nature were intended to describe man's behavior and were therefore viewed by him as experimental even though some of them were regarded by him as moral and therefore *not* experimental. In saying, for example, that men are motivated more strongly by passion or by self-interest than by reason, Publius thought he was saying something that required empirical observation of men. By contrast, when Hamilton said in his "Full Vindication" that because all men participate in one common nature, they have one common right, Hamilton did not think that this "because"-statement required empirical observation of men. For him it was either a self-evident primary truth which could be established on the basis of "internal evidence" or it was deducible from such a truth. There is little doubt, however, that most of Publius's statements about human nature were viewed by him as empirical. Indeed, *The Federalist* might appear to some readers as nothing more than a work in experimental politics and psychology because of the absence of any extended treatment of the moral philosophy which is kept, as it were, behind the arras and allowed to show itself only at critical junctures when Publius dealt with such fundamental matters as the tyranny of factions or of governments.

Because the authors of *The Federalist* held that virtually all descriptive statements about political matters of fact and existence are based on history or experience and *not* on an examination of the relations between ideas, their discussions of the inability of the government under the Articles of Confederation to preserve the Union, or of the need for a government at least as energetic as the one proposed at Philadelphia for the preservation of the Union, are discussions which are empirical insofar as they usually deal with the relationships between certain political means and ends while assuming the moral value of those ends. When Publius tried to show that a union would be more effective than thirteen separate states or three or four confederacies in keeping America at peace with foreign nations, he offered empirical arguments while he took for granted the moral value of international peace, not to speak of its value for a new republic. Publius's predominant view was that descriptive political science is experimental and therefore we can see why, after using rationalistic methods to establish a moral principle that forbids a certain kind of action, he used experimental methods to show that such a forbidden action could be prevented in a certain way. He followed a similar pattern when he first asserted the moral proposition that no government ought to be tyrannical and then claimed to know from experience that all governments which give the legislative, judicial, and executive powers to one individual or one group of individuals will be tyrannical. In addition, he was aware that he had to use experience in order to show how a government can avoid giving these three powers to one individual or group of individuals. And, finally, he knew that he had to appeal to experience in order to show how these three powers would remain separate in the real political world.

The Main Experimental Theses of *The Federalist*
From a Philosophical Point of View

Before I summarize the main experimental theses of *The Federalist* upon which I have concentrated, I want to make a purely terminological comment. I have been using the word "experimental" as a synonym of the word "empirical" although I realize that such a use may sound peculiar to some readers. In treating these words as synonymous, however, I am following the terminology of eighteenth-century British philosophy, especially that of Hume. In the Introduction to his *Treatise of Human Nature,* he says that although the science of man does not go beyond experience, it has a peculiar disadvantage which is not found in what we would today call physics, namely, that "in collecting its experiments, it cannot make them purposely, with premeditation, and after such a manner as to satisfy itself concerning every particular difficulty which may arise." He continues: "When I am at a loss to know the effects of one body upon another in any situation, I need only put them in that situation, and observe what results from it." By contrast, he says about the science of man or of human nature that if he were to try to clear up any doubt in it by putting *himself* in a situation that is analogous to that in which the physicist puts a body in the course of an experiment, this would so disturb the operation of his own behavior as to make it impossible to form any just conclusion from what would be observed. In short, as we might say, the very act of Hume's turning himself into an object of experimentation would alter him in such a way as to vitiate the conclusions of his experiment. On the basis of this reflection, Hume concludes: "We must therefore glean up our experiments in this science from a cautious observation of human life, and take them as they appear in the common course of the world, by men's behaviour in company, in affairs, and in their pleasures."[3] From this we can see that a scientist of man was regarded by Hume as one who could "glean up" experiments even though he did not perform "premeditated" experiments of the kind that a physicist might perform. According to Hume, a scientist of man would nevertheless depend on experience and might be said to arrive at experimental truths and engage in experimental reasoning of the kind that Publius engaged in while trying to defend certain parts of his argument in *The Federalist.*

In a summary view of the philosophy of *The Federalist,* two experimental or empirical theses deserve special mention. One is the psychological theory of motivation in which Publius compares the strengths of different motives; the other is a theory about the various and unequal distribution of property as the most common and durable source of factions. The first theory was implicit throughout *The Federalist* and was a part of what was sometimes called mental philosophy before it came to be known as psychology. The second was explicitly asserted in *Number 10* and has often been regarded as a speculative philosophy of history which allegedly anticipated that of Marx; but I have argued that it was a more modest effort in political science rather than a gran-

diose attempt at depicting the laws of all history in the manner of Hegel,
Marx, Vico, or Comte. Let me now recapitulate what I have said about these
two experimental or empirical theories.

Publius's most important assertions in the theory of motivation are about
the comparative strengths of different human motives. Because he thought
that the motive of reason was weaker than any of the other motives that he
considered, he was fearful that not only members of factions would violate
the rational dictates of moral duty but that members of the governing class
also would. He feared that their rationally established beliefs about what they
ought to do would, as a rule, be overcome by other motives that impelled
them and hence that they would act oppressively by violating the private
rights of other citizens. He also feared that rulers, however aware they might
be of their moral duty as enunciated in the principles of natural law, would
violate those principles by abridging the unceded and unalienable rights of
the people. Therefore he was anxious to check the impulses of an extra-legal
factious majority of the people and those of a constitutionally elected group
that would administer the government if the Constitution were adopted.

Let us now remind ourselves of the other central experimental thesis of
Publius that is sometimes called a philosophy of history. This thesis rests in
part on Publius's assertion that it is impossible to eliminate different economic interests among men living in civilized nations, an assertion which itself rests in part on the idea that men have different and unequal faculties of
acquiring things, an idea which can only be defended by appealing to experience. Some men, Madison believes, will be well equipped to acquire one kind
of thing, whereas others will be well equipped to acquire another kind of
thing; and within the class of men who are well equipped to acquire one kind
of thing, some will be better equipped than others. But then Madison makes
another empirical statement which is of fundamental importance in his theory. He says that once government enters upon the scene with the emergence
of civilized society, men who are gifted at acquiring things will be protected,
in which case the possession of different degrees and kinds of property will
result. Government will permit some men to specialize in the accumulation of
one kind of property whereas it will permit others to specialize in the accumulation of another kind of property. Furthermore, government will permit
some men to acquire lots of things of the kind that they are especially good
at acquiring, whereas others, although permitted by government to get hold
of as many things as they can, will in fact get hold of comparatively few
things. According to Madison, once government permits men of different abilities to exercise those different abilities, different sorts of group interests will
arise in society and therefore economic factions will arise. Such factions,
Madison says, will be impossible to eradicate because they arise from features of man and civil society that he regards as irremovable. In other words,
he does not think that it will be possible to eradicate certain differences in
abilities, nor does he think that governments in civilized societies will fail to
give the protection which permits those differences to manifest themselves.

In addition to maintaining that differences of economic interest will be irremovable in civilized nations, Madison maintains that this economic cause is the most common and most durable cause of factions. Madison clearly implies that there are other causes of factions, but unfortunately he was thought by some of his readers, most notably by Beard, to hold that difference of economic interest is the only cause of factional difference. In fact, however, Madison maintained that difference of passion and difference of opinion may also cause factional differences even though he devotes little space to these other causes. In any case, he seems to regard all of his assertions about the causes of factions as empirical or experimental even though he employs the word "faction" as a moral epithet. He not only appeals to general propositions about human nature when supporting his claim that the most common and durable source of factions has been the various and unequal distribution of property, but he also tells us that those who hold and those who do not hold property "have ever formed distinct interests in society." Madison seems to assume that if two groups have economic interests which are opposed *to each other,* they have interests which are adverse to the rights of other citizens, or to the permanent and aggregate interests of the community. Madison also holds that if one group is impelled by an economic interest which is different from that which rules another group, then members of one group may be impelled to invade the private rights of members of the other group; and since each group is impelled by a partial interest that unites it, this partiality will lead it to threaten the good of the whole community, the public good. However, Madison wanted society to be divided into lots of factions because he wanted to prevent any one faction from becoming a majority of the people. And this leads me to recapitulate some of the more important proposals in the practical or technological part of *The Federalist.*

The Technological Component of *The Federalist*

Technological knowledge is empirical knowledge for Publius, but it is different from the psychological empirical knowledge that he claims to have about the strength of man's various motives or the knowledge he claims to have about the causes of faction. I offer a homely example in order to make this point quite clear. A man who predicts that it will rain here today, or who tells us that it will rain here today because it rained to the west of us yesterday, is not giving us technological advice or advice about what to do. He is merely telling us what will happen in the atmosphere. We who listen to his prediction may carry umbrellas to work because we wish to remain dry, in which case we formulate and try to defend the proposition that carrying umbrellas will keep us dry. We seek such technological advice when we have a goal and wish to know how to achieve that goal. So, if our goal is to avoid the tyranny that a majority faction is likely to inflict on us—tyranny which is by definition the violation of our moral rights and therefore to be reprobated— we seek advice about how to ward off tyranny. In one of his capacities Publius predicts that under certain conditions there will be danger of what we may call a political downpour. He makes this prediction because he claims to know that there are factions and rulers who may well invade our rights, because, like most men, they are not impelled preponderantly by motives of reason but rather by interests and passions of certain kinds. Characteristically, Publius bases this claim to knowledge not only on general beliefs about man but also on the logically singular beliefs of history. To this extent, Publius resembles a meteorologist who supports his predictions not only by using general physical principles but also by looking out the window. In addition, however, Publius is in the business of telling us how to keep ourselves dry. He is, as it were, a political umbrella salesman as well as a political meteorologist, and it is in his capacity as political adviser that he recommends various kinds of divisions or separations in order to make sure that the republic contemplated in the Constitution will be administered on what Madison called just principles.

Some of the most revealing divisions recommended by Madison appear in his discussion of how to control factions. Before recommending these divisions, Madison considered the possibility that the dangerous motives of majority factions would be checked by motives that would serve as "internal restraints," but he denied that any such motives would be strong enough to overcome factious motives. He allowed that an enthusiastic form of religion might, by virtue of being passionate, do the job, but he did not approve of enthusiastic religion. Besides, he did not think it would last and he thought that it had too often, even in its coolest state, been a motive of oppression rather than a restraint upon it. The great desideratum, he said in his letter to Jefferson of October 24, 1787, was to modify sovereignty so as to make it sufficiently neutral to control one part of society—a factious majority—from invading the rights of another—a minority—and at the same time so control itself as not to set up an interest adverse to that of the entire society and the rights of the people who had conferred sovereignty upon it.

Madison's skepticism about the possibility of checking the immoral motives of majority factions by relying on appeals to prudence, reputation, and religious conscience led him to propose an external restraint upon factions which entailed certain divisions. And his skepticism about checking the immoral motives of governors in a similar way led him to propose another external restraint which required other divisions. As we know, the external restraint that he thought would check majority factions—the one sort of faction that worried him most—was to come about through making a republic large and populous.

At first blush this seems paradoxical. Let the people multiply and let them occupy a larger space, said Madison; but how, we may ask, would this check majority factions? It sounds as though Madison was recommending that a people divided into gangs of crooks should multiply, thereby increase the number of its gangs and therefore be given an even greater opportunity to do their dirty work. But this would be a superficial view of his intentions. According to Lovejoy, Madison was using a version of Bernard Mandeville's idea that private vices make public benefits, since Madison believed that the vices of factions could be turned against each other in order to protect the people.[4] Increase the number of competing gangs and extend the territory in which they operate, he said, and thereby diminish the probability that one of them will command a majority of the community. And if such an increase did not succeed in preventing one factious motive from uniting and actuating a majority, he continued, it would prevent a majority from acting tyrannically. One important division that Madison proposed, therefore, was the division of society into many competing factions; a second was the division or fragmentation of a majority in such a way as to prevent its being ruled by one factious motive; and a third was the division or separation of a factious majority's ruling motive and its opportunity to act on that motive.

Turning from the divisions that Madison wanted to use while checking factions, we may now make some summary observations on the division that Madison wanted to impose on the governing minority that he also feared. In effect, he wanted to separate or divide it into governmental entities which would stand in an adversarial relationship toward each other. First, there would be state governments and the national government glaring and snarling at each other when there was any chance that one might encroach on the rights or duties of the other. Then, within each state government and within the national government, there would be a separation of powers—executive, legislative, and judicial—that would also create a division within the government that would prevent it from tyrannizing over the people. Naturally, Madison shrewdly added while writing to Jefferson, the large and populous republic that would prevent majority factions from acting oppressively should not be so large as to prevent a majority from resisting oppression by those who administer the national government. And, of course, he did not wish federalism and separation of powers to sap the energies of the energetic national government that he thought the Constitution would install. The basic strategy in Madison's method for dealing with a factious majority and with a threatening ruling minority was neatly conveyed in his letter of October 24, 1787, to Jefferson: "Divide et impera, the reprobated axiom of tyranny, is under certain qualifications, the only policy, by which a republic can be administered on just principles."[5] Tyranny's vice became a republican virtue.

In sum, Madison, his fellow framers, and his fellow authors wanted to create a large and populous republic that would be divided into many interest groups that would check each other. They wanted, for a similar reason, to create a division between the many state governments and the one national government. They wanted to create a division by establishing three departments in each of the state governments and in the national government. They also wanted to divide the legislative department into two branches that would check each other. All of this division, I emphasize, rested on Publius's theory of motivation and on auxiliary theories about how to afford opportunities or to deny opportunities to those who were expected to have certain motives. Publius thought that the divisions he proposed would put obstacles in the way of men with factious tempers and in the way of would-be tyrants in the governing class. These obstacles would, he thought, impede men who were supposed by him to have motives which would lead to tyrannical actions if those men were not impeded. In the case of majority factions, he wanted to create such obstacles or external restraints because he thought, as we have seen, that certain internal restraints were not strong enough to overcome the impulse to tyrannize. However, the use of the words "internal" and "external" in this context may cause some confusion when we compare Madison's proposal for controlling factious majorities with his proposal for controlling the national government.

When Madison tells us that the motives which rule a majority faction will not be overcome by what he calls the inefficacious motives of prudence, reputation, and conscience, we know that although he thinks that these three internal restraints will not serve as checks upon a factious majority, he also thinks that the external restraint of a large, well-populated republic will very likely serve as a check upon such a majority. But when he proposes ways of checking governmental tyranny in *Number 51,* it may not be clear that he believes that these same internal restraints are just as inefficacious in controlling would-be governmental tyrants as they are in controlling members of majority factions. It may not be clear because, in a famous passage in *Number 51,* Madison says explicitly that a government can exercise "internal control" over itself. The passage, which I have quoted earlier, reads as follows: "If angels were to govern men, neither external nor internal controuls on government would be necessary. In framing a government which is to be administered by men over men, the great difficulty lies in this: You must first enable the government to controul the governed; and in the next place, oblige it to controul itself. A dependence on the people is no doubt the primary controul on the government; but experience has taught mankind the necessity of auxiliary precautions."[6]

This passage clearly indicates that Madison thinks that a government should and can impose internal restraints upon itself. However, when he implies in this passage that a government can control itself, he is not speaking of an individual human being who can, unlike members of a factious majority, restrain himself by paying due regard to the motives of prudence, reputation, or conscience. Madison is speaking here of the government as an artificial entity which has what he calls an "interior structure"; and it will control itself, he thinks, because it is divided into three powers—executive, legislative, and judiciary—which are contrived so as to check and balance each other. Madison's belief that this internal division of the government would be effective—to some extent—in controlling the government was therefore compatible with his belief that, generally speaking, the tyrannical impulses of individual administrators would not be restrained merely by the motives of prudence, reputation and conscience. The internal control which Madison thought would *not* restrain members of factious majorities was therefore quite different from the internal control that he thought *would*—to some extent—restrain tyrants by preventing one part of the interior structure of the government from dominating the others. According to Madison, what prudence, reputation, and conscience could not do *within the mind* of a man of factious temper, separation of powers might to some extent accomplish *within the government.* The internal control which would come about by separating powers and seeing to it that those who had such powers or opportunities had the motives to use them, would, in Madison's view, diminish the likelihood that the government would tyrannize over the people. The people's natural rights, he thought, would be protected because no one part of the interior structure of government would dominate any other and therefore be able to tyrannize over the people by violating rights which they had never ceded to the government when they established it.

Madison contrasted the internal control that a properly contrived government would exert upon itself with certain "exterior provisions" for control by the people that he questioned. Most notable among the latter was one suggested by Jefferson, namely, that the people should be called upon in constitutional conventions to keep the different departments of power within their constitutional limits if some dispute between them should arise. Although Madison granted that the people should exert the "primary" control on government, he thought that the government should also control itself internally through separation of powers; and his belief in the power of government to control itself by virtue of being divided stands in sharp contrast to his view that factions can be controlled only by the use of external restraints. The difference in his approach to administrative tyranny and factional tyranny arises, for one thing, because he did not regard factions as governmental entities which are "contrived" by the Constitution and, for another, because factions, unlike the government, are by definition composed of men with dishonorable purposes. Although Madison thought that a constitutional separation of powers would divide the government in a way that would allow it to control itself, he did not propose that factions be analogously divided or broken up. Obviously, he did not think that they could be subjected to anything that corresponded to constitutional division. Therefore, he wanted the people to be broken up into lots of factions so as to prevent any one faction from becoming a majority, and he also wanted any factious majority that might arise to be prevented from acting tyrannically by not allowing its ruling motive and its opportunity for such action to coincide.

The Role of Metaphysics and Theology
in *The Federalist*

The division or separation of a factious majority's motive and its opportunity is central in Madison's thought; it is the division of the cause of a foreseeable action so as to prevent that action from being performed. It is the division that occurs when a precipitant and a state are not "suffered to coincide." Whereas in *The Federalist* Madison's method of preventing the motive and the opportunity of a faction from coinciding was the creation of a large and populous federal republic, we know that in Philadelphia he had unsuccessfully proposed a national legislative veto over laws passed by state legislatures, a constitutional device that would have gone beyond space and population in checking the "ambition" and "personal interest" of state legislators who produced many different, mutable, and unjust statutes. Had his proposal been accepted by the Philadelphia Convention, it would have provided a legal instrument for denying an opportunity to men who were so dominated by ambition and interest as to bring about injustice by violating private rights or to cause public unhappiness by acting against the permanent and aggregate interests of the community.

If we generalize Madison's method of driving a wedge between motive and opportunity, we reach the idea that an action can be prevented from being performed by splitting what philosophers such as John Stuart Mill later called the entire cause of an event. In other words, we see that Madison implicitly accepted what was later formulated as a comparatively sophisticated version of the principle of universal causation. He held that every event has a cause, including psychological and political events, but his theory of action—to use a term of contemporary philosophers—rests on the more general idea that an entity of any kind, whether animate or inanimate, will behave in a certain way if and only if it is impelled or stimulated to behave in that way while it is in a certain state or in certain circumstances. The combination of that impulse and that state of an entity is a necessary and sufficient condition for the occurrence of a later event in the history of the entity, according to the principle of universal causation as conceived by Publius, even though, in company with many others who use ordinary language, he often says that a motive or impulse may itself be *the* cause of an action by an individual or by a group of individuals. Therefore, to prevent such an action from being performed, Publius is committed to holding that we must either eliminate the motive or see to it that it is outweighed by another motive; or else we must eliminate the opportunity; or, of course, we can eliminate both the motive and the opportunity. In *Number 10* Madison refers to the possibility of preventing a majority from having a factious motive when he says that "the existence of the same passion or interest in a majority at the same time must be prevented"; and he refers to the possibility that a majority which *does* have such a factious motive may be denied an opportunity to act when he says that such a majority "must be rendered, by their number and local situation, unable to concert and carry into effect schemes of oppression." In principle, therefore, he relies on the idea that a factious deed will be performed by a majority if the majority has a motive which is factious by definition and, in addition, has an opportunity to carry its motive into effect. He also seems to accept the converse of this proposition, namely, that if a factious deed has been performed by a majority, it must have had both a motive and an opportunity to perform it. Therefore, he accepts the corollary of the principle of universal causation that a majority will perform a factious deed if and only if it has a factious motive and an opportunity to carry it out.[7]

The principle of universal causation, or of causality, was not regarded by Publius as a principle of any special science such as psychology or politics;

it was a general principle of which Publius's theory of individual and collective action was a special case. In applying this theory of action, Publius uses the concepts of motive and of opportunity not only to show how objectionable actions might be prevented but also to show how actions of which he approved might be encouraged. Publius could give either kind of advice because his theory of action was neutral concerning the actions it treated. It stated the necessary and sufficient conditions under which an action would be performed and, by implication, the necessary and sufficient conditions under which an action would not be performed, whether Publius approved of the action or disapproved of it. When using his theory of action, therefore, Publius sometimes advises us how to prevent objectionable actions which might be performed by individual states under the influence of partial and immediate interests, or by rulers who might be moved to violate the rights of the people or act against their true interests, or by factions which would necessarily be moved to act similarly. Publius also advises us to give opportunities or powers to collective bodies or individuals whose motives will, in conjunction with those opportunities and powers, lead to the performance of actions of which he approves.

It should be borne in mind, therefore, that when Publius relied on the principle of causality as exemplified in his theory of action, he needed a moral philosophy which would help him determine which actions should be prevented and which should be brought about. Sometimes that moral philosophy leads him to advise that the pure and noble administrators of an energetic national government be encouraged to act for the good of the community; and sometimes that moral philosophy leads him to condemn tyrannical governments which violate natural rights by keeping the executive, the legislative, and the judicial powers all in their hands. When Publius argues in the first vein, he reveals the brighter component of his gray theory of human nature. But when he recommends putting impediments in the way of rulers, the darker component of that theory of human nature is more in evidence. He believes that even the noblest of men have to be watched and therefore, in his more watchful moods, Publius uses his theory of action to recommend external restraint, especially when he gives advice about how to check the violation of natural rights by those who must be *supposed* to be knaves, whether or not they really are knaves. Publius walks a fine line on the subject of promotion and prevention, as he does on so many others. When he argues for a federal union, he cannot be too praising of the motives of the national leaders whom he expects to answer the call of their country, but when he argues for separation of powers, he seems to treat these same national leaders as though they could not be trusted as far as the next corner. This helps us understand why he sometimes wants motive and opportunity to coincide and sometimes wants them divided. Since the promotion of the general welfare was a goal of the Constitution just as the protection of natural rights was, the former goal required the encouragement of noble action, according to Publius, whereas the latter required the prevention of ignoble action. We cannot say that Publius uses the principle of causality only to stop action that he deplored; he also uses it to encourage action that he admired.

Once we recognize that Publius's theory of action is a corollary of the principle of universal causation, we are tempted to ask how he thought the latter is to be defended, since that question was hotly debated by philosophers in the eighteenth century and was answered in very different ways by Publius's masters, Locke and Hume.[8] But because Publius does not say anything about the principle of causation beyond what Hamilton says in *Number 31* about the "primary truth" or "axiom" that "there cannot be an effect without a cause," we can say very little about Publius's view of the epistemological status of that principle. Hamilton's formulation of it turns it into a truism and therefore what Hume called "frivolous," because it makes the principle true merely by virtue of the definition of the word "effect." It would appear that the point of mentioning that version in *Number 31* was purely rhetorical. Hamilton thought it would lend dignity to other principles that Hamilton put in the same company with it, principles of much greater political importance because they helped Hamilton "demonstrate" the necessity of a national power of taxation.

Before completing this section I want to remind the reader that the principle of universal causation was not the only metaphysical belief that Publius accepted on rationalistic grounds. He also believed in the existence of man's essence, as we have seen in previous discussions of his moral views, and he thought that the law of nature was a law of nature's God. Man's nature or essence was presumably created by an omnipotent, wise, and beneficent being; and it was from this nature or essence that both Hamilton and Madison derived man's duties and corresponding rights in some of their writings. We have seen earlier that a view of this kind is present in some of Hamilton's earliest writing on natural law as well as in Madison's. And although the view was not made very explicit in *The Federalist,* I do not think that the authors could have defended their version of natural rights without some appeal to a Creator of man's essence even though the references to God in *The Federalist* are quite exiguous and perfunctory. At one point Madison says, as he calls attention to the difficulty of defining terms, that "when the Almighty himself condescends to address mankind in their own language, his meaning, luminous as it must be, is rendered dim and doubtful, by the cloudy medium through which it is communicated." And shortly thereafter, while expressing wonder about the fact that the Philadelphia Convention had reached so much agreement, Madison says: "It is impossible for the man of pious reflection not to perceive in it, a finger of that Almighty hand which has been so frequently and signally extended to our belief in the critical stages of the revolution."[9]

As I conclude this chapter, I should emphasize that the different kinds of statements—metaphysical, moral, epistemological, psychological, theological, and technological—that I have mentioned in this philosophical map or survey of *The Federalist* are not equally conspicuous in the work. As I have pointed out, those that appear most frequently are the descriptive statements of psychology and political technology to which Publius appeals when he advises the people of America how to prevent specific kinds of actions and to encourage others. If he had been pressed to say why they ought to perform either kind of action, Publius might well have put some of his moral, metaphysical, epistemological, and theological cards on the table while defending his recommendations in political technology. But since he usually keeps those cards close to his vest, his political technology and his psychology are the most visible parts of his doctrine. It is only on those rare occasions when Publius makes explicit appeals to the natural rights of man and the common good of the American people that his underlying but underdeveloped moral theory is exposed to his readers. In order to show what the structure of his theory would look like if he were to have been more explicit in presenting his moral theory, I shall presently compare the structure of the argument of *The Federalist* with that of the Declaration of Independence, despite the great difference between the fat volume that defended the Constitution and the few pages that defended the Revolution.

13

The Federalist and
the Declaration
of Independence Compared

Although the main aim of this study has been to focus on the philosophy of *The Federalist* itself, I want to try to cast further light on that philosophy by comparing it with the philosophy espoused in the Declaration of Independence. Gordon Wood, a distinguished student of the early history of the United States, has said that "the whole intellectual world of 1776 had become unraveled" by 1787, and so there is a special reason for asking whether the philosophy of the Declaration had undergone serious transformation at the hands of Publius.[1] Before trying to answer this question I should repeat that although the word "philosophy" is notoriously ambiguous, I have used it to designate ideas in ethics, in metaphysics, in epistemology, and in the theory of human nature. Therefore, ideas of that kind will be my main concern in this chapter.

The Moral Argument of the Declaration
and that of *The Federalist*

Like *The Federalist,* the Declaration of Independence contains both moral and descriptive statements which together lead to a moral conclusion. In words that are likely to be familiar to the reader, the first paragraph of the Declaration announces that the signers think that they should explain why they are dissolving the political bands which had connected them with Great Britain. The next paragraph then presents what may be called the moral propositions in their argument. They say that it is self-evident that all men have certain unalienable rights, among them life, liberty, and the pursuit of happiness. The signers also tell us that it is self-evident that governments are instituted among men in order to prevent these rights from being invaded or violated, and that the just powers of government are derived from the consent of the governed. They then go on to say that it is self-evident that whenever any form of government becomes "destructive of these ends," meaning the purposes for which it is instituted, the people have a right to alter or abolish it and to institute a new government, "laying its foundation on such principles, and organizing its powers in such form as to them shall seem most likely to effect their safety and happiness." And they conclude the moral part of their argument by asserting that when a long train of abuses and usurpations evinces a design on the part of a government to destroy the ends mentioned earlier by ruling a people despotically, it is the people's right—indeed their duty—"to throw off such government and to provide new guards for their future security." This conclusion is presented as the logical conclusion of the Declaration's allegedly self-evident premises, on the assumption that as soon as there is an observable design on the part of a government to destroy the ends for which it is instituted, the government may be regarded as having destroyed those ends.[2]

The next part of the Declaration's moral argument is devoted to showing that the government which was being thrown off *had* destroyed the ends for which governments are instituted among men. The revolutionaries recite "the history of the . . . King of Great Britain" and submit a number of "facts" in a long list of statements that make up the Declaration's indictment of the king, statements intended to show that he had aimed to establish an absolute tyranny over the United States. From their moral principles and their descriptive statements of fact, the revolutionaries move to a conclusion which they express as follows: "We, therefore, the representatives of the United States of America, in general Congress assembled, appealing to the Supreme Judge of the world for the rectitude of our intentions, do, in the name, and by the authority of the good people of these colonies, solemnly publish and declare, that these united colonies are, and of right ought to be, free and independent states: that they are absolved from all allegiance to the British Crown, and that all political connection between them and the state of Great Britain is, and ought to be, totally dissolved. . . ."

The reasoning by which the colonists derive their conclusion that the connection between them and Great Britain *ought to be* totally dissolved may therefore be represented as reasoning of the following form: (1) Whenever a people is treated by a government in a manner which shows that the government intends to tyrannize over them, the people have a duty to sever their connection with that government; (2) the American people have been treated in that manner by the British government; therefore, (3) the American people have a duty to sever their connection with the British government. As we can see from what I have said earlier, the first statement of moral duty in this schematic argument is supported by other statements made in the moral part of the Declaration, and the second statement in the argument is, because it is a conjunction of all the statements made in the Declaration's indictment of the British king, supported by those conjuncts. The author of the Declaration regarded some of his moral statements as self-evident or intuitively known, and others as derivable from such self-evident statements. Consequently, he arrived at statement (1) while subscribing to a view which was very like Locke's view that morality could be a demonstrative science whose axioms would be established merely by examining the relations between ideas and whose theorems would be established by deducing them from such axioms. By contrast, the conjunctive statement (2) was supported by appealing to experience or history.

When we turn from the Declaration to *The Federalist,* we can see that if the moral assumptions of the latter work had been made more explicit, it, like the Declaration, would have contained moral propositions which its authors would have declared to be self-evident truths or deducible from self-evident truths, as well as descriptive propositions which they would have, by contrast, declared to be historical or empirical. Furthermore, *The Federalist* could have been cast as one long argument for the moral conclusion "The Constitution ought to be ratified" just as the whole of the Declaration was an argument for the moral conclusion "The Revolution ought to be made." Of course, when stated more fully, the long argument of *The Federalist* would have been immensely more complicated than the short argument of the Declaration. The act of adopting the Constitution would require a more complicated defense than the defense of the Revolution if only because the former act would itself require a more elaborate description. Morover, the defenders of the Constitution would have had to cite much more empirical evidence than that cited in the Declaration, especially because they assert so many psychological, political, and technological propositions which contain terms such as "democracy," "republic," "faction," "motive," "interest," "passion," and "opportunity." If the authors of *The Federalist* had marshaled this empirical evidence more systematically, and if they had made their moral premise more explicit, they would have more clearly justified their moral conclusion that the Constitution ought to be adopted. The Declaration is almost a textbook model of moral argument by comparison to what we find in *The Federalist* by way of systematically articulated moral premises and relevant descriptive premises.

There is one allegedly self-evident premise in the Declaration which would have played a particularly important role in a more explicit version of Publius's argument. I mean the premise which says that whenever any government becomes destructive of the ends for which it is instituted among men, the people not only have the right to alter or to abolish it, *but also* "to institute a new government, laying its foundations on such principles, and organizing its powers in such forms as to them shall seem most likely to effect their safety and happiness." In this premise the Declaration prepared the way for a *con*structive act that might follow the *de*structive act of revolution—a *con*structive act of the sort that was preeminently illustrated by the adoption of the Constitution. This statement goes well beyond another one in the Declaration which says that people who see a design to rule them despotically not only have the duty "to throw off" such a government but also the duty "to provide new guards for their future security" or the security of their rights. From the viewpoint of a reader of the Declaration, the Constitution was an instrument which would create not only new guards for the security of natural rights but also effect the happiness of the people.

We must always remember that the Declaration criticized the king of Great Britain not only for violating the natural rights of the colonists but also for failing to increase their happiness and for making them positively unhappy in ways that were not immediately connected with his violation of their rights. The very first "fact" about the king that the signers of the Declaration "submitted to a candid world" was expressed as follows: "He has refused his assent to laws the most wholesome and necessary for the public good"; and at least some of these wholesome laws would not have been limited to guarding the unalienable rights of the people. We must therefore recognize that the Declaration, the Constitution, and *The Federalist* all distinguish the idea of natural rights on the one hand and the idea of public good, public interest, or public happiness on the other, even though it is true that each document implies that a violation of natural rights will of itself cause public unhappiness. Why would Madison have referred so often to the mischief of violating private rights *and* to that of acting in contravention to the public good if he had not distinguished between these two kinds of mischief? Why would the Preamble to the Constitution distinguish between the establishment of justice and the promotion of the general welfare if the framers had not had a similar distinction in mind? Why would Madison have spoken in *Number 51* of an ideal majority as a coalition based on the principles of justice *and* the general good if he had equated these two principles with each other?

Summing up this section, we may say that there is no fundamental philosophical difference between the Declaration and *The Federalist*. In both documents we find the same rationalistic ethics which derives unalienable rights from duties extracted from man's essence as created by God and formulated in the law of nature. In both documents we find the same epistemological doctrine that one must appeal to history and experience in order to support statements of fact. In both documents we find a concern for private rights and for the public good. And in both documents we even find an awareness that some men have tyrannical motives. All of these philosophical ideas were as current in 1787 as they were in 1776.[3]

Self-evident Truths, True Interests, and the Opportunities of Dictators

In the light of this, what shall we say about the thesis that the *whole* intellectual world of 1776 had become unraveled by 1787? I know that Professor Wood says that "under the severest kinds of political and polemical pressures old words had assumed new meanings" during these eleven years.[4] But did the words in any of the philosophical doctrines I have cited assume meanings in 1787 which were different from the meanings they had in 1776? I do not think that they did. I do not think that the principles of natural law asserted in the Declaration were different in meaning from their counterparts in *The Federalist*. "Life," "liberty," "security," and "happiness" were not reinterpreted or redefined by Publius; nor were the expressions "tyranny," "rights," "duties," and "public good." We may say the same thing about the phrase "self-evident truths" and about Hamilton's equivalent for it, the phrase "primary truths" as that was used in *Number 31*. In 1787 the terms "history," "experience," "motive," "cause," and "opportunity" continued to mean what they had meant in 1776. Consequently, many of the philosophical doctrines to which the signers of the Declaration subscribed were not radically different from those adopted in *The Federalist*. Even though Publius did not weave those doctrines into as explicit a moral argument as that contained in the Declaration, many of them are present in *The Federalist* and are called upon as needed in different parts of that work. Even if the philosophy of the Declaration had become unraveled by 1787, it would not have been impossible for Publius to reweave its doctrinal strands into an argument which was not fundamentally different from the more finished fabric presented in the Declaration.

This is not to say that Publius did not add propositions which were more needed in his argument than they were in the argument of the Declaration. Because there was obviously more need in *The Federalist* than there was in the Declaration to describe the impulses of men who would be officials and citizens in the new government, Publius made scattered remarks which constitute a theory of motivation that goes well beyond what we find in the Declaration. And because Publius had to answer critics of the Constitution who worried about the tyranny of factions, he used his theory of motivation to support a view of the causes of factions and he advanced a view of how to control majority factions. Moreover, since the authors of *The Federalist* had more need than the signers of the Declaration had to discuss the nature of self-evident truths and to point out that they might not seem true to disordered, biased, ignorant, or perverse minds, we find epistemological remarks in *The Federalist* which we do not find in the Declaration. Those remarks are not limited to observations on how we establish self-evident and demonstrable truths, since we also find Publius adopting a view about how the true interest of the community can be discovered. Here, as in other cases, the additional philosophy or psychology that we find in *The Federalist* is not incompatible with what we find in the Declaration. It merely supplements doctrines of the latter so as to defend the Constitution's method of instituting a new government by "laying its foundations on such principles, and organizing its powers in such form" as seemed to the framers most likely to bring about the safety and the happiness of the people.

Is this all that we can say about the view that the whole intellectual world of 1776 had become unraveled by 1787? Hardly. But in order to say something else that will be illuminating, I think we had better not speak of words having different meanings in 1776 from what they had in 1787 and speak rather of the different political applications of the same philosophical doctrines in these different years. The main philosophical doctrines I have in mind are (1) the moral doctrine of inviolable natural rights as well as the epistemological doctrine that man's possession of them is determined by examining the relations between ideas and (2) the moral doctrine that government ought to minister to the true interests of the people as well as the epistemological doctrine that such interests are determined experimentally. Once we look more closely at these doctrines, we shall see how they might be used differently under different circumstances, and in particular how they might be linked with the political elitism of *The Federalist*. In seeing this we shall see something that supports Wood's view "that the Constitution was in some sense an aristocratic document designed to curb the democratic excesses of the Revolution."[5] For we shall see that the idea of self-evident truth—which was so prominent in the defense of natural rights—and the idea of a true interest—which was so crucial in *The Federalist*'s pronouncements on the public good—were both used in ways that buttressed the political elitism that Wood had in mind when he called the Constitution an aristocratic document.

When I speak of political elitism in *The Federalist,* I refer to something to which I have alluded in earlier parts of this study. It is obvious to the least philosophical reader of Publius that he thought the people were subject to momentary passions which could lead them to make grave political mistakes; that rational, wise, and virtuous leaders could refine the people's passions and speak more effectively for them than they could for themselves; that demagogues could flatter the people while leading them into subjugation; that the people tend to focus on the immediate, short-term advantages of certain courses of action while disregarding the long-term advantages of different courses of action; that the people tend to be influenced by local, partial interests while disregarding the interests of the community as a whole; that discerning leaders would be better able than the people themselves to see what the people's true interests were; and last, but not least, that the people might not see the truth, much less the self-evidence or demonstrability of truths which served as the major moral premises of arguments advanced for the adoption of the Constitution. This is only part of the political elitism which is blatantly present in *The Federalist* in spite of the many genuflections that are made in the direction of the people. But now I wish to say something about the philosophy in *The Federalist* that supports and encourages this kind of elitism, the philosophy which did not change in meaning between 1776 and 1787 but which was, perhaps, put to more obvious elitist use in 1787 than it had been in 1776. I should add that certain parts of the philosophy I have in mind were potentially aristocratic even before it was used in the Declaration, so if *The Federalist* activated this potentiality, so to speak, more than the Declaration did, that was because of extraphilosophical developments between 1776 and 1787, developments that are so instructively treated by Professor Wood.

In order to clarify the matters that are of most interest to me, it will be well to begin by recalling one of the motives of Locke in his *Essay,* the book that portrayed a conception of morality which I think was in the minds of many who signed the Declaration and those who wrote *The Federalist*. Locke was determined to refute the doctrine of innate principles and also to show it to be politically dangerous. According to him, it discouraged men from using their own powers of reason and led them to take so-called innate principles upon trust and without further examination. Locke said that acceptance of the doctrine of innate principles made men blindly credulous and therefore more easily governed by those who might become what he called dictators of unquestionable principles. Such dictators, Locke went on, might make those they governed "swallow" whatever principles were supposedly innate and they might ultimately get them to swallow what he called a principle of principles, namely, that principles must not be questioned.

Ironically, however, Locke thought that his own doctrine of self-evident principles would not have this sort of political effect, since he believed that a self-evident principle would be seen to be true by the use of intuitive reason and therefore nobody could be made to swallow it merely on the say-so of an intellectual dictator. I say "ironically" because Locke also held that some men are unable to perceive the self-evidence or even the truth of self-evident principles. He held that all men are endowed with reason and that the natural law can be known by reason, but he also held that the natural law is not necessarily known to any and every man. Why? Locke answers: Because some men prefer not to know it, others have been corrupted to the point where they cannot know it, and still others are too dull to know it. Therefore, Locke says that in trying to discover what the law of nature is, "not the majority of the people should be consulted but those who are more rational and perceptive than the rest." It follows, whether Locke knew it or not, that his doctrine of self-evident principles was just as politically dangerous as the doctrine of innate principles that he attacked on political grounds. For if one maintains that certain people are in a better position to see the self-evidence of a principle than others, one espouses a doctrine which may easily lead to the elevation of some men as dictators of principles.

If they are supposed to be the only ones who can discover what the law of nature is because only they can perceive its self-evidence and therefore its truth, then they may well become dictators of principles. If only they can discover self-evidence merely by grasping the ideas expressed in the natural law and seeing how those ideas are related to each other, then they are in a privileged position. Such privileged persons might easily say to the majority who are not able to see the relations between ideas that they should not question the assertions of their betters about natural law. In doing so, the betters would set themselves up as dictators of principles. The doctrine that only the learned can see the self-evidence of self-evident principles need not change its meaning in order to be used by political elitists to curb democratic excesses. It can retain its original meaning and still be used by dictators of principles who claim that *they* can see self-evidence whereas the majority of the people are too ignorant to see it. From a democrat's point of view, such self-appointed dictators of principles *ab*use an epistemological doctrine without altering the meaning of any of its component terms. They seize an opportunity to make themselves dictators of moral principles and, as a conesquence, dictators of actions.

I think it very important to recall in this connection that Locke, who admitted that he had not constructed anything like the demonstrative science of morality he thought possible, held that "the greatest part of mankind" would not suffer because of this. They would not have been able to follow a proof in ethics, he said, even if it were available. Therefore, he went on, "hearing plain commands is the sure and only course to bring them to obedience and practice." The moral instruction of the people, Locke also said in *The Reasonableness of Christianity,* is best left to the precepts and principles of the Gospel, enunciated as they were by one who was a messenger of God. Whoever is persuaded that Jesus Christ was sent by God to be a king and a savior of those who believe in him, Locke concluded, would regard Christ's commands as principles; "there needs no other proof for the truth of what he says, but that he said it. And then there needs no more, but to read the inspired books, to be instructed: all the duties of morality lie there clear, and plain, and easy to be understood."[6]

This passage shows the political dangers of adopting the moral rationalism that Locke accepted. When Locke saw that he could not make good on his claim that all of morality could be deduced from self-evident axioms or primary truths, he was led to say that a demonstrative science of morality would never be missed by the vast majority of mankind because there was an authoritative source, the Gospel, in which all of the moral principles were clear for everyone to understand. In other words, when the limitations of ethical rationalism became evident, the next step was moral authoritarianism, so far as day laborers and dairymaids were concerned. It was the moral authority of the New Testament to which Locke appealed when trying to circumvent the difficulties created by his inability to do what his moral rationalism required him to do: present a demonstrative science of morality.

There is no doubt that Locke's epistemology of natural law influenced the views held by both Madison and Hamilton, but the further question is whether they exploited its aristocratic potentialities. An appeal to Locke's epistemology was certainly made in Hamilton's youthful "Full Vindication" and "Farmer Refuted" of 1774 and 1775; one was also made in Madison's *Memorial and Remonstrance* of 1784; and we know that Hamilton used that epistemology to political advantage in *Number 31.* Both Hamilton and Madison believed that the self-evidence of the Lockeian axioms of natural law and the consequent demonstrability of its theorems were analogous to the self-evidence and demonstrability of the axioms and theorems of mathematics; and both of them agreed with Locke that certain members of the community were better able—because of their learning or lack of bias and passion—to discover the truths of natural law than the majority of the people were. Consequently, the epistemological views of Hamilton and Madison about how to know the natural law were consonant with the political elitism they espoused in *The Federalist.* We must keep in mind, however, that their views on the self-evident truths of natural law directly affected only their views of how to test principles expressing moral duties and moral rights. By contrast, they did not hold that the discovery of the true interests of the community was made by using the sort of rational intuition or deduction used in mathematics; they believed that the discovery of true interests was supposedly made by the use of empirical or experimental reasoning. For them, the proposition that all men had a *right* to life, liberty, religious freedom, and even the pursuit of happiness could be discovered by Locke's rationalistic method of discovering the laws of nature, whereas the proposition that some course of action was in the interest of the whole community could only be discovered by experience or experiment.

It might be thought, therefore, that this would leave an epistemological opening for the majority of the people. After all, it might be argued, the least learned and least sagacious human beings can see and observe the external political world even if they cannot learn whether moral truths are axioms or theorems of natural law by examining the relations between ideas in a quasi-mathematical manner. Therefore, the majority of the people might be thought to be just as gifted as the few at discovering whether an action in fact contributed to the public good. So the question arises: Did Publius subscribe to any form of epistemological elitism with regard to the discovery of true public interest? The answer, I think, is "yes." At many places in *The Federalist* Publius says that only those who rise above the ambition, bias, prejudice, partial interest, and immediate interest of ordinary men will be in a position to see what the true interests of the community are. In other words, the true or real interest of the nation, like the truth of propositions which attribute natural rights to all men, is viewed by Publius as something objective which a few men are better able to detect than others because only a few men can rise above biased passions and interests. Consequently, it is hard to say that whereas general statements about natural rights are discoverable only by the learned, statements about what redounds to the *true* public interest are discoverable by an ordinary person. In other words, even though the discovery of what makes the people truly happy, or of what is really good for them, or of what is in their true interest is an empirical matter, such a discovery can only be made, according to Publius, by a special sort of person. Therefore, justice and the public good were on the same level in this respect. Both of them, Publius held, could be perceived only by the few. Even though the principles of natural law were supposedly seen to be true by examining the relations between *ideas* whereas statements about what contributed to the general welfare were seen to be true by examining what Hume called *matters of fact,* Publius thought that the detection of truth in both of these realms could require an expertise that not all men possessed.

It follows that Publius's epistemological elitism cut across a fundamental division in his theory of knowledge, the division between the method of testing statements in the demonstrative sciences and the method of testing statements in the experimental sciences. Because Publius held in *Number 31* that self-evident or primary truths contain "an internal evidence, which antecedent to all reflection or combination commands the assent of the mind," Publius was able to say that "where it produces not this effect, it must proceed either from some defect or disorder in the organs of perception, or from the influence of some strong interest, or passion, or prejudice."[7] Publius regarded the internal evidence for primary truths about natural rights as objectively impinging on the mind, so when that evidence failed to command a man's assent, Publius maintained that the man's mind was defective or that he was then in a state that prevented it from functioning properly. But the point I want to stress here is that Publius held something analogous about true statements concerning the real or true interest of the community. A man whose mind was dull or not functioning properly would fail to discover those experimental truths just as he would fail to discover the self-evidence of the law of nature.

An ordinary man might be stupid or he might be prevented by passion, selfish interest, or prejudice from seeing what would bring long-term happiness to the community, whereas his superiors would not be so disadvantaged. They, according to Publius, could see better than most men what the true interest of the community was, and their advantage over the majority of men in this respect was analogous to their advantage over them in demonstrating the law of nature which set forth man's rights. Just as Locke held that the greater part of mankind lacked the leisure and the capacity for moral demonstration and were therefore not expert in determining man's moral duties and rights, so Publius held that they were not expert at seeing what would serve the true interests of the whole community. He believed that they would have to carry in their minds a long train of causal connections in order to see that performing a certain action would lead, not by mathematical laws but by the laws of psychology and political science, to distant consequences in the whole country around them and in the future before them. For this reason, Publius was armed with a double-barreled epistemological elitism which was also potentially present in the doctrines that Americans of 1776 espoused. In 1787 this potential elitism was actively exercised, as we see in at least two numbers of *The Federalist.* In *Number 31,* as we know, Hamilton uses the epistemological doctrine of primary or self-evident principles to demonstrate the necessity of a national power of taxation and, in passing, to argue that only disordered minds and minds influenced by passion or interest would disagree with his view. And in *Number 17* Hamilton says that only "speculative men" who rise above "the mass of the citizens" can see the benefits *to that mass* which a national government will bring. According to Hamilton in these places, only a few persons can see that certain key actions of a federal union are in accord with so-called primary truths and with the true interests of the public.

After saying this, I must point out that there are places in *The Federalist* where the American people are credited with enough intelligence to know things which are said at other places to be knowable only by the few. *Number 26* presents us with an interesting example of what might be called the populistic side of Publius's theory of knowledge. This number should also

be of interest to those who think that the ideas of 1787 were more conserva-
tive than those of 1776. In the very first sentence Hamilton says that it was
"hardly to be expected that in a popular revolution the minds of men should
stop at the happy mean, which marks the salutary boundary between POWER
and PRIVILEGE, and combines the energy of government with the security
of private rights." Here Hamilton expressed his fear that a people imbued
with revolutionary fervor might *not* stop at this happy mean and therefore
might restrain the legislature from providing properly for the national defense
because of "a zeal for liberty more ardent than enlightened." But, Hamilton
goes on to say, only two states, Pennsylvania and North Carolina, had yielded
to this zeal for liberty by saying in their constitutions that standing armies in
time of peace are dangerous to liberty and therefore ought not to be kept up.
This shows, according to Hamilton, that the people were wiser than some of
the opponents of the Constitution. He writes: "The citizens of America have
too much discernment to be argued into anarchy. And I am much mistaken if
experience has not wrought a deep and solemn conviction in the public mind,
that greater energy of government is essential to the welfare and prosperity of
the community."[8]

This statement is characteristic of many that are made in *The Federalist*
about the people's capacity to discern that certain things contribute to the
public good, so we are faced with the following questions. Shall we say that
the work contained a logical inconsistency of which Publius was unaware?
Or shall we say that Publius was deliberately talking out of both sides of his
mouth, sometimes saying what he really thought about the people's meager
intellectual powers with regard to the welfare of the community and sometimes merely flattering them in order to win them over to his side? In my
opinion, Publius was quite prepared to grant that the people could discover
the truth of comparatively general propositions about what would contribute
to their welfare, for example, that any efficient, stable, and energetic government would do so under normal circumstances. However, I doubt that he
thought the mass of mankind could assess the truth of very specific propositions about what would contribute to the general good. And there certainly
are passages in *The Federalist* where he obviously plays to the gallery. Perhaps the most ingenious statement that Madison makes in this connection is
the following one in which he flatters some of his readers by telling them that
they cannot be flattered:

> To a people as little blinded by prejudice, or corrupted by flattery, as those
> whom I address, I shall not scruple to add that [a well constructed senate]
> may be sometimes necessary, as a defence to the people against their own
> temporary errors and delusions. As the cool and deliberate sense of the
> community ought in all governments, and actually will in all free govern-
> ments ultimately prevail over the views of its rulers; so there are par-
> ticular moments in public affairs, when the people stimulated by some
> irregular passion, or some illicit advantage, or misled by the artful mis-
> representations of interested men, may call for measures which they them-
> selves will afterwards be the most ready to lament and condemn. In these

critical moments, how salutary will be the interference of some temperate and respectable body of citizens, in order to check the misguided career, and to suspend the blow meditated by the people against themselves, until reason, justice and truth, can regain their authority over the public mind? What bitter anguish would not the people of Athens have often escaped, if their government had contained so provident a safeguard against the tyranny of their own passions? Popular liberty might then have escaped the indelible reproach of decreeing to the same citizens, the hemlock on one day, and statues on the next.[9]

This passage, I think, expresses the dominant view of Publius concerning the intellectual powers of the people. He did not rely on the public mind to be controlled consistently by reason, justice, and the truth, but he did think that temperate and respectable citizens in the senate would protect them against the tyranny of their own passions. This was the variety of parentalism against which Locke inveighed when he attacked Robert Filmer in the *First Treatise of Government* but which Locke encouraged when he denied that dairymaids and day laborers could do ethics or mathematics.

Epistemological Dualism and Madison's Concern for the Protection of Natural Rights

Despite Publius's willingness to say that there were only a few men who could determine what was objectively just and only a few men who could determine what was objectively good for the community, it might be wondered whether the alleged certainty of Locke's quasi-mathematical law of nature by comparison to the mere probability of any judgment about whether the people were happy might have led Publius to elevate the protection of natural rights above the promotion of the people's happiness in spite of his believing that only the few could see what those rights were or how the people's happiness was to be attained. If man's possession of natural rights was thought to be as certain as a mathematical truth whereas man's happiness could at best be established with the probability that some philosophers associate with empirical or experimental statements, then any conflict between protecting natural rights and promoting the public good might be regarded as automatically resoluble in favor of the former. If the wise man would always be more confident that we have certain natural rights than he would be that the public good has been promoted, would he not be bound to advise protection of those rights if a conflict between protecting them and promoting the public good should arise? If a man mounted to the highest level of certainty possible when theorizing about what was in the public interest, would he not inevitably be at a lower level than he would be while truthfully theorizing about natural rights? Would he not be more confident in his statements about natural rights than he could ever be in his statements about what contributed to the social good? Therefore, would he not be advised to protect natural rights even if protecting them would *not* be in the interest of the public?

This question presupposes a familiar epistemological dualism between the method of establishing our rights and the method of establishing what is in the public interest, a dualism according to which true moral principles of natural law are not subject to revision in the light of future experience whereas statements about the true interests or happiness of the people *are* subject to such revision. Future experience might lead to a change or abandonment of the latter statements, but the authors of *The Federalist* show no signs of believing that the moral principles of natural law could ever be overturned or revised by future experience. For a rationalistic moralist, that would be like altering an axiom or a theorem of mathematics on the basis of a new experience, something that was forbidden by the theory of knowledge accepted by Publius. So we may once again ask whether the acceptance of an epistemological dualism between the method of establishing natural rights and establishing the true interest of a people led all of the authors of *The Federalist* to put the protection of natural rights on a pedestal which was higher than that on which they put the public good or the happiness of the people.

It is extremely difficult to answer this question with confidence, and yet I think that epistemological considerations played some part in leading Madison to elevate the protection of natural rights above the promotion of the public good. Before I show why, I want to show that Madison *did* elevate the protection of natural rights above the promotion of the public good in some parts of *The Federalist,* no matter what he or his fellow authors said in other parts of the work, and quite apart from the role that epistemology played in this elevation. Even though Madison defines the ruling motive of a faction as one which is either adverse to private rights or to the public good, he lays more emphasis on the dangers posed by factions to private rights. I grant that he holds in *Number 10* that factions are not only enemies of justice but also enemies of stability—which he regards as an ingredient of good government and therefore as a contributor to the public good. And he bases his criticism of factions on the same two grounds when he says that complaints are constantly made "that our [state] governments are too unstable; that the public good is disregarded in the conflicts of rival parties; and that measures are too often decided, not according to the rules of justice, and the rights of the minor party; but by the superior force of an interested and over-bearing majority." However, after Madison acknowledges that "the evidence of known facts will not permit us to deny that [these complaints] are in some degree true," he indicates that when factions bear the major responsibility for the heaviest misfortunes of Americans, they do so *"particularly* [my emphasis], for that prevailing and increasing distrust of public engagements, and alarm for private rights, which are echoed from one end of the continent to another."[10]

Madison's "engagements," whether public or otherwise, are what Locke called compacts; and Madison, like Locke, thinks they ought to be kept because the undeniable law of nature says that they should be kept.[11] Moreover, Madison points out that the most important acts of legislation are "so many judicial determinations, not indeed concerning the rights of single per-

sons, but concerning the rights of large bodies of citizens," and that such determinations will not be just if the legislators who array themselves on different
sides are simultaneously judges *and* parties in these determinations. "Justice,"
he says, "ought to hold the balance between them. Yet the parties are and
must be themselves the judges; and the most numerous party, or, in other
words, the most powerful faction must be expected to prevail."[12] So once
again Madison's chief worry seems to be the violation of rights even though
he says at this point in *Number 10* that legislative factions work against the
public good as well as against justice when they act as judges in their own
cause. It is not surprising, therefore, that when Madison illustrates "improper
or wicked" projects on the part of factions, he mentions with special concern
"a rage for paper money, for an abolition of debts, [and] for an equal division of property." Such a rage would obviously lead majority factions to invade natural rights, and that is what I think worried Madison most about majority factions.

I come now to the part played by epistemology in Madison's tendency to
lay special emphasis on the protection of natural rights. His belief in the un-
deniability of quasi-mathematical moral principles which asserted that men
have these rights was at least part of his reason for defending them so adamantly against invasion, even if an invasion of them were to promote the
public good. It is hard to argue that he favored the protection of natural
rights over the promotion of the community's happiness merely on the basis
of epistemological considerations, but it is also hard to deny that Madison's
belief in an "undeniable" principle of natural law played some part in the argument of his *Memorial and Remonstrance*. There he confidently concluded
that the right to religious freedom was wholly exempt from the cognizance of
the institution of civil society and therefore not qualifiable by *any* reference
to the good of society. In effect, therefore, if he were confronted by the views
of those who were rational and perceptive enough to know what the principles of natural law or justice were and also by the supposedly opposed views
of those who were rational and perceptive enough to know what the true interests of society were, he would have unhesitatingly associated himself with
the former group of privileged minds. He rested his case for religious freedom
on an undeniable principle of natural law the violation of which could not be
justified by *any* appeal to the whole society's interests, however well supported by relevant evidence. In other words, he was not prepared to sur-
render the right to religious freedom by relying on an experimental statement
about what would make the people happy, partly because that statement
could not be as certain as the self-evident or demonstrable principle of natural
law which expressed man's right to religious freedom. Because *no* experience
could overturn a true principle of justice, whereas *some* experience could
overturn a statement that the public good would be served by an action, Madison seemed more inclined to favor the principle of justice.

Madison's attitude toward the right to religious freedom in his *Memorial
and Remonstrance* was very different from his attitude toward the right to liberty in *The Federalist*. When defending a Constitution which countenanced

slavery, he was forced to choose between the slaves' right to liberty and the slaveholders' right to property, and in favoring the latter he could, from a logical point of view, appeal to the permanent and aggregate interests of the community. This allowed him to remain comparatively silent about what he had once called the most oppressive dominion ever exercised by man over man, and to hold in effect that the slaves' inviolable right to liberty could be violated in the interest of the public good. This reveals a profound difficulty in an ethical theory which simultaneously asserts that rights are absolute and inviolable and at the same time that they may be violated in the interest of the public good. Such an ethical theory allowed Madison to insist in his *Memorial and Remonstrance* that the right of religious freedom was expressed in an undeniable principle of natural law which *could not be* suspended or violated out of concern for the public good and it also allowed him to say—with less insistence, to be sure—that the right of political liberty *could be* suspended or violated out of concern for the public good. In short, the alleged epistemological immunity of undeniable moral laws to refutation by an argument based on experience was not a real immunity. Even Madison, the great champion of justice to all *men,* could undo it in *Number 10* and in *Number 51* by using the word "citizen" in place of "men." Justice, *the* end of government in *Number 51,* was justice to citizens, not to slaves. And liberty in *Number 51* was liberty for citizens, not for slaves. In *The Federalist,* by carefully choosing "citizens," Madison managed to avoid attacking what he had once called the most oppressive dominion ever exercised by man over man.

By contrast, in the Virginia Debates on ratification of the Constitution, as we have seen earlier, Madison explicitly acknowledged that he was appealing to the public good in defending the "temporary permission" of trade in slaves. In his own defense he said that he would have conceived the clause attacked by George Mason as "impolitic, if it were one of those things which could be excluded without encountering greater evils," namely, the refusal of the southern states to enter the Union. The word "impolitic" is of special interest because it reminds us that in his letter to Jefferson of October 24, 1787, Madison criticized those who were too ready to forget a maxim that Madison himself accepted, namely, that "honesty is the best policy."[13] By "honesty" Madison meant virtue or virtuous action, that is to say, just action or action which respects the natural rights of others, and his maxim that honesty is the best policy was in accord with Locke's view that God had joined virtue and public happiness together by making the practice of virtue, honesty, or obedience to the law of nature conducive to the advantage or benefit of society.[14] But, Madison added as he commented on oppressive factious majorities, "they often proceed on the converse of the maxim" that honesty is the best policy since they hold "that whatever is politic is honest."[15] It might be argued, therefore, that when Madison replied to George Mason that it would be politic to countenance slavery, Madison was himself accepting the maxim that whatever is politic is honest. In doing so, he departed dramatically from the philosophy that dominated his *Memorial and Remonstrance* where he adamantly denied that the good of society—real or imagined—could be cited in defense of a violation of the natural right of religious freedom, a right which was supposedly absolute because it was expressed in a proposition that followed from an undeniable or self-evident principle of natural law.

Epistemological Dualism and Hamilton's
Concern for the Public Good

What I have just said shows that we must not exaggerate the role of epistemology in determining what position an author of *The Federalist* would take on the relative importance of natural rights and the public good. We must bear in mind that Madison and Hamilton accepted virtually the same epistemology of morals even though they occasionally assigned different degrees of importance to protecting natural rights and promoting the public good. With this in mind, let us briefly consider what differences they sometimes expressed on this fundamental issue. These differences do not emerge dramatically in *The Federalist,* where both men had to submerge their disagreement in order to stand united in their defense of the Constitution; as a consequence, their differences are expressed indirectly—by means of emphasis rather than by outright advocacy.

In *Number 37* the cautious Madison notes that among the difficulties encountered by the Philadelphia Convention was that of "combining the requisite stability and energy in Government, with the inviolable attention due to liberty, and the Republican form"; so it is evident in *Number 37* and elsewhere that Madison was torn by his commitment to the public good and to the private rights *of citizens.* When he compared energy and stability as "valuable ingredients" of good government with "the vital principles of liberty," he remarked characteristically on "the difficulty of mingling them together in their due proportions." And when he summarized his views on this difficulty, he said:

> The genius of Republican liberty, seems to demand on one side, not only that all power should be derived from the people; but, that those entrusted with it should be kept in dependence on the people, by a short duration of their appointments; and, that, even during this short period, the trust should be placed not in a few, but in a number of hands. Stability, on the contrary, requires, that the hands, in which power is lodged, should continue for a length of time, the same. A frequent change of men will result from a frequent return of electors, and a frequent change of measures, from a frequent change of men: whilst energy in Government requires not only a certain duration of power, but the execution of it by a single hand.[16]

In contrast to the judicious Madison, the flamboyant Hamilton was more agitated while praising the "energy and efficiency of government." In *Number 1* Hamilton wrote with passion when he anticipated what opponents of the Constitution would say:

An enlightened zeal for the energy and efficiency of government will be stigmatized, as the off-spring of a temper fond of despotic power and hostile to the principles of liberty. An overscrupulous jealousy of danger to the rights of the people, which is more commonly the fault of the head than of the heart, will be represented as mere pretence and artifice; the bait for popularity at the expence of public good. It will be forgotten, on the one hand, that jealousy is the usual concomitant of violent love, and that the noble enthusiasm of liberty is too apt to be infected with a spirit of narrow and illiberal distrust. On the other hand, it will be equally forgotten, that the vigour of government is essential to the security of liberty; that, in the contemplation of a sound and well informed judgment, their interest can never be separated; and that a dangerous ambition more often lurks behind the specious mask of zeal for the rights of the people, than under the forbidding appearance of zeal for the firmness and efficiency of government. History will teach us, that the former has been found a much more certain road to the introduction of despotism, than the latter, and that of those men who have overturned the liberties of republics the greatest number have begun their carreer [sic], by paying an obsequious court to the people, commencing Demagogues and ending Tyrants.[17]

It was typical of Hamilton to remark that zeal for the rights of the people would be more likely to mask ambitious despotic intent than would zeal for firmness and efficiency in government. That was his way of dealing with those who were, as he thought, excessively anxious about the aristocratic tendencies of the Constitution. "Firmness," "energy," "efficiency," and "stability" were the code words of those who laid greater stress on what they regarded as good government in the *true* interests of the people. And "the rights of the people" was the slogan of those who laid greater emphasis on the liberties which had been central in the rhetoric of 1776. It was clear from the start in *Number 1* where Hamilton stood on this substantive issue. But how was this connected with his views in epistemology?

Even though Hamilton believed that man's natural rights were expressed in self-evident truths whereas the public good could only be measured experimentally, he emerges in *The Federalist* as a more ardent champion of governmental energy and efficiency than of the people's natural rights. He adopts this position even though he agreed with Madison that the number of men who could accurately determine the true interest of the people was small, perhaps just as small as the number who could perceive self-evidence. So there would seem to be very little difference in the epistemologies of Hamilton and Madison which could explain their different views on the relative value of energy and liberty. Of course, one might argue that since Hamilton maintained that a few truths of political science were demonstrable, he might have believed that statements about the value of efficiency and energy in government were as demonstrable as any statement of natural law or mathematics. It might therefore be argued that Hamilton had less reason than Madison for preferring the protection of natural rights to the promotion of the public good, since both would be defended by Hamilton as though he were a political Euclid. But even Hamilton said in *Number 85* that a political truth could *rarely* be brought to the test of mathematical demonstration. Therefore, it is fair to say that Hamilton and Madison differed about the relative importance of protecting natural rights and promoting the public good even though they subscribed to a rationalistic theory of natural rights, to an empiricist theory of how to discover the public good, and to the view that very few people could accurately discover truths about natural rights or about the public good. So, although we can explain some things about *The Federalist* by referring to the epistemological views of its authors, we cannot, by referring to them *alone*, explain why Hamilton and Madison differed on one of the fundamental substantive issues in political ethics. Their agreement in epistemology does not entail agreement concerning all of the propositions whose method of verification they discuss. Two empiricists may disagree about the color of a desk and two rationalists may disagree about the truth of a mathematical proposition. Small wonder, then, that Hamilton and Madison might have disagreed about whether energy in government or natural rights should be favored even though both of them subscribed to the same hybrid theory of knowledge.

Final Remarks

We must not forget when we read *The Federalist* that Hamilton and Madison were lawyers and practical politicians who did not use what Hume called "a strict philosophic eye" whenever they came upon a profound philosophical problem. In saying this I do not wish to endorse the anti-intellectualism which has affected so many students of *The Federalist,* especially the kind I criticized at the beginning of this study. I hope that I have shown in the intervening pages that Publius's philosophy did not appear only in purple patches that served as mere ornamentation for the political technology that was his major concern. I hope that I have also shown that if we do not understand the philosophical ideas that I have tried to explain in this study, we will not fully understand the most important practical parts of *The Federalist.* The reader now knows—I hope—how misleading it is to say with Beard that Hamilton derived his "primary truths" merely from his studies of history and from the politics in which he participated; or to say with R. L. Schuyler that the prevailing view of the framers was expressed in John Dickinson's statement that "experience must be our only guide. Reason may mislead us." Even though Hamilton, Jay, and Madison were not closet philosophers, they read closet philosophers who pulled them in different directions, sometimes toward Locke's rationalistic theory of natural rights and sometimes toward Hume's empiricism in political science. Madison and Hamilton were so well read in philosophy that they sometimes lead us to think they will probe more deeply than they could possibly probe while pursuing their main object, that of successfully defending the Constitution of the United States. Still, as I hope I have shown, there is a good deal of philosophy in *The Federalist*—both explicit and implicit—and I believe that by extracting it and analyzing it we can improve our

understanding of what may be the most influential work in the history of political technology. In the misleading jargon of our time, Publius was not only
a pragmatist but an ideologist, and we can understand Publius the pragmatist
better if we know more about what Publius the ideologist thought. His ideology, or what I call his philosophy in this study, was fundamentally the same
as the philosophy we find in the Declaration of Independence even though
The Federalist was a long argument in favor of constructing a union of states
whereas the Declaration argued for dissolving the bands that connected those
states with Great Britain. But the guidance given by that philosophy was not
enough to solve all politico-philosophical problems, especially those that required pitting different private rights against the public good. In this respect
The Federalist leaves much to be desired, but then so do the works of many
great philosophers who did not have to defend a constitution while discours-
ing on justice and the good of the community.

So far in this chapter I have focused on Publius's idea that principles
about natural rights are tested by examining the relations between ideas,
whereas statements asserting that firm and efficient government would be in
the true interest of the people are tested by experience. And I have pointed
out that this epistemological difference between these two kinds of statements
did not of itself determine what position an author of *The Federalist* would
take on the question whether one should favor republican rights or good government. One may, while comparing *The Federalist* with the Declaration of
Independence, pose a related but different philosophical question to which
neither the men of 1776 nor those of 1787 had any clear answer. The question I have in mind is prompted by the fact that both documents assert or
imply that life, liberty, and the pursuit of happiness are, *all of them,* rights
which are expressed in self-evident, undeniable propositions. Consequently,
we may well ask how subscribers to both documents dealt with a case in
which two of these rights could not be simultaneously and successfully exercised. It is obvious that Madison virtually asked this question when he was
wrestling with his conscience over slavery. To insist that the slaves be given
their liberty, he seems to have said in reply, would violate the right of the
American people to pursue happiness by avoiding the dismemberment of the
Union, and therefore he accepted the continuation of slavery.

The reader should realize that I am trying to understand what may have
gone on in Madison's mind but that I am certainly not congratulating him on
his willingness to accept the continuation of slavery. Here I am mainly concerned to point out how vulnerable the moral rationalism of the Declaration
and of *The Federalist* was. Both documents attribute self-evidence or un-
deniability to each of a number of moral principles that were obviously in
danger of clashing with each other, and yet Madison, the other authors of
The Federalist, and the signers of the Declaration insisted that each of these
principles was as self-evident and as unconditionally true as they took the
principles of mathematics to be. Ironically, then, the authors of *The Federalist* were realists about man and politics who prided themselves on their
Humeian skill in balancing "a large state or society . . . on general laws,"

but they were not realistic enough about the Lockeian moral philosophy they accepted to see that it might get them into trouble of the kind I have just described. Having said this, I wish to point out that my main task in this work has been to clarify the philosophy of *The Federalist* and not to bury it. Justice Holmes once said in another connection: "When you get the dragon out of his cave on to the plain and in the daylight, you can count his teeth and claws, and see just what is his strength." In this work I do not think that I have pulled a philosophical dragon from the pages of *The Federalist*, but instead a philosophical hybrid, an offspring of Lockeian rationalism in morals and Humeian empiricism in politics.[18]

NOTES

Chapter 1. The Role of Philosophy in *The Federalist*

1. Letter to T. M. Randolph, Jr., May 30, 1790, *Papers of Thomas Jefferson,* ed. J. P. Boyd (Princeton, 1950–   ), Volume 16, p. 449.

2. Charles A. Beard, *The Enduring Federalist* (New York, 1948; reprinted in 1964), p. 9.

3. Ibid., p. 13.

4. Ibid., pp. 19–20.

5. Ibid., pp. vi–vii.

6. See note 1, above.

7. Beard, op. cit., p. 13. Also see my book *The Philosophy of the American Revolution* (New York, 1978), esp. pp. 78–94.

8. Robert L. Schuyler, *The Constitution of the United States: An Historical Survey of Its Formation* (New York, 1923), pp. 90–91. This view of Schuyler is criticized by Douglass Adair in his essay " 'Experience Must Be Our Only Guide': History, Democratic Theory and the United States Constitution," reprinted in Adair's *Fame and the Founding Fathers,* ed. Trevor Colbourn (New York, 1974), esp. pp. 109–111.

9. Max Farrand, ed., *Records of the Federal Convention* (New Haven, 1911–1937), Volume II, under date of August 13, 1787, p. 278.

Chapter 2. Hume's Experience and Locke's Reason

1. *Enquiry Concerning the Human Understanding,* in Hume's *Enquiries,* ed. L. A. Selby-Bigge (sec. ed., Oxford, 1902), Section IV, Part II.

2. Ibid., Section XII, Part III, p. 163.

3. Ibid., Section VII, Part I, note at end of Part I, p. 73.

4. Incidentally, it should not be supposed that, according to Hume, only the truths of mathematics are established by reason or reasoning. For when Hume distinguished between the demonstrative sciences of geometry, algebra, and arithmetic on the one hand and the experimental sciences on the other, he spoke of the objects of these two different kinds of sciences—relations of ideas and matters of fact—as comprising "all the objects of human reason or enquiry."

5. The passage I have been summarizing may be found in Hume's *Enquiry Concerning the Human Understanding,* Section V, Part I, note 1, pp. 43–45.

6. J. S. Mill, "On the Definition of Political Economy; and on the Method of Investigation Proper to It," *Collected Works,* Volume IV (Toronto, 1967), pp. 324–325. It may be of interest to observe that in his *Considerations on Representa-*

tive Government (1861), Mill called *The Federalist* "the most instructive treatise we possess on federal government" (*Collected Works,* Volume XIX, p. 555).

7. See reference in note 5, above.

8. Ibid.

9. Ibid.

10. Ibid., Section XII, Part III, p. 165. Hume used the term "natural philosophy" for physics, the term "physic" for medicine, and the term "politics" for political science in the passage cited. See Chapter 5, note 3, below.

11. Ibid., Section VIII, Part I, pp. 83–84. On Hume's distinction between what he calls "premeditated" experiments as used in physics and other sorts of experiments, see his *Treatise of Human Nature,* ed. L. A. Selby-Bigge (Oxford, 1888), pp. xxii–xxiii. Also see Chapter 12, below.

12. Hume, *Essays: Moral, Political and Literary* (Oxford, 1963; first published in the years 1741 and 1742), p. 561.

13. Ibid., p. 562.

14. See Hume's *Enquiry Concerning the Principles of Morals,* Appendix I, Selby-Bigge edition of Hume's *Enquiries,* pp. 288–289; also Appendix IV, p. 322. Also see my book *What Is and What Ought to Be Done* (New York, 1981), pp. 109–118, for an extended discussion of Hume's moral views. Hume believed that *experimental* reasoning might be used in establishing moral statements, but not *demonstrative* reasoning.

15. Hume, *Enquiries,* p. 293; Section V of *An Enquiry Concerning the Principles of Morals.*

16. Ibid.

17. C. D. Broad, *Five Types of Ethical Theory* (London, 1930), pp. 114–115. Also see D. F. Norton, *David Hume: Common-Sense Moralist, Sceptical Metaphysician* (Princeton, 1982), for a careful study of Hume's views on this question, esp. Chapter 3.

18. John Locke, *Essay Concerning Human Understanding,* ed. P. H. Nidditch (Oxford, 1975), Book IV, Chapter II, Section 1, p. 531; also see my *Philosophy of the American Revolution* (New York, 1978), pp. 17–18. The first two chapters of the latter work contain an extended discussion of many aspects of the doctrine of intuitive knowledge and self-evident truth as it affected the philosophy used by several American revolutionaries.

19. Locke, op. cit., Book I, Chapter III, Section 4.

20. Hume, *A Treatise of Human Nature,* ed. L. A. Selby-Bigge (Oxford, 1888), Book III, Part I, Section I, p. 463. In his *Enquiry Concerning the Human Understanding,* Section XII, Part III, p. 163, Hume criticized one of Locke's examples of a supposedly demonstrable moral proposition, namely, "Where there is no property there is no injustice." Locke presents this example in his *Essay,* Book IV, Chapter III, Section 18, pp. 548–550. For a discusion of the views of Locke, Hume, and Thomas Reid on this issue, see my *Science and Sentiment in America: Philosophical Thought from Jonathan Edwards to John Dewey* (New York, 1972), pp. 58–62, and esp. p. 60. Also see below, Chapter 6, note 6.

21. On the appeal to axioms in *The Federalist,* see Roy P. Fairfield's comments in his edition of *The Federalist Papers* (sec. ed., Baltimore, 1981), pp. xxii–xxiii; also p. 285, note 55. Fairfield remarks in the second passage that "Hamilton's discussion of geometrical, ethical, and political axioms is reminiscent of Spinoza's *Ethics,* though there is no necessary influence." Fairfield, like many other commentators on *The Federalist,* does not mention Locke in this connection. Such a

failure is often due to what Henry Sidgwick called a "complete misapprehension" which originates in the idea that "the founder of English empiricism must necessarily have been hostile to 'intuitional' ethics" [*Outlines of the History of Ethics for English Readers* (first ed., 1886; repr. Boston, 1968), p. 175]. For further discussion of this matter, see the material connected with note 11, Chapter 13, below.

Chapter 3. Using Abstract Reason in Morals and Politics

1. A. O. Lovejoy, *Reflections on Human Nature* (Baltimore, 1961), p. 46.

2. *The Federalist*, ed. J. E. Cooke (Middletown, Conn., 1961, p. 8). Throughout this work I shall cite this excellent edition of *The Federalist*.

3. Ibid., p. 297.

4. Ibid.

5. Ibid.

6. It might help to remark here that Madison says this while discussing Article VII of the Constitution, namely, "The ratification of the conventions of nine States shall be sufficient for the establishment of this Constitution between the States so ratifying the same."

7. I think it worth remarking parenthetically on the passage in Locke which is probably the model on which the Declaration rests when it mentions the "long train of abuses and usurpations" that imposes a duty on the colonies to revolt. The passage in Locke, unlike the corresponding passage in the Declaration, is descriptive rather than normative. Locke begins his discussion of the topic by saying that as a matter of fact a little mismanagement in public affairs, great mistakes by rulers, many wrong and inconvenient laws, and all the slips of human frailty "will be *born by the People,* without mutiny or murmur." But when he continues this discussion, he writes: "But if a long train of Abuses, Prevarications, and Artifices, all tending the same way, make the design visible to the People, and they *cannot but feel* [my emphasis], what they lie under, and see, whither they are going; 'tis not to be wonder'd, that they should then rouze [*sic*] themselves, and endeavor to put the rule into such hands, which may secure to them the ends for which Government was at first erected" [see John Locke, *The Second Treatise of Government,* Section 225 in *Two Treatises of Government* (Cambridge, 1970), ed. P. Laslett, p. 433]. Now, although the Declaration of Independence *begins* a discussion of the same topic by asserting *descriptively* that men are "more disposed to suffer, while evils are sufferable, than to right themselves by abolishing the forms to which they are accustomed," the Declaration shifts from a descriptive to an ethical gear in the very next sentence. For the Declaration reads at this point: "But, when a long train of abuses and usurpations, pursuing invariably the same object, evinces a design to reduce them under absolute despotism, it is their right, it is their duty, to throw off such government. . . ." Therefore, Jefferson and Madison, when he appealed to the "absolute necessity" of superseding a compact, were not asserting the psychological necessity expressed in Locke's words "they cannot but feel, what they lie under, and see, whither they are going"; rather, Jefferson and Madison were asserting a moral necessity or duty.

8. *The Federalist*, p. 352; Locke, *The Second Treatise of Government,* Section 123, p. 368.

9. Ibid., Section 13, p. 293.

10. *The Federalist*, pp. 59–60.

11. "A Full Vindication of the Measures of the Congress, etc.," *The Papers of*

Alexander Hamilton, ed. H. C. Syrett (New York, 1961), Vol. I, p. 47; also "The Farmer Refuted," ibid., p. 104.

12. Locke, *Second Treatise,* Section 6, p. 289.

13. Ibid., Section 4, p. 287.

14. Ibid.

15. Ibid., Section 54, p. 322.

16. Ibid., Section 89, p. 343.

17. *The Papers of Alexander Hamilton,* Vol. I, p. 46.

18. Ibid., p. 51.

19. Ibid., p. 86. I have modernized the spelling of proper names.

20. Ibid., pp. 86–87.

21. Ibid., pp. 87, 88–89.

22. Ibid., pp. 104–105.

23. Ibid., p. 122.

24. Ibid., p. 136. Much of what I report in the foregoing pages about Hamilton's views is discussed in my *Philosophy of the American Revolution* (New York, 1978), pp. 78–94.

25. *The Federalist,* p. 178. There is irony here. Hamilton the revolutionary appealed to the law of nature when justifying insurrection against Britain, but Hamilton the federalist appealed to it when justifying the actions of a people whose representatives failed to put down insurrection.

26. Ibid., pp. 193–194.

27. Ibid., p. 194.

28. See note 23, above.

29. *Papers of James Madison,* ed. R. A. Rutland et al. (Chicago, 1973), Volume 8, p. 299; also the note of the editors, ibid., p. 296, on Madison's role in drafting the Virginia Declaration of Rights; for Article XVI of the last, see R. L. Perry, ed., *Sources of Our Liberties* (New York, 1972), p. 312.

30. See my *Philosophy of the American Revolution,* p. 73.

31. Ibid., Chapters 1–3.

32. *Papers of James Madison,* Volume 8, p. 299. Notice that religion is *identified* with the duty we owe to our Creator and the manner of discharging or performing that duty. And when Madison says that the religious duty and the manner of discharging it *can* be directed only by reason and conviction, I think he uses the word "can" to refer to a psychological fact. In other words, Madison thought it would be psychologically impossible for a man to arrive at a religious belief by using anything but his own faculties. In this respect he agreed with something Locke said in *A Letter concerning Toleration:* ". . . such is the nature of the understanding, that it cannot be compelled to the belief of any thing by outward force. Confiscation of estate, imprisonment, torments, nothing of that nature can have any such efficacy as to make men change the inward judgment that they have framed of things. . . . It is only light and evidence that can work a change in men's opinions; and that light can in no manner proceed from corporal sufferings, or any other outward penalties" [*Works of John Locke* (London, 1823), Volume VI, pp. 11–12].

This creates a difficulty for both Locke and Madison. If a man's religious duty must, from a *psychological* point of view, be discovered only by his reason, and if the manner in which he discharges that duty is also psychologically necessitated in the manner described, then how can Madison go on to say that it is the *right* of every man to exercise religion as conviction and conscience may dictate? If a man's belief can only be caused by evidence and therefore cannot be caused by what Locke calls "outward force" and what Madison calls "force and violence," then any belief about God's existence, any belief about his attributes, and any belief about how he should be worshipped will be psychologically necessitated by the evidence. In that case, why does Madison say, in effect, that every man has a right to do what he cannot help doing, namely, use his own understanding or reason to support his religious beliefs? I have discussed this matter at length in my *Philosophy of the American Revolution*, pp. 197–202.

33. Compare Francis Hutcheson's comment on the statement "that our *Right* of *serving* GOD, in the manner which we think acceptable, is not *alienable.*" Hutcheson says that this right is not alienable "because it can never serve any valuable purpose, to make Men worship him in a way which seems to them displeasing to him." I quote this to support the view that when Madison says that "it is the duty of every man to render to the Creator such homage and such only as he believes to be acceptable to him," the word "him" refers to God, as it does in Hutcheson's statement. See Francis Hutcheson, *"Inquiry Concerning the Original of our Ideas of Virtue or Moral Good,* which is Treatise II of Hutcheson's work entitled *An Inquiry into the Original of our Ideas of Beauty and Virtue; In Two Treatises* (sec. ed., London, 1726). The passage I quote appears on p. 283 of this edition. I should add that in quoting Hutcheson's remark I do not mean to suggest that in his *Memorial and Remonstrance against Religious Assessments* Madison adopted Hutcheson's doctrine of moral sense. Hutcheson believed in the existence of unalienable natural rights even though he did not accept certain rationalistic views about what such rights were.

34. *Papers of James Madison*, Volume 8, p. 299.

35. Locke, op. cit., p. 11.

36. See my *Philosophy of the American Revolution*, pp. 195–213. C. N. Stockton has argued that "there is no clear and significant appeal to natural rights in *The Federalist*" [*Ethics*, Volume 82 (1971–72), pp. 72–82], even though he recognizes that some passages point in the other direction.

37. *The Philosophy of the American Revolution*, pp. 81–94.

38. *Enquiry Concerning the Human Understanding*, Section XII, Part III, p. 163.

39. Ibid., Section IV, Part I, p. 25.

40. *The Federalist*, p. 594.

41. Ibid., p. 591.

42. Ibid., p. 592.

43. Ibid., p. 594. The passage from Hume appears in his *Essays*, p. 125. Hamilton diverges slightly from Hume's text when quoting him. I present Hume's text.

44. Hume, *Essays*, p. 14.

45. At least one commentator on *The Federalist* has failed to see the gulf between Hume's philosophy of science and Hamilton's view that a political truth can be mathematically demonstrated. Garry Wills seizes upon Hume's remark that "consequences almost as general and certain, as any which the mathematical sciences afford us" may be "deduced" from "the force of laws, and of particular forms of government," and says that it expresses Hamilton's "ideal" when the latter announces his rationalistic Lockeian views on "primary truths or first principles" and their consequences in *Number 31*. Nothing could be further from Hume's epistemological views on morals or politics than the doctrine advocated in that number. See Garry Wills, *Explaining America: The Federalist* (New York

1981), pp. 90–91; also see note 25, above. I should add that Douglass Adair cites this same passage from Hume in the course of expounding the philosopher's view that politics may, to some degree, be reduced to a science. However, Adair does *not* argue that Hume was here expressing Hamilton's "ideal" in *Number 31*. See Adair, *Fame and the Founding Fathers*, p. 96.

Chapter 4. Using Experience and History in Politics

1. Madison writes: "Hence the number of Representatives in the two cases [small and large republics], not being in proportion to that of the Constituents, and being proportionally greatest in the small Republic, it follows, that if the proportion of fit characters, be not less, in the large than in the small Republic, the former will present a greater option, and consequently a greater probability of a fit choice" (*The Federalist*, pp. 62–63).

To make the matter more concrete, let us suppose that the small republic has 1,000 constituents or citizens and that the large one has 10,000. Let us also suppose that the minimum number of representatives is 200, in accordance with Madison's desire to guard against cabals of the few, and that the maximum number is 500, to avoid the confusion of a multitude. Finally, let us suppose that the proportion of fit characters among the constituents is 10 percent in both cases, thereby satisfying Madison's requirement that the proportion of fit characters in the large republic is *not less* than in the small republic. It follows that the small republic will have 100 fit characters as constituents, whereas the large republic will have 1,000.

Using these illustrative statements, we can see, first of all, why Madison says that the number of representatives in the two cases—that of a small republic and that of a large republic—is not proportional to the number of constituents. Because we have established an absolute minimum and an absolute maximum for the number of representatives—namely, 200 and 500—a small republic of 1,000 constituents in all would probably have 200, the smaller number of representatives, while the large republic of 10,000 constituents would have 500, the larger number of representatives. Therefore, the ratio of representatives to constituents in the smaller republic would be 200/1,000 whereas it would be 500/10,000 in the larger republic. Obviously, the first ratio of 1/5 is greater than the second ratio of 1/20. I should say in passing that given our illustrative numbers, the ratio would always be greater in the small republic. For even in the unlikely event that the small republic had the maximum number of 500 representatives while the large republic had the minimum number of 200 representatives, the ratio would be 500/1,000 or 1/2 for the small republic whereas that ratio would be 200/10,000 or 1/50 for the large republic. In short, the ratio of representatives to constituents in the case of the small republic would range between 1/5 and 1/2 whereas it would range between 1/20 and 1/50 in the case of the larger republic; and hence it would always be greater in the smaller republic, as Madison says.

The next point of Madison's to illustrate through the use of our numbers is that "if the proportion of fit characters, be not less, in the large than in the small Republic, the former will present a greater option, and consequently a greater probability of a fit choice." We have to show how, given the previous conclusion that the proportion of representatives to constituents is greater in the smaller republic *and the assumption that the proportion of fit characters is not less in the large than in the small republic,* that the large republic "will present a greater option, and consequently a greater probability of a fit choice" of representatives. Let us recall that we have assumed so far that the proportion of fit characters to the total number of constituents is equal, namely, 10 percent, in both republics and therefore not less in the large than in the small republic. Concretely, we have assumed that the small republic will have exactly 100 fit characters whereas the large republic will have exactly 1,000 fit characters. In that case, whether the small republic has 200 (the minimum) or 500 (the maximum) representatives, it will not even have a chance to fill all of the representatives' seats with fit characters. On the other hand, since the large republic has 1,000 fit characters available, it can easily fill all of the representatives' seats with fit characters. So, clearly, the larger republic will have a greater chance of producing a superior body of representatives in the first case, where the larger republic and the smaller republic have an *equal* proportion of fit characters. Now let us turn to the second case, where the larger republic has a *greater* proportion of fit characters than the smaller republic has, that is, more than 1,000. A fortiori, the larger republic will in this second case have a greater chance of producing a superior body of representatives.

2. Ibid., p. 62.

3. Ibid., p. 428.

4. Ibid., p. 429. Earlier in this number, Madison had said that the arguments in favor of having a senate are "suggested by reason, illustrated by examples, and enforced by our own experience" (ibid., p. 428).

5. Ibid., p. 429.

6. See above, Chapter 2, note 6.

7. *The Federalist,* p. 429.

8. Ibid.

9. See above, Chapter 2, note 5.

10. *The Federalist,* pp. 429–430.

11. Ibid., pp. 430–431.

12. Ibid., p. 431.

13. Ibid., p. 594.

14. Ibid., p. 535.

15. Ibid., p. 30. See Chapter 7, note 7, below, on Madison's use of the word "axiom" in *Number 44.*

16. Ibid., pp. 29–30.

17. Ibid., pp. 30–31. Hamilton says something similar in *Number 70* after trying to attack the idea of a plural executive by appealing to history. He says, characteristically: "But quitting the dim light of historical research, and attaching ourselves purely to the dictates of reason and good sense, we shall discover much greater cause to reject than to approve the idea of plurality in the executive, under any modification whatever." But when he tells us what the dictates of reason are, we can see that they are what Hume would have called experimental truths, for example, "Wherever two or more persons are engaged in any common enterprize or pursuit, there is always danger of differences of opinion" (*The Federalist,* p. 474).

18. Ibid., p. 31.

19. Ibid.

20. See note 4, above, on Madison's reference to reason, examples, and "our own experience." The relevant passages in *Number 63* show that his appeals to reason and examples were based on "experience in its broadest sense," by contrast to what he calls "our own experience."

21. See Farrand's *Records of the Federal Convention of 1787,* Volume II, under date of Aug. 13, 1787, p. 278. Also see Douglass Adair, " 'Experience Must Be Our Only Guide,' " *Fame and The Founding Fathers,* ed. Trevor Colbourn (Williamsburg, 1974), pp. 107–123.

22. See above, Chapter 1, note 8.

23. Farrand, loc. cit.

24. Hume, *Essays,* p. 125.

25. Hume, *Enquiry Concerning Human Understanding,* Section V, Part I, note 1, p. 44.

26. Hume, *Essays,* p. 125.

27. Hume, *Enquiry Concerning the Human Understanding,* Section X, Part I, pp. 110–111. Note that he says that *experience* is *our only guide in reasoning* concerning matters of fact, thereby showing not only that he made a statement very like Dickinson's "Experience must be our only guide," but also that he did not treat experience and reasoning as mutually exclusive where matters of fact are involved. Incidentally, Dickinson refers to "the elegant and ingenious Mr. Hume" and to "this great man, whose political reflections are so much admired," in the ninth of his *Letters from a Farmer in Pennsylvania;* and in his eleventh letter Dickinson calls Hume one "of the best writers" as he quotes from the latter's essay "Of the First Principles of Government." See Dickinson's *Letters,* ed. with an introduction by R. T. H. Halsey (New York, 1903; Kraus Reprint Co., New York, 1970), p. 88; p. 120, note C. See T. Draper, "Hume and Madison," *Encounter* 58 (February 1982), p. 38, for a reference to these passages in Dickinson's *Letters.* Also compare the phrase "elegant and ingenious" with Hamilton's reference in *Number 85* to Hume as "a writer, equally solid and ingenious" (*The Federalist,* p. 594).

28. Locke, *Essay,* Book IV, Chapter XII, Sections 9–10, p. 645.

29. *The Federalist,* p. 5.

30. Ibid., p. 6.

31. Ibid., pp. 21–22.

32. *Enquiry Concerning the Human Understanding,* Section VIII, Part I. Douglass Adair remarked on "the constant and reiterated appeal to Greek and Roman 'experience,' both during the Philadelphia Convention and in the state ratifying convention," " 'Experience Must Be Our Only Guide,' " *Fame and the Founding Fathers,* p. 114. Also see H. Trevor Colbourn, *The Lamp of Experience* (Chapel Hill, 1965), esp. pp. 4–6 and Chapter VI, for the colonial view of history's utility; and Carl Becker, *The Heavenly City of the Eighteenth-Century Philosophers* (New Haven, 1932), p. 95, where he cites not only Hume but also Charles Pinot Duclos in the latter's *Histoire de Louis XI.* On the same point, see the remarks by the editors of *The Papers of James Madison* (Chicago, 1975), Volume 9, pp. 3–4.

33. *The Federalist,* p. 27.

34. Ibid., p. 96. Adair has caught many of the appeals to experience in the *Records of the Federal Convention of 1787,* ed. Max Farrand (New Haven, 1911–1937); see Adair's " 'Experience Must Be Our Only Guide,' " op. cit., esp. p. 110, n. 5, where Adair gives deserved praise to Trevor Colbourn, *The Lamp of Experience.*

35. *The Federalist,* p. 128. The seemingly misplaced commas are Madison's.

36. Ibid., p. 159.

37. Ibid., p. 241.

38. Ibid., p. 349.
39. Ibid., p. 355.
40. Ibid., p. 51.
41. See above, Chapter 1, note 8.
42. Adair, op. cit., pp. 109–110; p. 111, n. 8.

Chapter 5. Causes of Factions and
the Question of Economic Determinism

1. For an extended presentation of some views on the speculative philosophy of history, see my *Foundations of Historical Knowledge* (New York, 1965; reprints, New York, 1969, and Westport, Conn., 1982), Chapters I and II.

2. Charles A. Beard, *An Economic Interpretation of the Constitution of the United States* (New York, 1913; reprint, New York, 1944), pp. 13–16. Beard does not attribute "the hypothesis of economic determinism" to Marx or Engels, but refers to "the theory of the economic interpretation of history" as formulated by E. R. A. Seligman in the latter's *The Economic Interpretation of History* (New York, 1902), p. 3. However, Seligman says that "Marx must be recognized as in the truest sense the originator of the economic interpretation of history" (ibid., pp. 52–53). Interestingly enough, when Beard takes occasion to mention European authors whom Madison had anticipated, Beard (op. cit., p. 14) mentions Ferdinand Lassalle but not Marx, whereas Seligman (op. cit., p. 54) says: "it is now conceded by the ablest students of socialism that Lassalle originated none of the important points" in the theory of the economic interpretation of history.

3. Hume, *Enquiry Concerning the Human Understanding*, Section XII, Part III, p. 165. This is the passage in which Hume singles out reasoning concerning general as opposed to particular facts. The important phrase in the quotation is "a whole species of objects." It is a whole species, therefore, which is examined by "politics, natural philosophy, physic, chemistry, etc.," whereas "disquisitions in history, chronology, geography, and astronomy" are said by Hume to be concerned with particular facts. See Chapter 2, note 10, above.

4. *The Federalist,* p. 57. One is led to regard this as a definition because of Madison's use of the word "understand." In other words, one supposes that he is presenting the meaning of "faction."

5. Ibid., pp. 56–57.
6. Beard, op. cit., p. 15.
7. *The Federalist,* p. 59.
8. See below, Chapter 11.
9. Madison's idea that there is more than one source of faction is emphasized by Douglass Adair, who rightly points out that when Beard tries to show that Madison subscribed to economic determinism, Beard does not quote enough from *Number 10* to make it evident that Madison believed that there are noneconomic as well as economic causes of faction. This is obvious if one reads pp. 58–59 of Cooke's edition of *The Federalist*—the seventh paragraph of *Number 10*—and then reads what Beard quotes from Madison on pp. 14–15 and 156–157 of *An Economic Interpretation of the Constitution* as well as Beard's exposition of Madison's views on the sources of faction. See Adair, "The Tenth Federalist Revisited," first published in 1951 and reprinted in *Fame and the Founding Fathers*, p. 86 and note 25 thereon. In fairness to Beard, one should note that in *The Enduring Fed-*

eralist, published in 1948, he says, for what it is worth, that Madison "was no 'economic determinist' in the strict Marxian line" (p. 15). And in fairness to Irving Brant, one should note that in *James Madison: Father of the Constitution* (Indianapolis, 1950), p. 173, Brant pointed out (without explicitly criticizing Beard) that in *Number 10* Madison "recognized the influence of differing opinions in religion, contrary theories of government, attachment to rival leaders and many other points which stir the human passions and drive men 'into mutual animosities.' " In this connection, see also A. T. Mason, "The Federalist—A Split Personality," *American Historical Review* 57 (April 1952), p. 634, note 32, where Mason rightly complains about Harold Laski's writing as follows in *A Grammar of Politics* (London, 1925), p. 162: ". . . as Madison wrote, 'the only durable source of faction is property.' " Laski seems to take the cake in the competition to misinterpret Madison's views for he baldly *mis*quotes Madison whereas Beard errs by omitting certain passages in *Number 10*. Mason properly credits B. F. Wright with having caught these errors in his paper *"The Federalist* on the Nature of Political Man," *Ethics* 59 (January 1949), p. 22. And, of course, we must remember that Adair, in his unpublished Yale doctoral thesis of 1943 (see note 52, below), had caught Beard's errors. Robert E. Brown, *Charles Beard and the Constitution* (Princeton, 1956), p. 29, also notes Beard's omissions in quoting from *Number 10*. For all I know, many other readers of Madison and Beard may have caught Beard's misleading quotations of Madison before Adair had in 1943; they seem so obvious.

10. *The Federalist,* p. 58.

11. David F. Epstein, *The Political Theory of* The Federalist (Chicago, 1984), p. 67, remarks that Madison's liberty to exercise reason is not identical with the political liberty he mentions earlier in *Number 10*.

12. In *Number 10,* Madison tried to account for the existence of *different* opinions and not for the existence of opinion *as such* when he cited the fallibility of man's reason and his freedom to exercise it. "Opinion" has sometimes been used in the history of philosophy to refer to what would better be called "mere opinion," that is, to opinion or belief which necessarily falls short of knowledge for various reasons. On the other hand, "opinion" is sometimes used neutrally, so that it may or may not refer to a true belief which meets other conditions that permit us to say that the holder of the opinions knows that his opinion is true. Because Madison is concerned to account for the existence of *different* opinions, we may question, as Oscar Handlin has pointed out, a statement by Garry Wills about this matter. Wills says that, according to Madison in *Number 10,* "opinion . . . is the result of reason's fallibility; if all knew perfectly, they would agree." It seems to me that in *Number 10* Madison is not trying to account for the fact that everyone inevitably lacks knowledge and therefore that everyone has no more than *mere* opinion on any subject. Madison thought that some men might have opinions for which they could supply evidence that would be sufficient to support their claims to knowledge, and therefore a factional difference between two groups could exist where one group subscribed to an opinion that constituted knowledge whereas another subscribed to a false opinion. In such a case the two groups would have different opinions even though one of them had a substantiated opinion and therefore knowledge whereas the other had "mere opinion." See Garry Wills, *Explaining America* (New York, 1981), p. 29; also Oscar Handlin's review thereof, *Reviews in American History* (December 1981), p. 426. The

interpretation of Madison I am inclined to support is borne out by the following statement that he makes in *Number 50:* "When men exercise their reason coolly and freely, on a variety of distinct questions, they inevitably fall into different opinions, on some of them" (*The Federalist,* p. 346). A typical use of the word "opinion" in *The Federalist* is illustrated in *Number 3,* where Jay considers the "opinion which the people of America have so long and uniformly entertained of the importance of their continuing firmly united under one Federal Government, vested with sufficient powers for all general and national purposes." Immediately after saying this, Jay adds: "The more attentively I consider and investigate the reasons which appear to have given birth to this opinion, the more I become convinced that they are cogent and conclusive" (*The Federalist,* p. 13). It would seem, therefore, that the opinion mentioned by Jay is not a "mere opinion" for him, since he thinks that cogent and conclusive reasons have given birth to it and may be adduced in support of it. I think Jay would not have hesitated to say that he *knew* that the people of America should be firmly united under one federal government vested with sufficient powers for all general and national powers, just because the mentioned opinion was supportable by cogent and conclusive reasons. Jay, along with his fellow authors, did not maintain that no opinion could attain the status of knowledge.

13. *The Federalist,* p. 58.

14. Locke's illustration concerning acorns appears in *The Second Treatise of Government,* Chapter V, Section 28. In *Number 10* Madison may be departing from Locke's view that an acorn becomes the property of a man as soon as he picks it up in a state of nature. By contrast, Madison seems to say that a difference in the amount of *property* in acorns that you and I hold arises only after government comes into existence.

15. *The Federalist,* p. 58.

16. Ibid.

17. See David F. Epstein, op. cit., p. 72.

18. *Papers of James Madison,* Volume 10, pp. 212–213.

19. For an extended discussion of Burlamaqui's views, see my *Philosophy of the American Revolution,* esp. pp. 213–221.

20. See my *Social Thought in America: The Revolt Against Formalism* (original ed., New York, 1949; most recent reprint, New York, 1976), pp. 121 and 123–124, where I misleadingly—as I now think—equate the statement that Madison's property-based factions are rooted in the diversity of human faculties with the statement that such factions are permanent.

21. The Marxian use of the word "ideology" varies. See T. B. Bottomore and M. Rubel in their *Karl Marx: Selected Writings in Sociology and Social Philosophy* (London, 1956), p. 5, n. 2. The use I have in mind may be found in Marx's Preface to *A Contribution to the Critique of Political Economy,* in Bottomore and Rubel, op. cit., p. 52.

22. Beard quotes this in *An Economic Interpretation of the Constitution of the United States,* p. 15, n. 1. The passage appears in Seligman, op. cit., p. 3.

23. Beard, op. cit., pp. 15–16.

24. See note 9, above.

25. Beard, op. cit., p. 157.

26. Ibid., p. 156. Also see Beard, *The Economic Basis of Politics* (New York, 1945), p. 17.

27. As we have seen earlier in this chapter, there is more to Madison's definition. Here I quote only that part of it which bears on the issue now under consideration, and I emphasize the word "or."

28. Although I agree with Adair about Beard's lamentable failure to quote certain passages from *Number 10* which bear on Madison's view of factions based on "opinions," I think that, in fairness to Beard, we must recognize the feature of *Number 10* to which I have been calling attention. Other aspects of this issue will be considered later in this chapter when I discuss the relationship between the views of Madison on faction and those of Hume on the same subject.

29. See Chapter 2, above, especially the material to which note 5 of that chapter is attached.

30. See Adair, *Fame and the Founding Fathers,* pp. 103–106.

31. Hume, *Essays,* p. 55.

32. Ibid., pp. 55–56.

33. Ibid.

34. Ibid., pp. 56–57.

35. Ibid., p. 58.

36. Ibid. Theodore Draper maintains that Douglass Adair was only "partly right" in giving Madison so much credit for going beyond what Hume had said about economic factions in "Of Parties in General." However, Draper does not show, nor does he even try to show, that we can find in Hume's essay the *thesis* of Madison that the most common and durable source of factions has been the various and unequal distribution of property. Rather, Draper asserts that "Madison's emphasis on 'the various and unequal distribution of property' could have come right out of Hume." See Draper's "Hume and Madison," *Encounter* 58 (1982), pp. 34–47, esp. p. 45. Draper supports his speculation by first pointing out that Hume, in his essay "Of the First Principles of Government," regarded the influence of property in politics as a commonplace idea, since Hume had pointed out there that James Harrington had "made property the foundation of all government." Draper tries to offer further support for his speculation about the possible source of Madison's "emphasis" on the various and unequal distribution of property by citing Hume's essay "Whether the British Government inclines more to Absolute Monarchy or to a Republic," in which Hume once again refers to Harrington's thesis. Draper acknowledges, however, that in neither essay did Hume accept without qualification Harrington's thesis that "the balance of power depends on that of property"; in fact, Hume denied the thesis. In any case, however, even if Hume had wholeheartedly accepted Harrington's thesis in both essays, Hume would not have been aserting Madison's thesis or proposition that the most common and durable source of factions has been the various and unequal distribution of property. Draper's observation that these essays showed an awareness on Hume's part of *some* connection between economics and politics, or of the influence of property in politics, hardly persuades one that Madison's full-fledged thesis "could have come right out of Hume." Indeed, I do not think that Draper adequately supports even his guarded speculation that Madison's "emphasis" on the various and unequal distribution of property—where "emphasis" need not refer to anything about factions—could have come right out of Hume. In this connection, it might be noted that in 1913 Charles Beard had given Harrington credit for anticipating the economic interpretation of history or the theory of economic determinism in politics. See *An Economic Interpretation of the Constitution,* p. 14, n. 3, where, curiously enough, Beard does not cite a work by Harrington but

rather H. A. L. Fisher's *Republican Tradition in Europe* (New York, 1911), p. 51. However, in Beard's *The Economic Basis of Politics,* first published in 1922 and republished several times, there is a quotation from Harrington. See p. 13, n. 3, of the edition published in New York in 1945.

I should like to make one more point about Draper's effort to minimize the difference between Madison and Hume on economic factions. In "Of Parties in General," Hume says that in despotic governments "the distinct orders of men, nobles and people, soldiers and merchants, have all a distinct interest." Draper, in trying to erase any difference between Madison and Hume, contends that "Hume's 'orders of men' became Madison's landed, manufacturing, mercantile and monied interests and classes." But Draper does not seem to be moved by the fact that only one of Hume's "orders of men" is prima facie economic in nature, namely, the merchants. Nor does Draper point out that in the very next paragraph Hume denies that "the landed" and "trading" parts of the England of his day— which *did* constitute economic orders of men—had distinct interests.

37. Hume, *Essays,* pp. 55 and 58.

38. Ibid., p. 58. Unlike Adair, op. cit., pp. 105–106, I stress the difference between (1) Hume's seemingly noncausal statement that factions from interest are the most reasonable and the most excusable and (2) Madison's obviously causal statement that economic interest based on the various and unequal distribution of property is the most common and durable cause of factions. Hume's view that factions in a free society may be eradicated, when it is contrasted with Madison's view in *Number 10* that they cannot be eradicated, serves to reveal a related contrast between the two thinkers on the subject of factions. However, it must be recognized that Madison thought that the Constitution was defective for not having given the national legislature a veto over the laws of state governments as a way of curbing factions. See his letter to Jefferson of October 24, 1787, *Papers of James Madison,* Volume 10, p. 212.

39. Hume remarks, however, that he can more easily understand factions based on "political principles" than factions based on "abstract speculative principles." Normally, he says, a difference about abstract speculative principle does not create a factional difference, but when different political principles "beget a contrariety of conduct," factional differences do occur and are more easily explained. If one citizen thinks that the true right of government lies in one man or family, he cannot readily agree with a fellow citizen who thinks that another man or family has that right. Each naturally wants his practical view to prevail and will, presumably, form a faction with others who share his view. By contrast, those who disagree about speculative principles—which contain no such words as "true right" or "ought"—and who form opposed factions on this basis, strike Hume as insane. He looks at their speculative doctrines, finds that their intellectual difference "is attended with no contrariety of action," and asks about all such speculative religious controversies: "What madness, what fury, can beget such . . . unhappy and such fatal divisions?" I cannot pursue Hume's reflections on this subject even though they are especially interesting as I write these words in 1984, when religious factionalism seems to be sweeping parts of the world. Instead, I must stick to my main task and return to Madison's *Number 10.*

Even though Madison may have had Hume's two kinds of parties from principle in mind when he spoke of factions based on "a zeal for different opinions" concerning religion and concerning government, Madison did not in *Number 10* express views as acidulous as Hume's on the subject of religious factions. However, Madison writes in the penultimate paragraph of *Number 10:* "a religious sect may degenerate into a political faction in a part of the Confederacy; but the variety of sects dispersed over the entire face of it, must secure the national Councils against any danger from that source." This shows that Madison explicitly allowed for noneconomic factions insofar as he allowed for the transformation of a religious "sect," which is based on a noneconomic principle, into a faction which would also be based, I presume, on a noneconomic principle.

40. It should be noted that in "Of Parties in General," Hume regarded Christianity, when it became an established religion, as a faction of *principle* so far as the people were concerned, and that he spoke of the philosophically minded teachers of this "sect" as having been "obliged to form a system of speculative opinions." My main point here is that Hume regards the words "opinion" and "principle" as equivalent. On this matter see Hume, *Essays,* p. 61. There he also remarks that after Christianity became the established religion, its principles of priestly government "engendered a spirit of persecution" which became "the source of the most inveterate factions in every government." He goes on to say, in a passage that Adair (op. cit., p. 105, n. 16) does not, in my opinion, interpret quite accurately, that "such divisions, therefore, on the part of the people, may justly be esteemed factions of *principle;* but, on the part of the priests, who are the prime movers, they are really factions of *interest.*" Hume's point here is that the same pair of factions—the Christians and their opponents—was based on differences of principle from the point of view of the people, but based on differences of interest from the point of view of the priests. By contrast, Adair interprets this passage in Hume as follows: "Hume, in keeping with his reputation as the great skeptic, feels that while the congregations of persecuting sects must be called 'factions of principle,' the priests, who are 'the prime movers' in religious parties, are factions out of 'interest.'" It seems to me that Adair fails to see that, according to Hume, the Christians constitute one and the same faction which is viewed in different ways by the people and their priests. The former think they are persecuting their opponents on the basis of speculative differences, but their priests, who are the prime movers, stimulate factional strife out of their own interest. In his essay "Of the Parties of Great Britain," Hume noted that the heads of factions are commonly most governed by interest, whereas the inferior members of factions are governed by principle (*Essays,* p. 65). I might add that Hume's skepticism is not involved here but rather his anticlericalism. Furthermore, Madison revealed a considerable degree of anticlericalism when he wrote in his *Memorial and Remonstrance Against Religious Assessments:* ". . . experience witnesseth that ecclesiastical establishments, instead of maintaining the purity and efficacy of Religion, have had a contrary operation. During almost fifteen centuries has the legal establishment of Christianity been on trial. What have been its fruits? More or less in all places, pride and indolence in the Clergy, ignorance and servility in the laity, in both, superstition, bigotry and persecution" (*Papers of James Madison,* Volume 8, p. 301). Compare this with Hume's statement "that, in all ages of the world, priests have been enemies to liberty; and, it is certain, that this steady conduct of theirs must have been founded on fixed reasons of interest and ambition" (*Essays,* p. 65).

41. For the moment we may content ourselves with observing that if action from interest is action in pursuit of advantage—as it was often construed at the time—and if there are noneconomic advantages, then it is obvious that a person or a group of persons may have noneconomic interests. See Chapter 7, below.

42. This is treated by Hume in the last and very brief paragraph of his essay "Of Parties in General" (*Essays*, pp. 61–62).

43. Ibid., p. 61.

44. Adair, op. cit., p. 105, n. 16.

45. Ibid., n. 17.

46. Garry Wills (*Explaining America*, pp. 211–212) sees more clearly than Adair how Hume's parties correspond to Madison's factions in *Number 10*, but Wills, like Adair, seems to have difficulty understanding the difference between Hume's personal parties and Hume's parties from affection. I repeat that the crucial difference is that *personal parties* for Hume differ or oppose each other because of "personal friendship or animosity among such as *compose* [my emphasis] the contending parties," whereas *real parties* from affection differ or oppose each other because they have different attachments toward certain individuals or families. For Hume, two differing parties from affection need not be composed of persons who are friendly to their fellow party members or hostile to members of the opposing party.

47. Adair, op. cit., pp. 103 and 105. In his essay "Hume and Madison," cited above, Draper says that Madison deliberately covered up his obligation to Hume in *Number 10*, and speculates that Madison may have done so out of deference to Jefferson's and John Adams's hostility to Hume. Madison, according to Draper, "must have been well aware that Hume was regarded as 'poison' in his own circle and even in that of Adams" (Draper, op. cit., p. 40). I am not convinced that Draper's speculation is supported by what little evidence there is that bears on the subject. I note that Publius, like many eighteenth-century authors, is not always scrupulous about citing authors upon whom he seems to depend; for example, Locke is never cited by him. I note that Madison did not hesitate to criticize Jefferson in *Number 49* on a fundamental issue. I also note that it is dangerous to rely on the general principle that one author will not cite another author favorably because the other author is "poison" to a third person who is a friend of the first author. For a discussion of how one student of Jefferson—Adrienne Koch—may have been misled by Jefferson's supposed intellectual animus toward Hume, see Lucia White's paper "On a Passage by Hume Incorrectly Attributed to Jefferson", *Journal of the History of Ideas* 37 (1976), pp. 133–135. Finally, I note that Jefferson himself was quite willing to write to T. M. Randolph, Jr. in 1790 that "several of Hume's political essays are good" (*Papers of Thomas Jefferson*, Volume 16, p. 449).

48. Hume, *Essays*, p. 58.

49. The point is that men disagreed about speculative principles before "modern times" without dividing into factions. Hume sometimes calls such groups "sects," as in "Of the Dignity or Meanness of Human Nature," *Essays*, p. 81.

50. Hume, *Essays*, p. 55.

51. See Chapter 11, below.

52. *Papers of James Madison*, Volume 9, p. 355.

53. Ibid., Volume 10, p. 213.

54. See Adair, *Fame and the Founding Fathers*, p. 102, n. 10, for a relevant reference to Madison's letter to Jefferson of October 24, 1787.

55. Hume, *Essays*, pp. 61–62.

56. *Papers of James Madison*, Volume 10, p. 213; Hume, *Essays*, pp. 55–56.

57. Farrand, *Records*, Volume I, p. 135 (June 6); I reproduce this passage exactly as it appears.

58. Ibid., pp. 422–423.

59. Ibid., p. 431. For a different version of Madison's speech of June 26, see the so-called Lansing version in *The Papers of James Madison,* Volume 10, p. 78.

60. The phrase "speculative philosopher of history" might also be applied to Hume and Mill because they urged that the effort to support laws of history by direct induction may be supplemented by the use of the a priori method of deducing these laws from more general propositions. To the extent to which Madison made such a use of the a priori method, he too might be called a speculative philosopher of history; for we have seen that Madison sometimes appealed to principles of human nature in this manner. However, I want to emphasize that while advancing his most distinctive causal thesis in *Number 10,* Madison tries to explain the existence of factions alone.

61. Adair, op. cit., pp. 87–88.

62. See Theodore Draper, op. cit., p. 37, n. 11.

Chapter 6. The Essence of Ideal Man and the Nature of Real Men

1. For an illuminating discussion of Hume's similar view of the study of human nature, see Barry Stroud, *Hume* (London, 1977), Chapter I. Hume makes it quite clear in the Introduction to his *Treatise of Human Nature* that "human nature" is studied by what he called "the science of man," and that "the only solid foundation we can give to this science itself must be laid on experience and observation." Hume also says in that Introduction: "to me it seems evident, that the essence of the mind being equally unknown to us with that of external bodies, it must be equally impossible to form any notion of its powers and qualities otherwise than from careful and exact experiments." See Selby-Bigge ed., p. xxi.

2. *The Philosophy of the American Revolution,* especially Chapters 2, 4, 5.

3. Ibid., pp. 78–94.

4. See above, Chapter 3, note 11.

5. Locke, *Essay,* Book IV, Chapter III, Section 18, p. 549.

6. See Chapter 2, note 20, above. The curious reader might consult T. L. Heath's translation of *The Thirteen Books of Euclid's Elements* (New York, 1956), Volume I, pp. 349–350.

7. See *Passive Obedience,* in *The Works of George Berkeley,* ed. A. A. Luce and T. E. Jessop (London, 1953), Volume VI, p. 35; also my *Philosophy of the American Revolution,* esp. pp. 150–152.

8. A. O. Lovejoy, *Reflections on Human Nature* (Baltimore, 1961), p. 6.

9. I doubt whether Lovejoy, when using the phrase "essential folly," intended to use the word "essential" so as to suggest that man's folly did not have to be discovered by the use of experience because it could be discovered merely by studying ideas and the relations between them.

10. Lovejoy, op. cit., p. 6. The passage is from Voltaire's *Dieu et les hommes,* published in 1769.

11. Bertrand Russell once wrote: "That this should be announced from Sinai would be as fruitless as Hamlet's report of the ghost's message: 'There's ne'er a villain, dwelling in all Denmark, but he's an arrant knave.' " See Russell, "The Elements of Ethics," *Philosophical Essays* (London, 1910), p. 20.

12. See Wright's Introduction to his edition of *The Federalist* (Cambridge, Mass., 1961), p. 27.

13. *Reflections on Human Nature,* p. 47.

14. *The Enduring Federalist* (New York, 1948), p. 15. Also see Richard Hofstadter, *The American Political Tradition* (New York, 1948), Chapter I, passim.

15. Gerald Stourzh believes that this essay by Hume exerted a strong influence on Hamilton; see Stourzh's *Alexander Hamilton and the Idea of Republican Government* (Stanford, 1970), pp. 101–102, where he deals with aspects of Hume's essay that are different from those on which I focus here. However, see note 23, below. Garry Wills, in Chapter 22 of his *Explaining America,* cites this essay by Hume in order to show that Publius, while not being obliged to accept Hume's estimate of human nature in toto, agreed with it to some extent (pp. 190–192). In this context, Wills is concerned to show, among other things, that Publius did not accept certain "Hobbesian" psychological axioms, as maintained by Robert A. Dahl in *A Preface to Democratic Theory* (Chicago, 1956), p. 8. On this point, see notes 41 and 42, below. Also see Chapter 11 below, where I criticize Dahl's interpretation of Madison's view of human nature on grounds similar to those adduced by Wills in *Explaining America,* Chapter 22.

16. Hume, *Essays,* pp. 82–83.

17. Ibid., p. 83.

18. Ibid., p. 84. In passing, Hume remarks that this favorable assessment is also attacked "by making an unfair representation of the case, and insisting only upon the weakness of human nature."

19. Ibid.

20. Ibid., pp. 84–85.

21. Ibid., p. 85. Here Hume appends a footnote in which he observes "what has been proved beyond question by several great moralists of the present age, that the social passions are by far the most powerful of any, and that even all the other passions receive from them their chief force and influence." Hume adds: "Whoever desires to see this question treated at large, with greatest force of argument and eloquence, may consult my Lord Shaftesbury's Enquiry concerning Virtue." Hume was referring to Shaftesbury's *An Inquiry Concerning Virtue, or Merit,* which appears in Shaftesbury's *Characteristics.* See note 24, below; also see below, Chapter 7, note 14.

22. Hume, *Essays,* p. 81.

23. See note 21, above. Hume's statement about the great power of the social passions by comparison to the selfish passions distinguishes his psychology—in this essay—from that of Publius, as we shall see in the next chapter. In this essay Hume argues that two things have led astray those who insist "so much on the selfishness of man." First of all, having observed that every act of virtue or friendship is attended with "a secret pleasure," they fallaciously concluded "that friendship and virtue could not be disinterested." They failed to see, Hume argues, that one feels a pleasure in doing good to a friend because one loves him, and that one does not love the friend for the sake of that pleasure. Second, Hume says, because it has always been found that the virtuous are far from being indifferent to praise, they have been represented fallaciously as having nothing in view but the applause of others. However, Hume thinks it unjust to depreciate a laudable action when we find any tincture of vanity in it, or to ascribe the action "entirely to that motive" on that account. Vanity, Hume thinks, is very different from other passions. Where avarice or revenge enters into any seemingly virtuous action, it is difficult to determine just how far it enters "and it is natural to suppose" that avarice or

revenge is "the sole actuating principle" of the action. However, Hume continues, "vanity is so closely allied to virtue, and to love the fame of laudable actions approaches so near the love of laudable actions for their own sake, that these passions are more capable of mixture, than any other kinds of affection; and it is almost impossible to have the latter without some degree of the former. . . . To love the glory of virtuous deeds is a sure proof of the love of virtue" (Hume, *Essays,* pp. 87–88).

Lovejoy, with characteristic learning and acuteness, observes that although "Hume liked to dilate in this edifying manner on the close kinship" between the love of glory and the love of virtue, Hume could also be more "realistic" about mankind in other places. See Lovejoy, op. cit., p. 186. We need not enter into the details of Lovejoy's views on Hume. However, it is worth repeating here that Stourzh, op. cit., pp. 101–102, argues that Hume's view in his essay "Of the Dignity or Meanness of Human Nature" influenced Hamilton's views on the love of glory. It is worth emphasizing that Hume advocated two distinguishable views in "Of the Dignity or Meanness of Human Nature": a psychological view on the comparative strength of the selfish and social motives or principles, and a moral view according to which selfish motives are vicious whereas social motives are virtuous. Because Publius was more concerned with psychology than with morals, Hume's psychological view is the one that merits comparison with that of Publius; and I think it fair to say that in the essay I have been discussing, Hume assigned less weight to the selfish motives than did Publius.

24. Lovejoy, op. cit., p. 25. On p. 53 of the same work Lovejoy denies a generalization set forth in Becker's *The Heavenly City of the Eighteenth-Century Philosophers,* where it is said that the following were essential articles of the religion of the Enlightenment: "(1) Man is not natively depraved; . . . (3) Man is capable, guided solely by the light of reason and experience, of perfecting the good life on earth. . . . The Philosophers . . . knew instinctively that 'man in general' is natively good, easily enlightened, disposed to follow reason and common sense, generous and humane and tolerant, easily led by persuasion more than compelled by force; above all, a good citizen and a man of virtue." Becker's full statement may be found on pp. 102–103 of the book which Lovejoy quotes.

25. Lovejoy, op. cit., pp. 51–52. Lovejoy makes clear that he attributes to Madison the view that the people *as voters* had depraved motives, but he does not emphasize sufficiently that there is an important difference between attributing such motives to people who are voters and attributing them to mankind as a whole.

26. Ibid., p. 41.

27. Even if one accepts Lovejoy's view (op. cit., p. 52) that for Madison "the total electorate was made up wholly of 'factions,' " it is doubtful that the community was, according to Madison, composed only of voters. Surely Madison included nonvoting women and children in the community for whose good the Constitution was being constructed. And since they were not necessarily members of factions, they did not necessarily have whatever objectionable motives were entailed by membership in factions.

28. Lovejoy, op. cit., p. 51. Madison's teacher John Witherspoon defended this principle, which he calls "overpoise." See below, Chapter 7, note 31.

29. Lovejoy, op. cit., p. 49. Also see note 28, above.

30. Ibid., p. 57. See Farrand, *Records of the Federal Convention,* Volume I, p. 512. I reproduce Madison's notes as printed in Farrand's *Records.*

31. Farrand, *Records,* Volume I, p. 584.

32. Madison's remark on July 11, 1987, about Morris's views on human nature has given rise to a comedy of historical errors in which Lovejoy—to his credit—had no part. The comedy seems to begin with the idea of Morris's biographer, Theodore Roosevelt, that Madison was trying on July 11 to disassociate himself from Morris's pessimism. Roosevelt writes "[Morris] throughout appears as *advocatus diaboli;* he puts the lowest interpretation upon every act, and frankly avows his disbelief in all generous and unselfish motives." Then Roosevelt continues: "[Morris's] continual allusions to the overpowering influence of the baser passions, and to their mastery of the human race at all times, drew from Madison, although the two men generally acted together, a protest against his 'forever inculcating the utter political depravity of men, and the necessity for opposing one vice and interest as the only possible check to another vice and interest' " [Theodore Roosevelt, *Gouverneur Morris* (Boston, 1898), p. 121]. Roosevelt does not cite the records of the Convention when he makes this misleading remark. But if one reads them, one can see that Madison was not protesting against Morris's "forever inculcating the utter political depravity of men." Madison was protesting against what he thought was an *inconsistency* between a position taken by Morris on a matter before the Convention on July 11 and Morris's tendency to assert the political depravity of men "on all [previous] occasions." Madison was not disassociating himself from Morris's views; on the contrary, Madison seems to have been trying to get Morris to agree on a certain political issue by reminding Morris what Morris had previously said about the political depravity of men.

If Theodore Roosevelt had seen this point more clearly, he would not have misled Charles Beard. In *An Economic Interpretation of the Constitution,* Beard appears to have relied exclusively on Theodore Roosevelt's statement about Madison's "protest" and did not cite the *Records of the Convention* on this matter even though Beard had been deeply immersed in the *Records* while writing his own book. Because he relied exclusively on Roosevelt's remarks about Madison's "protest," Beard was led to write: "This protest from Madison, however, betrays inconsistency, for on more than one occasion in the Convention he expounded principles substantially identical with those which he reprobated in Morris" (Beard, op. cit., p. 209). The result is ironical. Because Roosevelt, Beard's source, did not know that Madison was merely charging *Morris* with inconsistency, Beard was led to charge *Madison* with inconsistency. It should be noted that there is a difference between Roosevelt's quotation of Madison and what Madison says in the passage previously quoted from Farrand, *Records,* Volume I, p. 584. Roosevelt seems to have initiated a tradition of misquoting Madison as saying that Morris was "forever inculcating the utter political depravity of men," whereas what Madison had said (according to his own notes on the proceedings) was that Morris was "a member who on all [previous] occasions, had inculcated So strongly, the political depravity of men." Not only does Beard misquote in the manner of Roosevelt, but so does Richard Hofstadter, *The American Political Tradition* (New York, 1948), p. 7; like Roosevelt and Beard, Hofstadter does not cite the *Records of the Convention* or any other source for the passage about Morris that he attributes to Madison. On the other hand, Gerald Stourzh correctly cites the source in his *Alexander Hamilton and the Idea of Republican Government,* p. 245, in footnote 141 of Chapter III of that work. Stourzh, unlike the other commentators I have mentioned, sees the point of Madison's criticism of Morris. However, Stourzh shows no awareness of the remarks and therefore no awareness of the errors which had been made earlier by Roosevelt, Beard, and Hofstadter in accusing Madison of inconsistency when commenting on Morris's views of human nature.

33. *The Federalist*, p. 349. Lovejoy does not quote this passage in full; he omits the material in the first paragraph that begins with the words "if men were angels." I might add that Beard and Hofstadter had both cited *Number 51* in order to show Madison's alleged inconsistency in criticizing Morris's view of human nature. See Lovejoy, op. cit., p. 55.

34. "Of the Independency of Parliament," *Essays*, p. 40. Professor Sebastian de Grazia has called my attention to a similar thought of Machiavelli in his *Discourses*, Book I, Chapter 3: ". . . it is necessary for whoever prearranges a republic and institutes laws in it to presuppose all men criminal (*presuppore tutti gli uomini rei*)." See Niccolò Machiavelli, *Il Principe e Discorsi*, ed. S. Bertelli (Milan, 1960), p. 135. Also see Adair's reference to this passage in Hume as influencing Madison (*Fame and the Founding Fathers*, p. 102).

35. Hume, *Essays*, p. 42.

36. Ibid., pp. 42–43.

37. It is surprising that Lovejoy, who was so interested in what he calls approbativeness, should not have recognized the role that it played in Madison's thinking. In order to summarize what Lovejoy means by "approbativeness," he quotes the following from a phrenological textbook: "Love of praise; desire to excel and be esteemed; ambition; desire to display and show off; . . . desire for a good name, for notoriety, fame . . . and to be well thought of, sensitiveness to the speeches of other people, and love of popularity" (op. cit., p. 90). Approbativeness, one might say, was the desire that overcame honor when men joined in factious behavior, but this does not mean that it replaced honor according to Hume or Madison. Adair (op. cit., p. 102) recognized the impact of Hume's views of *political* knavery on Madison.

38. *The Federalist*, p. 96.

39. Stourzh, op. cit., Chapter III, calls attention to the influence on Hamilton of Hume's essay "Of the Independency of Parliament."

40. What Hume, Hamilton, and Madison emphasized more than some of the pessimists mentioned by Lovejoy emphasized was the role that membership in a group could play as a source of objectionable behavior. So important was this for Madison that he emphasized it not only when describing the behavior of men linked by a common passion or a common interest but also when describing the behavior of men who try to use their reason in arriving at opinions. He says in *Number 49* that "the strength of opinion in each individual, and its practical influence on his conduct, depend much on the number which he supposes to have entertained the same opinion. The reason of man, like man himself is timid and cautious, when left alone; and acquires firmness and confidence, in proportion to the number with which it is associated. When the examples, which fortify opinion, are *antient* as well as *numerous*, they are known to have a double effect" (*The Federalist*, p. 340). Although this point about *opinion* is not stressed by Madison in *Number 10*, it might well have been if Madison had not been so preoccupied there with the gathering of citizens into factions actuated by common impulses of *passion* and of *interest*. This is a convenient place at which to call attention to Hume's remark that "the influence of faction is directly contrary to that of laws. Factions subvert government, render laws impotent, and beget the fiercest animosities among men of the same nation, who ought to give mutual assistance

and protection to each other" ("Of Parties in General", *Essays,* p. 55). In that essay, however, Hume does not seem to *define* a faction as bad in itself, whereas Madison does in *Number 10.* For an interesting and relevant comparison between Madison's views on factions and those of Edmund Burke, see Benjamin Wright's Introduction to his edition of *The Federalist,* p. 33.

41. *The Federalist,* p. 378. See E. M. Burns, *James Madison: Philosopher of the Constitution* (New Brunswick, 1938), pp. 30–32. On p. 31 Burns correctly calls attention to the fact that Madison "did not really believe in the *total* depravity of man's political nature." In his notes on the Federal Convention, after presenting his remarks on Morris's views on the political depravity of men (see above, note 31), Madison may have shown how he could wobble about human nature. Farrand's *Records,* Vol. I, p. 584, show him saying, "The truth was that all men having power ought to be distrusted to a certain degree." But in a passage that Madison had crossed out, he had evidently written that the truth was that all men having power ought to be "both distrusted & confided in to a certain degree." See Farrand, Vol. I, p. 584, n. 7.

42. See Adair, op. cit., p. 302. I must acknowledge that in spite of making several statements which portray Madison as an extreme pessimist, Lovejoy also says, as it were, parenthetically that Madison "sincerely believed, as apparently did many of his colleagues, that they themselves were disinterestedly constructing a scheme of government which would make for the good of the people as a whole and in the long run" (op. cit., p. 52, and also p. 52, n. 16). And Hamilton, after saying at the Convention that mankind "in general" was vicious and governed by passion, also said in the same speech that "there may be in every government a few choice spirits, who may act from more worthy motives" (Farrand, *Records,* Vol. I, p. 381). Stourzh, op. cit., pp. 78–79, notes Hamilton's tendency to avoid saying that *every* man is corrupt and Hamilton's willingness to acknowledge that sometimes human nature rises above itself, in acts of bravery and heroism, as in "The Farmer Refuted," *Papers,* Vol. I, p. 156. Furthermore, Hamilton said in *Number 76* that "the supposition of universal venality in human nature is little less an error in political reasoning than the supposition of universal rectitude" (*The Federalist,* pp. 513–514). See also Garry Wills, *Explaining America,* Chapter 22.

43. James P. Scanlan, "*The Federalist* and Human Nature," *Review of Politics* 21 (1959), p. 659.

Chapter 7. Reason, Passion, and Interest

1. For a relevant example of Hamilton's use of a mechanical metaphor, see *Number 15,* where, in speaking of the difficulty of uniting a number of lesser sovereignties which have their own power, Hamilton writes that "there will be found a kind of excentric [*sic*] tendency in the subordinate or inferior orbs, by the operation of which there will be a perpetual effort in each to fly off from the common center. This tendency is not difficult to be accounted for. It has its origin in the love of power" (*The Federalist,* pp. 96–97). Also see Lovejoy, *Reflections on Human Nature,* pp. 39–47, where the notion of counterpoise is said to have been illustrated in mechanical terms by several seventeenth- and eighteenth-century writers. According to Lovejoy, they held that the centrifugal force acting on planets would, if not counteracted, mischievously send them off on tangents into space, whereas the equally mischievous centripetal force of the sun

would, if not balanced, pull them into it. The fact that both forces acted simultaneously on the planets to produce their happy rotary motion was, Lovejoy says, viewed as a mechanical version of counterpoise, whereas a psychological version of it was discussed by Pascal and Hooker, and a political version of it was presented by Mandeville, Pope, Vauvenargues, Helvétius, and others before it was advocated in Madison's *Number 10*.

2. See, for example, Hume's *Enquiry Concerning the Human Understanding*, Section VIII, Part I, passim, especially a passage such as "The same motives always produce the same actions: The same events follow from the same causes" (p. 83), in which Hume seems to view the statement before the colon as a special case of the statement after the colon. For Hume, therefore, the motive that produces the action causes the action in the same sense as any mechanical force causes an effect.

3. Samuel Johnson, *A Dictionary of the English Language* (first published, London, 1755; reprint, New York, 1979).

4. *The Federalist*, pp. 235–237.

5. For an illuminating discussion of the history and vicissitudes of this trio of motives, see Albert O. Hirschman, *The Passions and the Interests: Political Arguments for Capitalism before Its Triumph* (Princeton, 1977) esp. pp. 28–31, 43–44, and 46.

6. For a discussion of Jefferson's views on the rational power of blacks, "their rank in the scale of beings," and therefore their right to be emancipated, see my *Philosophy of the American Revolution*, pp. 115, 281–282. In his *Notes on Virginia*, Query XIV, Jefferson regarded the question as one in natural history and therefore as an empirical or experimental question; see *The Life and Selected Writings of Thomas Jefferson*, ed. A. Koch and W. Peden (New York, 1944), esp. pp. 260–262.

7. *The Federalist*, pp. 193–194. Hamilton says of an intuitive or self-evident first principle that it "contain[s] an internal evidence, which antecedent to all reflection or combination commands the assent of the mind," also that it is a truth that "carries its own evidence along with it" (p. 147). Madison agrees with Hamilton on the relation between required ends and authorized means but, characteristically, I think, makes his point with a minimum of philosophical machinery. In *Number 44* Madison writes: "No axiom is more clearly established in law, or in reason, than that wherever the end is required, the means are authorised; wherever a general power to do a thing is given, every particular power necessary for doing it, is included" (pp. 304–305). The use of the word "axiom" is enough to show the closeness of Madison and Hamilton on this issue, but Madison eschews the use of some of Hamilton's Lockeian epistemology while enunciating the "axiom" in question.

8. Ibid., p. 6.

9. Ibid. It is worth remarking that the authors of *The Federalist* did not express agreement with Hume's view that "reason alone can never be a motive to any action of the will." In spite of Publius's occasional brief forays into technical philosophy, he was, in Hume's words, "one that does not examine objects with a strict philosophic eye" (*Treatise of Human Nature*, Book II, Part III, Section III, pp. 413, 417). Indeed, Hume himself did not always examine objects with a strict philosophic eye, since we know that in his essay "Of Parties in General" he says that "different principles beget a contrariety of conduct" without bothering to qualify this statement by mentioning his view that reason alone cannot

cause an action. Like Hume in his *Essays*, Publius spoke with the vulgar on such topics; certain fine points of Hume's *Treatise* were not made in his *Essays* and they are even more foreign to the concerns of those who wrote *The Federalist*. For a very helpful discussion of Hume's view on reason as a motive, see Barry Stroud, *Hume*, pp. 155–170. For Hume's remark in "Of Parties in General," see Hume, *Essays*, p. 58. It is obvious from the context that the principles which beget—that is, cause—conduct are beliefs and, to that extent, rational.

10. See entries on "affection" and "passion" in Johnson's *Dictionary*.

11. See Johnson on "interest" as a noun.

12. *The Federalist*, p. 57. Lovejoy writes that "the 'passion' which Madison regarded as the chief source of the 'spirit of faction' is economic self-interest" (op. cit., p. 48, n. 13). Although Lovejoy therefore believes that Madison regards interest as a species of passion, the fact that Lovejoy puts "passion" in quotation marks suggests that he may have found the view or the terminology odd in some way. Perhaps he (incorrectly, as I think) believed that Madison's "or" in a "common impulse of passion, or of interest" was appositive.

13. Scanlan, in *"The Federalist* and Human Nature," *Review of Politics* 21 (1959), p. 662, cites *Number 71*, where Publius speaks of occasions on which "the interests of the people are at variance with their inclinations," where inclinations are passions. On the basis of this passage, Scanlan maintains that interests are motives which are "distinguishable from passions." My point, which will become clearer below, is that such distinguishability is compatible with the view that interests are a species of passions when passions are viewed broadly.

14. Anthony Ashley Cooper, Third Earl of Shaftesbury, *An Inquiry Concerning Virtue, or Merit* (Introduction by D. Walford, Manchester, England, 1977), p. 96.

15. Hume, *Treatise*, Book III, Part II, Section II: "All the other passions, beside this of interest. . ." (p. 491). Incidentally, in this same section Hume seems to hold a view about the comparative strength of self-interest which is different from the one he advances in his essay "Of the Dignity or Meanness of Human Nature." In the *Treatise* he views it as a very strong motive.

16. See Joseph Butler, *Sermons* in *Works*, ed. J. H. Bernard (London, 1900), Volume I, especially Butler's Preface and his Sermon XI, paragraphs 5–8, which appear on pp. 138–140.

17. See Francis Hutcheson, *An Essay on the Nature and Conduct of the Passions and Affections* (London, 1742; facsimile reproduction, with an Introduction by Paul McReynolds, Gainesville, Fla., 1969), Section II, Part II, pp. 29–34, where Hutcheson distinguishes between the general calm desire of private good and the particular selfish passions. It is worth noting that Hutcheson identifies the distinction with one made by "the Schoolmen" between *appetitus rationalis* and *appetitus sensitivus;* he also connects the distinction with things said in the ninth book of Plato's *Republic;* and, like Butler, he was very anxious to refute Hobbes's view that all of the particular passions can be reduced to self-interest. In the latter connection, see C. D. Broad, *Five Types of Ethical Theory* (London, 1930), p. 63–65.

18. Butler, *Works*, Volume I, p. 138.

19. Ibid., pp. 138–139.

20. Ibid., pp. 139–140.

21. Hume, "Of the Dignity or Meanness of Human Nature," *Essays*, p. 87.

22. Butler, op. cit., p. 139.

23. Hirschman, op. cit., p. 43.

24. Butler, op. cit., p. 139.

25. John Witherspoon, *Lectures on Moral Philosophy*, ed. V. L. Collins (Princeton, 1912), p. 12. See pp. 142–143 for references to works by Hutcheson and Butler.

26. *The Federalist*, p. 58.

27. See above, Chapter 5, note 42.

28. David F. Epstein, unlike many commentators, properly emphasizes this point (*The Political Theory of* The Federalist, p. 86).

29. *Papers of James Madison*, Volume 9, pp. 140–141.

30. In *Number 17* Hamilton uses the word "counterpoise" when describing certain relationships between the states and the Union (*The Federalist*, p. 108). In *Number 73* Hamilton speaks of "the counterpoising weight of the executive" in contrast with that of the legislature (p. 498). Incidentally, there are extended entries on "counterpoise" as a verb and noun in Johnson's *Dictionary;* they are illustrated by interesting and relevant passages in Bacon, Shakespeare, Milton, Swift, and Boyle. Some uses are physical, some economic, some political. Not all of these passages accord with Lovejoy's use of the word when he says that it refers to "accomplishing desirable results by balancing harmful things against one another" (op. cit., p. 39). Often it is used neutrally so that it does not refer to a balancing of harmful things which produces *desirable* results.

31. Witherspoon, op. cit., p. 94.

Chapter 8. On the Strength of Different Motives

1. *The Federalist*, p. 31.

2. Ibid., p. 142.

3. Ibid., p. 340.

4. Ibid., p. 374. Madison here adds his much-quoted observation that "had every Athenian citizen been a Socrates; every Athenian assembly would still have been a mob."

5. Ibid., pp. 395–396.

6. Ibid., p. 488.

7. Ibid., p. 505.

8. Lovejoy, *Reflections on Human Nature*, p. 52; also note 16 thereon. Also see Chapter 6, note 42, of the present work. In connection with Lovejoy's remark on competent historians of his day, it should be recalled that his book was published in 1961.

9. See my *Philosophy of the American Revolution*, pp. 78–96.

10. *The Federalist*, p. 195.

11. See Chapter 6, note 5, above.

12. In my discussion of this topic I am indebted to Scanlan, "*The Federalist* and Human Nature," cited in Chapter 7, n. 13, but my analysis of the important subdivisions diverges from Scanlan's in certain respects.

13. Hutcheson, *An Essay on the Nature and Conduct of the Passions and Affections*, pp. 29–30.

14. See Scanlan, op. cit., p. 663, who refers to relevant remarks by Jay in *Number 5* (pp. 24–25), by Madison in *Number 62* (p. 420), and by Hamilton in *Number 1* (p. 5), *Number 5* (p. 27), and *Number 6* (p. 32). It may be noted here that in *Number 62* Madison explicitly acknowledges the fact that we may

attribute passions—which he calls "emotions" here—to nations as well as to individuals, saying: "One nation is to another what one individual is to another; with this melancholy distinction perhaps, that the former with fewer of the benevolent emotions than the latter, are under fewer restraints also from taking undue advantage of the indiscretions of each other" (p. 420). It should be added that although Madison makes a possible distinction between, as it were, the emotional life of a nation and that of an individual, he never tells us how an attribution of an emotion to a nation is linked with statements about the individuals who compose the nation.

15. Witherspoon, op. cit., p. 13. Witherspoon's statement that he was here making a distinction while examining "our nature as it really is," as opposed to discussing "the nature of virtue," may be contrasted with Hume's conflation of a psychological and a moral issue in a passage we have met in the previous chapter: "Were our selfish and vicious principles [motives] so much predominant above our social and virtuous, as is asserted by some philosophers, we ought undoubtedly to entertain a contemptible notion of human nature." As we have seen, Hume's use of the epithets "vicious" and "virtuous" imports a moral issue which is distinguishable from the issue as to the predominance of the selfish over the social motives; and it was the latter issue that was of major concern to Publius as well as to Witherspoon when he was discussing "our nature as it really is." See Hume, *Essays,* p. 85; also Chapter 6, note 23, above.

I say that Publius's subdivision of an individual's particular passions into those that are public and those that are selfish was *not unlike* Witherspoon's subdivision of them into harmonious and hostile passions, merely because a distinction may be drawn between selfish passions that are hostile and those that are not. Since the gratification of a selfish passion such as the love of fame may bring pleasure or happiness to the person who has the passion without necessarily bringing pain or unhappiness to another person, a selfish passion need not be a hostile passion. By contrast, revenge is a passion which is both selfish and hostile because gratification of it not only brings some sort of pleasure to the person who takes revenge but also brings pain to the person upon whom revenge is taken. Insofar, then, as a passion is selfish but not hostile, it may be called "nonsocial" as opposed to "antisocial" because it gratifies the selfish person without harming others in society.

16. In *Number 72* (p. 488), Hamilton presents us with an example of an individual who may be motivated by his own interest and also by a sociable or public interest in the good of the community, namely, the president of the United States. His own interest would be illustrated by his "desire of reward," which Hamilton calls "one of strongest incentives of human conduct." On the other hand, the president may "plan and undertake extensive and arduous enterprises for the public benefit," in which case he might be said to be motivated by a sociable or public interest.

17. Scanlan, op. cit., p. 663.

18. *The Federalist,* pp. 28–29. Here, it should be noted, Hamilton seems to say that private interests are private passions, since those interests are listed as passions, along with attachments, enmities, hopes, and fears.

19. *The Federalist,* p. 4.

20. Ibid., p. 31.

21. Ibid., p. 62.

22. Jeremy Bentham, *An Introduction to the Principles of Morals and Legis-*

lation, ed. J. H. Burns and H. L. A. Hart (London, 1970), p. 12. In passing, we may observe that Bentham writes as follows in a footnote to the last passage quoted: "Interest is one of those words, which not having any superior *genus,* cannot in the ordinary way be defined."

23. *The Federalist,* p. 57.

24. Ibid., p. 318.

25. Ibid., p. 283.

26. Bentham, loc. cit.

27. *The Federalist,* pp. 6 and 62.

28. Farrand, *Records of the Federal Convention,* Volume I, p. 422.

29. At a certain point in Scanlan's discussion of immediate interests, op. cit., he begins by giving the impression not only that true and immediate interests motivate individuals alone—a view I have already questioned—but also that true interests are "those which, objectively and in the long run, are of greatest importance to the individual: that is, permanent benefits, comprehensive benefits, and benefits which are ultimate or distant results of present action." On the other hand, according to Scanlan, immediate interests "are any benefits which pertain directly to the individual's present situation, and for that reason most easily gain his attention." From this one *might* conclude that, according to Publius, an interest which is true cannot be immediate, and conversely. Yet Scanlan writes: "An interest, of course, may be both true and immediate. But the authors make the distinction because they find that very often this is not the case: in a given situation, immediate interests may be of no great or lasting importance, and are likely to conflict with true interests."

The passages cited by Scanlan in support of what he says about this distinction all seem to treat immediate interests as those which motivate men who have their eyes on short-term gains. One passage comes from *Number 6,* where Hamilton comments on the weakness of a nation's "momentary passions and immediate interests" (*The Federalist,* p. 31) by comparison with general and remote considerations of utility—which we may identify with true interest. The coupling of *momentary* passions and *immediate* interests suggests that the latter not only involve benefits that are in the near future but also that they are short-lived benefits. A second passage comes from *Number 10,* where Madison contrasts "indirect and remote considerations, which will rarely prevail over the immediate interest which one party [faction] may find in disregarding the rights of another, or the good of the whole" (*The Federalist,* p. 60). Here the immediate interest, because it is contrasted with "remote considerations," seems to be an interest in benefits that will not only come quickly but also disappear so quickly as not to exist in the remote future. A third passage comes from *Number 15,* where Hamilton argues that one cannot depend on treaties "which oppose general considerations of peace and justice to the impulse of any immediate interest and passion" (*The Federalist,* p. 94). The use of the word "impulse" here suggests that the immediate interest involves a benefit that arrives quickly and leaves quickly. A fourth and final passage in *Number 15* puts "immediate interests or aims" into apposition with "momentary conveniences" (*The Federalist,* p. 97), where the word "momentary" clearly refers to a convenience that is short-lived.

I wonder whether we can consistently say that, according to Publius, (1) a true interest involves, among other things, a benefit which is a distant result of present action and (2) an interest may be both true and immediate. I say this because it would appear that, for Publius, an immediate interest moves us to perform an action if and only if we think it will bring us benefits in the immediate future, which is to say, in the *near* future. In that case, how can a true interest, which involves benefits in the distant future, also be an immediate interest? According to Publius, action from immediate interest often involves looking forward to temporally immediate gains or benefits, and we are motivated to perform an action by an immediate interest if and only if we are motivated by the prospect of a benefit which comes directly after the action, without anything intervening. But can such a benefit continue beyond the moment, or is it necessarily brief? Strictly speaking, immediate arrival leaves open the question as to how long the benefit can last, but it seems to preclude *arrival* of the benefit at a distant point in the future. My own view is that Publius was not thinking very carefully about the possibility that an immediate benefit, when viewed literally, *could* last forever; therefore, he regarded action from an immediate interest as one in which an individual foresees a quick *and* short-term gain. When he refers to immediate interests, he is likely to refer to it in a deprecatory manner as something short-lived and therefore not to be followed by a nation with a desire to endure and to prosper. See Scanlan, op. cit., pp. 663–664.

30. In the foregoing I have concentrated on contexts in which Publius contrasts true interests with immediate interests and therefore on benefits that are expected to follow immediately in a temporal sense. But readers of eighteenth-century British philosophy know that Hutcheson, for example, distinguishes between (1) goods which are perceived to be immediately pleasant or good, such as *"Meats, Drink, Harmony, fine Prospects, Painting, Statues,"* and (2) *"Riches and Power,"* which our reason shows us to be mediately good. Both of these kinds of goods are said by Hutcheson to be "pursued from *Interest, or Self-Love.*" See Hutcheson, *An Inquiry Concerning the Original of Our Ideas of Virtue or Moral Good,* which is Treatise II of *An Inquiry into the Original of our Ideas of Beauty and Virtue* (sec. ed., London, 1726), pp. 113–114. If fine prospects and riches are both said to be pursued from interest, then we may speak of an *im*mediate interest in fine prospects and a mediate interest in riches. Here the immediacy of the interest in fine prospects depends on the fact that reason is not used in perceiving it to be a means to something else, and not on the fact that the pleasure gained from fine prospects occurs quickly after looking at them. It should be noted that there are passages in *The Federalist* where "immediate interest" is used in this nontemporal manner, as when it is said in *Number 73* that the executive has an "immediate interest in the power of his office" (*The Federalist,* p. 497).

31. *Papers of James Madison,* Volume 10, p. 213.

32. *The Federalist,* p. 61.

33. Ibid., p. 283.

34. Ibid., p. 31.

35. *Papers of James Madison,* Volume 8, p. 299. Here Madison might well have called upon at least part of what Locke wrote in the *Second Treatise:*

> For when any number of Men have, by the consent of every individual, made a *Community,* they have thereby made that *Community* one Body, with a Power to Act as one Body, which is only by the will and determination of the *majority.* For that which acts [i.e., actuates] any Community, being only the consent of the individuals of it, and it being necessary to that which is one body to move one way; it is necessary the Body should move that way whither the greater force carries it, which is the *consent of the majority:* or else it is impossible it should act or continue one Body,

one Community, which the consent of every individual that united into it, agreed that it should; and so every one is bound by that consent to be concluded by the *majority.* And therefore we see that in Assemblies impowered to act by positive Laws where no number is set by that positive Law which impowers them, the *act of the Majority* passes for the act of the whole, and of course determines, as having by the Law of Nature and Reason, the power of the whole (*Two Treatises of Government,* Chapter VIII, Section 96, pp. 349–350).

However, it must be realized that Madison does not seem to sanction a majority's invading the natural rights of an individual, no matter how much a society might gain by such an invasion.

36. *The Federalist,* p. 107.
37. Ibid.
38. Ibid.
39. Ibid.
40. Ibid.
41. Ibid., p. 108.
42. Ibid.
43. See my *Philosophy of the American Revolution,* Chapters 1 and 2.
44. *The Federalist,* p. 590.
45. Ibid., p. 194.
46. Scanlan, op. cit., p. 669.
47. Jonathan Elliott, ed., *The Debates in the Several State Conventions on the Adoption of the Federal Constitution* (Washington, 1836), Volume III, pp. 536–537.

Chapter 9. Motive, Opportunity, and Action:
The Principle of Causality at Work

1. *The Federalist,* p. 60.
2. Ibid. See David F. Epstein, *The Political Theory of* The Federalist, p. 89; Epstein rightly observes that a faction's "effects" are its deeds.
3. *Papers of James Madison,* Volume 10, p. 214.
4. Ibid., p. 213.
5. Ibid.
6. Ibid.
7. Ibid., pp. 213–214. Similar observations on inefficacious motives appear in Madison's *Vices of the Political System of the United States, Papers of James Madison,* Volume 9, pp. 355–356. In his speech to the Convention on June 6, he seems to associate what he calls "Conscience" with "Religion" when dismissing inefficacious motives (Farrand, *Records of the Federal Convention,* Volume I, p. 135). For an expression of Locke's views on enthusiasm, which he says abandons reason and revelation and "substitutes in the room of it, the ungrounded Fancies of a Man's own Brain," see his *Essay,* Book IV, Chapter XIX. Also see my *Science and Sentiment in America* (New York, 1972), pp. 26–27. Also compare Madison's deprecation of enthusiasm with Hume's in the latter's "Of Superstition and Enthusiasm," *Essays,* pp. 75–80.
8. *The Federalist,* p. 60.
9. Ibid., pp. 60–61.
10. Ibid., p. 61.

11. Ibid.

12. It is interesting to observe that Hamilton referred to "powers and opportunities" to act in what he contributed to Washington's Farewell Address. Hamilton speaks there of "the powers and opportunities of resistance of a numerous and wide extended nation," saying that they "defy the successful efforts of the ordinary military force or of any assemblages which wealth and patronage may call to their aid" [V. H. Paltsits, *Washington's Farewell Address* (New York, reprint ed., 1935), pp. 189–190]. I cite this passage only to show that at least one author of *The Federalist* saw the need to refer to powers or abilities, as well as opportunities, when discussing the conditions of action. Also see *Number 33,* where Hamilton writes: "What is a power, but the ability or faculty of doing a thing?" (*The Federalist,* p. 204).

13. *The Federalist,* p. 61.

14. Ibid., p. 64.

15. Ibid., p. 61.

16. Ibid., p. 64.

17. Ibid., p. 62.

18. Ibid., p. 251.

19. Ibid., p. 63.

20. Ibid., p. 84.

21. Ibid., p. 52.

22. Ibid., p. 84.

23. *Papers of James Madison,* Volume 10, p. 214.

24. *The Federalist,* p. 85.

25. *Papers of James Madison,* Volume 10, p. 212.

26. *The Federalist,* p. 64.

27. Ibid., pp. 351–352.

28. Ibid., p. 64.

29. Ibid.

30. Ibid.

31. Ibid., p. 63.

32. Ibid., p. 194.

33. Hume, *Treatise of Human Nature,* Book I, Part III, Section III (Selby-Bigge ed., 1888, p. 82).

Chapter 10. Combining and Separating Motives and Opportunities

1. *The Federalist,* p. 14.

2. Ibid., pp. 14–15.

3. Ibid., p. 15.

4. Ibid.

5. Ibid., pp. 15–16.

6. Ibid., p. 16.

7. Ibid.

8. Ibid.

9. Ibid.

10. Ibid., p. 17.

11. Ibid.

12. Ibid.

13. Ibid.

14. Ibid., p. 18.
15. Ibid., p. 20.
16. Ibid., p. 22.
17. Ibid., p. 26.
18. Ibid., p. 28.
19. Ibid., p. 36.
20. Ibid., p. 43.
21. Ibid., p. 50.
22. Ibid., p. 52.
23. Ibid.
24. Ibid., p. 53.
25. Ibid., pp. 50, 52, and 54.
26. Ibid., pp. 53–54.
27. Ibid., p. 54.
28. Ibid., p. 96. See Hume's *Essays,* p. 55. B. F. Wright says that Hamilton's use of the word "suppress" distinguishes his view of factions from that of Madison, but then seems to withdraw the idea that there was a great difference between them. See Wright's Introduction to his edition of *The Federalist,* pp. 17–18.
29. *The Federalist,* p. 131. Hume observed something like this in "Of Parties in General" when he said that "in despotic governments, indeed, factions often do not appear; but they are not the less real; or rather, they are more real and more pernicious upon that very account" (*Essays,* p. 58).
30. *The Federalist,* p. 141.
31. Ibid., p. 173.
32. Ibid., p. 402.
33. Ibid., p. 413.
34. Ibid., p. 439.
35. Ibid., p. 444.
36. Ibid., pp. 481–482.
37. A. T. Mason, "The Federalist—Split Personality," *American Historical Review* 57 (1952), pp. 625–643; J. Q. Adams, *An Eulogy on the Life and Character of James Madison* (Boston, 1836), p. 32.
38. *The Federalist,* p. 471.
39. Mason, op. cit., pp. 636–638.
40. Ibid., pp. 636–637.
41. *The Federalist,* p. 523.
42. Ibid., p. 526.
43. See Farrand, *Records of the Convention,* Volume I, pp. 146–147, where Hamilton's notes are reproduced. Also see Douglass Adair's Yale Ph.D. dissertation, *The Intellectual Origins of Jeffersonian Democracy* (1943), pp. 275–276, for some comments on these notes.
44. *The Federalist,* p. 349.
45. Ibid., p. 96.
46. Ibid., p. 349. See Chapter 6, above, p. 160.
47. Ibid., pp. 350–351.
48. Ibid., p. 8.
49. Ibid., pp. 347–348.
50. Ibid., p. 348.
51. Ibid., pp. 348–349.

52. Ibid., p. 324.
53. Ibid., p. 204.
54. Ibid., p. 349.
55. Ibid., p. 351.
56. Ibid.
57. Ibid., p. 352.
58. Ibid.
59. Ibid., p. 351.
60. Ibid., p. 353.
61. Ibid.
62. Ibid.
63. For an illuminating discussion of this point, see J. P. Scanlan's Ph.D. dissertation, *The Concept of Interest in* The Federalist: *A Study of the Structure of a Political Theory* (University of Chicago, August 1956), pp. 131–132.
64. *Papers of James Madison,* Volume 10, pp. 212–214, 205–206. Also see Chapter 9, above, material connected with note 29.
65. *Papers of James Madison,* Volume 10, p. 212.
66. Ibid., p. 214.
67. David F. Epstein, *The Political Theory of* The Federalist, pp. 103–104; Farrand, *Records,* Volume I, pp. 135–136.
68. Farrand, op. cit.
69. Epstein, op. cit., pp. 135–136 and 214, n. 125.
70. *The Federalist,* p, 294.
71. The view of Madison I have been discussing is also present in his *Vices of the Political System of the United States, Papers of James Madison,* Volume 9, pp. 350–351. See also Epstein, op. cit., p. 104.
72. Jonathan Elliott, *Debates,* Volume III, p. 453, under date of June 15, 1788.

Chapter 11. The Nonnaturalistic Ethics of Natural Rights

1. *A Preface to Democratic Theory* (Chicago, 1956).
2. Ibid., p. 5.
3. Ibid., p. 6, n. 1.
4. See Chapter 6, above, especially the sections "Realism and Pessimism" and "Man as a Knave in Politics"; also notes 15, 41, and 42 therein.
5. *Papers of James Madison,* Volume 9, p. 357.
6. Farrand, *Records,* Volume I, pp. 135–136. See my earlier discussion of these matters in Chapter 9, above.
7. Dahl, op. cit., p. 7.
8. Ibid., p. 6. It is of interest to note that in "Of Parties in General" Hume says that in free governments only the legislature can eradicate factions "by the steady application of rewards and punishments" (*Essays,* p. 55).
9. *The Federalist,* p. 60.
10. Dahl, op. cit., p. 6.
11. *The Federalist,* p. 324.
12. *Ibid.,* p. 335; Jefferson, *Notes on Virginia,* Query XIII; also see Garry Wills, *Explaining America,* pp. 111–112.
13. Dahl, op. cit., pp. 6–7.

14. *The Federalist,* pp. 235–237; I also refer to this in Chapter 7, note 4, above.

15. *The Federalist,* p. 333. This passage, with its causal word "lead," is quoted by Dahl himself, op. cit., p. 9.

16. *The Federalist,* p. 334.

17. Dahl, op. cit., p. 6.

18. Ibid., pp. 6–7.

19. Ibid., p. 6. I quote the language in which Dahl presents Madison's views.

20. Ibid., p. 7.

21. *The Federalist,* pp. 61, 64–65.

22. For a discussion of Burlamaqui's mode of distinguishing primitive and adventitious natural rights, see my *Philosophy of the American Revolution,* pp. 213–221. For a reference to Burlamaqui by Hamilton, see the latter's *Papers,* Volume I, p. 86, which I quote above, Chapter 3, note 20. According to Irving Brant, *James Madison: The Nationalist* (New York, 1948), p. 410, Jefferson sent Madison some works of Burlamaqui that Madison would have received prior to the Philadelphia Convention. On examples of natural rights in colonial thought, see Clinton Rossiter, *Seedtime of the Republic* (New York, 1953), pp. 375–381.

23. Dahl, op. cit., p. 10.

24. Ibid.

25. Ibid., p. 11.

26. Ibid., p. 5.

27. Ibid., p. 11.

28. Ibid., p. 22.

29. See my *Philosophy of the American Revolution,* pp. 161–163.

30. Dahl, op. cit., pp. 22–23.

31. Ibid., p. 23.

32. Ibid.

33. Ibid.

34. Ibid., p. 24.

35. *Papers of James Madison,* Volume 9, p. 357.

36. *The Federalist,* p. 62.

37. *Papers of James Madison,* Volume 8, pp. 298–304; *Papers of Thomas Jefferson,* Volume 2, pp. 545–547.

38. Hume, *Essays,* p. 55.

39. Ibid., p. 30.

40. Ibid., p. 64, n. 1. On this passage, see Duncan Forbes, *Hume's Philosophical Politics* (Cambridge, England, 1975), p. 185. Forbes says that the passage was withdrawn in the edition of 1768.

41. Hume, *Enquiry Concerning the Human Understanding,* Section XII, Part III, p. 165.

42. Dahl, op. cit., p. 26.

43. *The Federalist,* pp. 193–194. See Martin Diamond, "Democracy and *The Federalist:* A Reconsideration of the Framers' Intent," *The American Political Science Review* 8 (1959), p. 56, where he remarks that "the Founding Fathers believed that true knowledge of the good and bad in human conduct was possible."

44. *The Federalist,* p. 194. See my *Philosophy of the American Revolution,* pp. 78–96.

45. *The Federalist,* p. 62.

Chapter 12. A Philosophical Map of *The Federalist*

1. *The Federalist,* pp. 352 and 419. Also see *Number 45,* p. 309, and *Number 43,* p. 297, where Madison says that the safety and happiness of society are the objects at which all political institutions aim. Safety I take to be the same as the security of the people's rights.

2. Unlike many commentators, Epstein emphasizes this point (op. cit., pp. 109–110).

3. Hume, *Treatise of Human Nature,* pp. xxii–xxiii.

4. Bernard Mandeville's *The Fable of the Bees* was subtitled "Private Vices, Public Benefits." See F. B. Kaye's edition thereof (Oxford, 1924), esp. Volume I, pp. 17–37. Also see Lovejoy, *Reflections on Human Nature,* pp. 41 and 42–45, for a discussion of relevant views in Alexander Pope's *Essay on Man.* In addition, see Chapter 6, above, material connected with notes 27–29.

5. *Papers of James Madison,* Volume 10, p. 214.

6. *The Federalist,* p. 349.

7. Ibid., p. 61. On Mill's view of this question, see *A System of Logic,* Book III, Chapter V, Section 3 in *Collected Works,* Volume VII, pp. 327–334. Also see H. L. A. Hart and A. M. Honoré, *Causation in the Law* (Oxford, 1959), pp. 12–20, for a comparison of Mill's views with those of Hume. The authors point out that Mill laid more emphasis than Hume did on the fact that causes are complex, but they recognize that Hume was aware of this complexity. Although not cited by them, a passage in Hume's discussion of free will shows that he believed that actions are caused by a combination of "motives, inclinations, and circumstances" (*Enquiry Concerning Human Understanding,* Section VIII, Part I, p. 95). Hume's word "circumstances" includes what Madison meant by "opportunities." By manipulating such circumstances, Hume implied, one could prevent the action by putting impediments in the way of the would-be agent. Madison had something like this in mind when he said that a factiously motivated majority "must be rendered, by their number and local situation, unable to concert and carry into effect schemes of oppression." It might be argued, therefore, that Madison modeled his theory of how to control majority factions on a theory of free action that Hume and, of course, Hobbes before him had defended while analyzing the free actions of individuals rather than those of groups. According to this theory, an individual is free to perform an action if and only if that individual would perform the action if he had the motive to perform it. This implies that the individual is *not* free to perform an action if and only if *it is false* to say that he would perform it if he had the motive to perform it. And it would be false to say that just in case the individual did not have the opportunity to perform the action—if he were impeded by circumstances. By parity of reasoning, Madison thought that a factious majority would not be free to carry into effect its schemes of oppression just in case it lacked the opportunity to do so. Hobbes defended his views at length in his spirited debates with Bishop Bramhall. See Thomas Hobbes, "The Question Concerning Liberty, Necessity, and Chance," *The English Works of Thomas Hobbes,* ed. W. Molesworth, Volume V (London, 1840), passim; also see Hobbes's shorter work, "Of Liberty and Necessity," op. cit., Volume IV, pp. 229–278. We must bear in mind that Madison's method of denying freedom of action in this sense to factious majorities was, in his view, compatible with not destroying the *political* liberty of majority factions,

since his proposal in *Number 10* would supposedly allow the control of their actions while preserving "the spirit and the form of popular government" (*The Federalist*, p. 61).

This is a convenient place at which to point out that the version of the principle of causality to which Madison seems committed is compatible with what is sometimes called the plurality of causes. It is worth emphasizing this because Madison held that more than one cause may produce a factional difference. It is also worth emphasizing because it might appear that if one says that an action will be performed if and only if a motive and an opportunity are present, one denies the plurality of causes. One says, it might be argued, that there is exactly one whole cause, consisting of a motive and an opportunity, which is a necessary and sufficient condition for the performance of the action, whereas the doctrine of plurality of causes allows that "many causes may produce mechanical motion: many causes may produce some kinds of sensation: many causes may produce death" (Mill, op. cit., Book III, Chapter X, Section I, p. 435). The fact is, however, that any one of the many whole causes of killing, for example, is complex if it consists of a precipitant as well as circumstances which constitute the opportunity of a killer, an individual who brings about the death. Therefore, there is no inconsistency in accepting both the version of the principle of causality that I think is implicit in Madison's view *and* the pluralty of causes.

8. See Hume, *Treatise*, Book I, Part III, Section III, pp. 80–81, where Hume criticizes the views of Locke, Hobbes, and Samuel Clarke.

9. *The Federalist*, pp. 236–238.

Chapter 13. *The Federalist* and the Declaration of Independence Compared

1. Gordon S. Wood, *The Creation of the American Republic 1776–1787* (first published, 1969; reprint, New York, 1972), p. 524. Martin Diamond, "Democracy and *The Federalist*," pp. 52–68, has emphasized the continuity between the Declaration and *The Federalist*.

2. Concerning this assumption, see *Papers of James Madison*, Volume 8, p. 300 and editor's note 5 thereon, and p. 305; also *Papers of Thomas Jefferson*, Volume I, p. 194.

3. In my *Science and Sentiment in America*, Chapter 3, I discussed the philosophy of the Declaration from a point of view that changed between the completion of that work in 1971 and the completion of my *Philosophy of the American Revolution* in 1977. The latter contains a more extended and, as I now think, a more accurate treatment of this subject.

4. Wood, op. cit., p. 524.

5. Ibid., p. 626.

6. For an extended discussion of Locke's views on this matter, see my *Philosophy of the American Revolution*, pp. 15–32, where I cite relevant passages in Locke's *Essay Concerning Human Understanding* and his *Essays on the Law of Nature*, and his *Reasonableness of Christianity*.

7. *The Federalist*, pp. 193–194.

8. Ibid., pp. 164–165. Also see Jay in *Number 2* on the intelligence of the people (ibid., p. 10).

9. Ibid., pp. 424–425.

10. Ibid., p. 57. See Epstein, op. cit., p. 109.

11. See Henry Sidgwick's *Outlines of the History of Ethics for English Readers*, pp. 175–178. These few pages on Locke are remarkably illuminating.

12. *The Federalist*, pp. 59–60.

13. *Papers of James Madison*, Volume 10, p. 213.

14. See my *Philosophy of the American Revolution*, pp. 42–44, for further discussion of Locke's view and for citations of the relevant texts of Locke.

15. *Papers of James Madison*, Volume 10, p. 213.

16. *The Federalist*, pp. 233–234.

17. Ibid., pp. 5–6.

18. I take the opportunity in this paperback edition to cite Geoffrey Marshall's article, "David Hume and Political Scepticism," *The Philosophical Quarterly*, Volume 4 (1954), esp. pp. 255–257. In it, Marshall had called attention to Hume's impact on Madison's *Number 10* before Adair had done so in his published work but not before Adair had discussed this impact in his unpublished doctoral thesis, "The Intellectual Origins of Jeffersonian Democracy" in 1943. It is worth adding that when Marshall summarizes Hume's statement of what Marshall calls "the elements of all that is respectable in the philosophy of conservatism," Marshall concludes by quoting the very passage of Hume that Hamilton had quoted so favorably in the final number of *The Federalist*, (p. 594) but Marshall does not note that it had been quoted by Hamilton.

INDEX